The Book of Lists

LONDON

Also by Nick Rennison

The London Blue Plaque Guide

The Bloomsbury Good Reading Guide

The Bloomsbury Good Reading Guide
to Crime Fiction

Sherlock Holmes: An Unauthorised Biography

The Book of Lists
LONDON

by

Nick Rennison

CANONGATE
Edinburgh · New York · Melbourne

First published in Great Britain in 2006 by
Canongate Books Ltd, 14 High Street,
Edinburgh, EH1 1TE

This paperback edition published by Canongate Books in 2007

1

Inspired by *The Book of Lists*, edited by Amy Wallace and David Wallechinsky

British Library Cataloguing-in-Publication Data
A catalogue record for this book is available on request from the British Library

ISBN 978 1 84195 934 4

Designed and Typeset by Sharon McTeir, Creative Publishing Services
Printed and bound by Clays Ltd, St Ives plc

www.canongate.net

ACKNOWLEDGEMENTS

Many people contributed to this book. Anyone who has lived in London, or even just visited it regularly, knows at least one curious fact or intriguing story about the city. When I spoke to friends about the proposed *Book of Lists: London*, nearly all had thoughts about what should be included in it. If I listed all of them, I would begin to sound like an actor on Oscar night thanking his entire lifetime acquaintance for assistance with his career. The following, however, were particularly helpful. Andrew Holgate is a mine of information on London's history and he was always happy to share his knowledge. Over the last few years, Niamh Marnham, Andy Walker, Hugh Pemberton, Susan Osborne and Jacqui Vines have, at various times, accompanied me on walks in search of London curiosities past and present. Some of the fruits of those walks can be found in the pages of this book. When we both worked for Waterstone's, Paul Baggaley asked me to compile a guide to London writing for the company and working with Paul and other people in Waterstone's on the guide introduced me to many of the books which have been useful in creating *The Book of Lists: London*. During a week's shared holiday in Germany, David Jones and Linda Pattenden devoted nearly as much time to devising London-related lists as they did to continental sightseeing. All of these people have helped, directly or indirectly, with the compilation of this book.

At Canongate, who publish the original inspiration for this book, *The Book of Lists* by David Wallechinsky and Amy Wallace, Jamie Byng and Andy Miller provided plenty of suggestions for lists and for entries to include in them. My biggest debt, though, is to Helen Bleck whose editing skills, ideas and patience in dealing with an author who was rarely as organised as he should have been were much appreciated. Without her help there would have been no *Book of Lists: London* and I am very grateful.

Finally, I would like to thank my partner, Eve Gorton, who has had to live with an obsessive list-maker for the past fifteen months. Her love and support have been, as always, much valued.

PERMISSIONS FOR IMAGES
USED IN THE TEXT

CONTENTS

INTRODUCTION

Hundreds of books are written and published on London past and present each year. Some are weighty volumes which provide scholarly surveys of its two-thousand-year history or which analyse in enormous detail its social structures. This is not one of them. *The Book of Lists: London* is unashamedly lighter in weight. If readers are looking for profound historical insights or careful exercises in urban geography, they should go elsewhere. If, on the other hand, they would like to know why London Underground once employed a one-legged man to ride up and down the escalators at Earl's Court tube station, who gave her name to a rhyming slang term for a banana, why Beckton Gasworks once masqueraded as the killing fields of Vietnam, which symbol of American liberty was built in Whitechapel and what Hitler planned to do with Nelson's Column, then this is the book to consult. In the dozens of lists in it, they will learn about the Bengal tiger that once seized a small boy in the Commercial Road, London's only medieval mummy, a prostitute named Clarice la Claterballock, seven Cherokee chiefs who met King George II, a plan to stand the Crystal Palace on its end, a hotel suite in Mayfair that was once Yugoslav territory, a beer flood in Tottenham Court Road that drowned nine people and where tourists can see a pair of Queen Victoria's knickers. London is full of stories, curiosities and echoes of its past. I have tried to include as many of them as possible in the lists that make up this book.

1

BUILDINGS AND STREETS

15 CURIOUS LONDON STREET NAMES

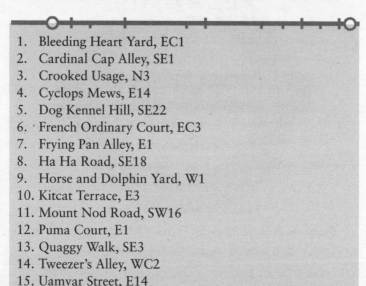

1. Bleeding Heart Yard, EC1
2. Cardinal Cap Alley, SE1
3. Crooked Usage, N3
4. Cyclops Mews, E14
5. Dog Kennel Hill, SE22
6. French Ordinary Court, EC3
7. Frying Pan Alley, E1
8. Ha Ha Road, SE18
9. Horse and Dolphin Yard, W1
10. Kitcat Terrace, E3
11. Mount Nod Road, SW16
12. Puma Court, E1
13. Quaggy Walk, SE3
14. Tweezer's Alley, WC2
15. Uamvar Street, E14

10 WELL-KNOWN LONDON STREET NAMES AND WHAT THEY MEAN

1. **Pall Mall**

   Pall Mall is named after a popular game, not unlike an extended version of croquet, which was played on the site of the present thoroughfare. In Pall Mall, a mallet was used to drive a ball down a course, several hundred yards long, towards a hoop at the end. Whoever took the fewest shots to reach the hoop and propel the ball through it was the winner. The name derives from the Italian words 'palla' ('ball') and 'maglio' ('mallet'). Samuel Pepys wrote in his diary for 2 April 1661: 'So I went into St James's Park, where I saw the Duke of York playing at Pelemele, the first time that ever I saw the sport.' Pepys saw the game being played on the site of the present Pall Mall but, soon after he wrote in his diary, the course was moved, allegedly because the dust from the carriages passing by disrupted play too often. The phrase 'pell-mell' is sometimes said to have derived from the game, referring to the speed with which players moved to strike the ball with their mallets, but the derivation is an invented one. 'Pell-mell' actually comes from the old French 'pêle-mêle', meaning 'mixed together'.

2. Piccadilly

'Pickadils' were small squares of material used in Tudor costumes either to disguise the stitching around the armholes of doublets and bodices or to help support the stiff, starched collars known as ruffs. In 1612 a wealthy London tailor called Robert Baker built a house on what was then open country to the west of the city. The house was mockingly nicknamed Piccadilly Hall, in reference to the pickadils which had helped to make Baker his fortune. As the city expanded and buildings spread westwards, Baker's house was soon surrounded by others and eventually demolished, but the name 'Piccadilly' was retained for the new thoroughfare.

3. Houndsditch

Today this is a street running between Bishopsgate and St Botolph Street but, in the Middle Ages, it was the name given to the ditch that ran beneath the city walls from the Tower to the old River Fleet. First recorded in the thirteenth century as 'Hondesdich', it was said by the Tudor chronicler John Stow to take its name from the dead dogs that were so often thrown into it. Others have suggested that it simply referred to a place where dogs were kept or that it derives from 'Hunes-dic', meaning a defensive ditch raised against the 'Huns', those who dwelt in the marshes and forests outside the city.

4. **Crutched Friars**

   Called 'Crouchedfrerestreete' or 'Chrocit Friars' in the medieval records, the street takes its name from the House of the Friars of the Holy Cross which was situated in it. In Middle English, the word often used for 'cross' was 'crouche', derived from the Latin 'crux', and this was corrupted to 'crutched'.

5. **Soho Square**

   The name 'Soho' is usually said to have derived from a hunting cry. In the years before the Great Fire, the area was open country with only a handful of cottages close to what is now Wardour Street. The land, much of it owned by the Palace of Westminster, was used for hunting and 'So-Ho!', like the better known 'Tally-Ho!', was called out when the prey was spotted. According to an old manual of field sports, 'When a stag breaks covert the cry is "tayho!" ... when a hare it is "soho!"' After the Great Fire of 1666, land was needed for the building of new houses and Soho Fields were covered by developments in the last decades of the seventeenth century but the old connection to the chase was preserved in the name. Some etymologists have disputed the traditional derivation.

6. **Threadneedle Street**

   There are several suggestions as to how the street in which the Bank of England stands got its name. Some say that it refers to the 'three needles in fesse argent' that appeared on the coat of arms of the Needlemakers' Company which is traditionally supposed to have had premises on the street, others that it is a corruption of 'Thryddanen' or 'Thryddenal' Street, meaning the third street that ran between Cheapside and the road from London Bridge to Bishopsgate. However the street got its current name there can be little doubt that it is an improvement on the one it had in the Middle Ages. It was then part of the medieval red-light district of London and, as the haunt of prostitutes, rejoiced (if that is the right word) in the name of 'Gropecuntelane'.

7. **Poultry**

Variously recorded in the Middle Ages as 'Polettar', 'Poletria', 'Puletrie', 'Le Pultree' and 'Poultrie', it took its name from the poulterers' market that was held in it.

8. **Old Jewry**

First recorded as 'The Jewry' in 1181, it was so called because it was the area in which London's Jewish population lived. Most of the Jews in London in the early Middle Ages descended from a group invited to the city in 1070 by William the Conqueror who wished to make use of their capital and commercial expertise. These Jews had settled in the street off Cheapside which still bears the name 'Old Jewry'. The Jewish population was expelled from London, and from England, by Edward I in 1290 and were not to return until the time of Cromwell.

9. **Seething Lane**

Few street names in the City have more variants in the records or more disputes about their meaning than Seething Lane. In 1257 it is documented as 'Shyvethenestrat'. A few decades later it has become 'Synchenestrate' and, a century later, in 1386, it has been transmuted into 'Cyvyndonelane'. One suggestion about its origin is that it owes its name to an Anglo-Saxon called Seofeca and that Seofeca's Lane was gradually corrupted via 'Siveken' and 'Seevin' to Seething. Samuel Pepys was living in Seething Lane when he wrote his diary in the 1660s.

10. **Minories**

The street is named after the Abbey of the Minoresses of St Mary of the Order of St Clare, which stood on the site from the thirteenth century until the dissolution of the monasteries under Henry VIII. When the abbey was dissolved the last abbess, a woman called Elizabeth Salvage, was given a life pension of £40 a year. The nuns were less generously treated. They received pensions varying between £2 and £3 3s 8d a year.

THE 32 LONDON BOROUGHS AND WHAT THEIR NAMES MEAN

1. **Barking and Dagenham**
   Both come from Anglo-Saxon personal names. Barking is the 'place of Berica's people' and Dagenham is 'Daecca's homestead' or 'Daecca's village'.

2. **Barnet**
   The name, first recorded in the eleventh century, denotes 'land cleared by burning'.

3. **Bexley**
   Bexley comes from two Old English words – 'byxe', meaning 'a box tree' and 'leah', meaning 'a woodland clearing'.

4. **Brent**
   Brent derives its name from the River Brent, which flows through the borough. The river takes *its* name from the Celtic goddess Brigantia.

5. **Bromley**
   First recorded in the ninth century as 'Bromleag', it means 'a clearing where broom bushes grow'.

6. **Camden**
   Charles Pratt, the first earl of Camden, started the first development in Camden Town in the late eighteenth century and gave his name to it.

7. **The City of Westminster**
   Dating back to the tenth century, the name means 'western monastery'.

8. **Croydon**
   Another name of Anglo-Saxon origin, Croydon means either 'valley of wild saffron' or 'crooked valley'.

9. **Ealing**
   First known as 'Gillingas' in the eighth century, Ealing derives from an Anglo-Saxon personal name and means 'the place of Gilla's people'.

10. **Enfield**
    Another borough name that comes from an Anglo-Saxon personal name, Enfield means 'Eana's open land'.

11. **Greenwich**
    First recorded in the tenth century, Greenwich means 'green (or grassy) port'.

12. **Hackney**
    The borough probably takes its name from the Anglo-Saxon personal name Haca and means 'the island in the marshland belonging to Haca' but it is possible that it owes its name to the Anglo-Saxon verb 'haccan' ('to kill with a sword or axe') and recalls an ancient battle site.

13. **Hammersmith and Fulham**
    Hammersmith, unsurprisingly, refers to a place with a forge or 'hammer smithy' and dates back to the thirteenth century. Fulham is an earlier name derived from an Anglo-Saxon personal name and means 'Fulla's land by the river'.

14. **Haringey**
    First recorded in 1201, Haringey means 'enclosure in the grey wood'.

15. **Harrow**
    'Hearg' is an Anglo-Saxon word for a temple or altar to pre-Christian gods and 'Harrow' derives from it.

16. **Havering**
Another borough that owes its name to an otherwise forgotten Anglo-Saxon petty chieftain, Havering means 'the land belonging to Haefer's people'.

17. **Hillingdon**
First recorded in the eleventh century, the name probably means 'Hilda's hill'.

18. **Hounslow**
'Hundeslawe', meaning 'hill belonging to Hund' appears in the Domesday Book and Hounslow is the modern form of it.

19. **Islington**
First recorded in Anglo-Saxon times as 'Gislandune' meaning 'the hill belonging to Gisla', the place name transmuted to 'Isendone' and then finally 'Islington'.

20. **The Royal Borough of Kingston upon Thames**
The name means simply 'the king's estate on the Thames'.

21. **Lambeth**
Lambeth takes its name from a 'hithe' or 'small port' where lambs were landed.

22. **Lewisham**
Lewisham comes from an Anglo-Saxon personal name and means 'Leofsa's homestead'.

23. **Merton**
The name comes from two Anglo-Saxon words meaning 'farm' and 'pool'.

24. **Newham**
The name was given to the borough when it was formed from the old boroughs of East and West Ham. Ham was an Anglo-Saxon word for a settlement.

25. **Redbridge**

Astonishingly, the name, dating from the eighteenth century, comes from a bridge across the River Roding which was built of red brick.

26. **Richmond upon Thames**

Originally called Shene, the present name dates from the end of the fifteenth century when Henry VII, owner of the manor, called it after his Richmond earldom in Yorkshire.

27. **The Royal Borough of Kensington and Chelsea**

Kensington derives its name from an Anglo-Saxon nobleman Cynesige who had a 'tun' or estate in the area in the eighth century. Chelsea, originally 'Chelcehithe', meant 'a landing place for chalk'.

28. **Southwark**

The name derives from Anglo-Saxon and means 'southern defensive work'.

29. **Sutton**

The name is first recorded in the Domesday Book and means 'southern farm'.

30. **Tower Hamlets**

First coming into use around the time of the English Civil War, the name referred to the hamlets, the collections of houses and buildings, surrounding the Tower of London.

31. **Waltham Forest**

Prior to the seventeenth century, Epping Forest was known as Waltham Forest and the name was revived for the borough when it was created in 1965.

32. **Wandsworth**

In Anglo-Saxon times it was known as 'Waendelsorde', which meant 'the enclosure belonging to Waendel', and the name has metamorphosed over the centuries.

9 UNUSUAL LONDON PUB NAMES

1. ### The Essex Serpent, Covent Garden
    Known as such in the mid-eighteenth century, the name derives from the sighting of what a pamphlet first published in 1669 describes as a 'Monstrous Serpent which hath divers times been seen at a Parish called Henham-on-the-Mount within four miles of Saffron Walden'. Recent research suggests that the serpent may have been the creation of a local practical joker called William Winstanley who created a dragon made of wood and canvas that could be activated by a man inside. Winstanley probably wrote the pamphlet himself.

2. ### The Hand and Shears, EC1
    The name refers back to Bartholomew Fair which was held in Smithfield for centuries. The night before the fair tailors would gather in the pub and, once suitably lubricated, would parade the streets waving their tailors' shears in their hands and crying out that the fair should begin.

3. ### I Am the Only Running Footman, Mayfair
    In the eighteenth century running footmen were employed by the wealthy to run ahead of their carriages to clear the way and pay any tolls.

    Original pub sign: I am the only running footman

4. ### The King of Corsica, Soho
    Named after the Frenchman Theodor von Neuhoff, who became involved in the Corsican struggle for

independence from Genoa in the mid-eighteenth century and was briefly proclaimed king of the island. In 1756 he was obliged to flee to London and died, penniless, in Soho. Several people, including Horace Walpole, paid for his funeral at St Anne's, Soho and for his tombstone. Walpole wrote an epitaph: 'The grave, great teacher, to a level brings/Heroes and beggars, galley-slaves and kings/ But Theodore this moral learn'd e're dead/ Fate pored its lesson on his living head/Bestow'd a kingdom, and denied him bread.'

5. **The Prospect of Whitby, Wapping**
   Parts of the building date back to 1520 when it was known as the Devil's Tavern but the name comes from an eighteenth-century coal boat, called the *Prospect* and registered at the Yorkshire port of Whitby, which was moored outside it.

6. **The Queen's Larder, Queen's Square**
   The pub takes its name from the story that, while George III was receiving treatment for his madness from doctors in Queen's Square, his Queen, Charlotte, rented premises to store his favourite foods.

7. **Spaniards Inn, Hampstead**
   There are at least two theories to explain the name. Either the property was named after two Spanish brothers who owned it in the seventeenth century and killed each other in a duel, or its name recalls the Spanish ambassador to the court of James II.

8. **The Sun and 13 Cantons, Soho**
   The pub was named after Swiss woollen merchants who had their premises nearby, and the thirteen cantons are those that made up the country of Switzerland.

9. **The Widow's Son, E3**
   The name of the pub refers to a story, possibly apocryphal,

that the pub was once a cottage owned by the mother of a sailor who failed to return from a voyage. Each year, on Good Friday, the day on which her son had been scheduled to return, the widow made hot cross buns to welcome him home. In the years since the cottage became a pub, the tradition of making hot cross buns has continued and they hang in the pub, unappetising mementoes of a mother's grief. Every Good Friday a Royal Navy sailor adds another to the collection.

6 LONDON PUBS NAMED AFTER PEOPLE YOU'VE NEVER HEARD OF

1. **The Ship and Shovell, Craven Passage, WC2**
   The improbably named Cloudesly Shovel rose from cabin boy to admiral. Although, in his day, he was one of the most famous sailors in the Royal Navy, he is now remembered today, if at all, for the manner of his death. His ship was wrecked off the Isles of Scilly in 1707 and eight hundred men were lost, including the admiral. It has been claimed that he was alive when he was cast ashore on one of the islands but that a local woman murdered him on the beach for his emerald ring. The woman confessed to the crime on her deathbed many years later. The immediate consequence of the disaster was an urgent reconsideration of the system of navigation in the navy and the government offered an enormous prize, later won by the clock-maker John Harrison, for an accurate method of determining longitude at sea.

2. **The John Snow, Soho**
   In 1834 the clergyman and wit Sydney Smith wrote in a letter to a friend that, 'He who drinks a tumbler of London Water has literally in his stomach more animated beings than there are Men, Women and Children on the face of

the Globe.' One of the consequences of the impurity of London water was that the capital was regularly ravaged by outbreaks of cholera, although no one at the time believed that the disease was carried in the drinking water. John Snow was a physician who was the first person to realise that contaminated water was causing the cholera to spread. During an outbreak of the disease in Soho in 1854, he analysed the mortality statistics and mapped them against the sources of water supply. He was able to prove that a single pump in Broad Street (now Broadwick Street) was the site of infection. The pub, once known as The Newcastle-upon-Tyne, was renamed in his honour to mark the centenary of his discovery, although, since Snow was a vegetarian teetotaller, a pub isn't the most appropriate monument to him.

3. **Dirty Dick's, Bishopsgate**
'Dirty Dick' was the nickname of an early nineteenth-century ironmonger called Nathaniel Bentley. A kind of male version of Dickens's Miss Havisham, Bentley became a recluse when his fiancée died the day before their wedding. Nothing in his house was touched or cleaned for decades. When Bentley died the landlord of the pub that stood here bought up the contents of his shop and house. The mummified bodies of Bentley's dead cats were still on display in the pub in the early 1980s. The present building is a newer one.

4. **Crocker's Folly, Aberdeen Place**
Frank Crocker was a nineteenth-century entrepreneur who built the pub as a hotel called The Crown at what he believed would be the site for a new rail terminus for lines from the Midlands. It has been claimed that, when the terminus was built at Marylebone instead, Crocker, deciding he was a ruined man, committed suicide by throwing himself off the roof of the hotel but he died a natural death in 1904. Soon after it was built, the pub

was nicknamed Crocker's Folly and it was officially re-named in the 1980s.

5. **Old Dr Butler's Head, Mason's Avenue, EC2**

The pub takes its name from a physician in the reign of James I. More quack than scientist, William Butler had a reputation for unconventional cures (once firing a pistol near an unsuspecting patient to scare him out of his epilepsy) and was the creator of Dr Butler's Purging Ale, a medicinal brew with a powerful laxative effect. The ale, surprisingly popular for many years, was sold at houses displaying the sign of 'Butler's Head'. The pub in Mason's Avenue is on the site of one of these, destroyed in the Great Fire and rebuilt and renovated several times since.

6. **Marquis of Granby, Chandos Place, WC2**

There are pubs of this name all over England (there are nearly a dozen in London alone) but few people have any idea who the Marquis of Granby was. John Manners, Marquess of Granby, was a hero of the Seven Years' War, a general who was victorious against the French at the Battle of Warburg in 1760. This particular Marquis of Granby in Chandos Place, then called the Hole in the Wall, was allegedly the pub in which the Bow Street Runners finally cornered the gentleman highwayman, Claude Duval. (*See also* **8 London Highwaymen**, p.114)

10 LONDON BUILDINGS THAT MIGHT HAVE BEEN

The following are London buildings and landmarks that were proposed but never built.

1. **Watkin's Tower**

   Soon after the building of the Eiffel Tower in 1889, a patriotic railway tycoon and MP called Sir Edward Watkin, convinced that anything the French could do, the British could do better, proposed the construction of a tower in Wembley Park that would be 150 feet taller than its Parisian counterpart. The tower would accommodate restaurants, theatres, a ballroom and a Turkish bath. Unfortunately Watkin's faith in British technology was, in this instance, unjustified. The tower reached a height of only 200 feet before money and the will to continue with the project ran out. The tower was abandoned and eventually dynamited out of existence in 1907. Its foundations were re-discovered when the foundations for the new Wembley Stadium were being dug.

2. **Wren's Giant Pineapple**

   Sir Christopher Wren had already been involved in plans to renovate St Paul's Cathedral before the Great Fire destroyed the building and made a completely new edifice possible. Six days before the fire broke out in Pudding Lane, Wren presented a design for St Paul's which included a dome to replace the dangerously dilapidated spire. On top of the dome was an elongated stone pineapple, more than 60 feet high. The fruit had only recently been introduced to England and Wren was clearly struck by its shape and texture. The 'Pineapple Design', as it has come to be known, was dropped from all future Wren blueprints for the cathedral.

3. **The Primrose Hill Necropolis**
    In the early decades of the nineteenth century, London faced a crisis in the management of its dead. The population was rising so steeply that the city's existing churchyards and burial grounds were unable to cope with the numbers dying each year. New solutions had to be found. One was proposed by an architect called Thomas Willson in 1829. Willson's idea was to build a gargantuan pyramid on Primrose Hill which would house more than five million corpses. With a base the same size as Russell Square, the pyramid would have 94 storeys and access to them would have been via a large number of steam-powered lifts.

4. **The Greenwich Britannia**
    In 1799, the sculptor John Flaxman published a short pamphlet in which he proposed the building of a naval monument in Greenwich Park. The monument was to take the shape of a gigantic, 230-foot tall figure of Britannia who would stand in the park looking out over the Thames. An illustration in the pamphlet, engraved by Flaxman's friend William Blake, showed the huge statue, holding spear and shield, with a lion peeping out from behind her skirts. 'It is a work,' Flaxman wrote, 'intended to last as long as the Trajan Column, the Amphitheatre or the Pyramids of Egypt.' In the event, few people shared his confidence. The statue of Britannia was not even built.

5. **The Trafalgar Square Pyramid**
    One of the busiest advocates of grand schemes to 'improve' London in the first half of the nineteenth century was Colonel Sir Frederick William Trench MP. If Trench had had his way, Trafalgar Square would have been adorned not with Nelson's Column but with a twenty-two tier pyramid taller than St Paul's. The edifice would have cost a million pounds to build, which Trench considered

'an expense not burthensome to the nation'. The nation begged to differ. The pyramid got no further than the drawing-board of the architects Philip and Matthew Cotes Wyatt.

6. **Trench's Elevated Railway**

Undeterred by the failure of his Trafalgar Square plans, Sir Frederick Trench was on hand in the 1840s to propose an elevated railway running along the Thames from London Bridge to Hungerford Bridge. A grand colonnade would be built by the river. On its upper level carriages would travel, drawn by a power-driven cable. Beneath its shade, sheltered from both sun and rain, pedestrians would stroll, impressed by what Trench called 'a feature of utility amid magnificence not to be equalled in any capital in Europe'. This was the decade of 'railway mania' but even the most maniacal of investors realised that Trench's plan was a financial non-starter and he was unable to raise the money to build it.

7. **The Great Victorian Way**

In 1855, the designer of the Crystal Palace, Sir Joseph Paxton, presented a proposal to a parliamentary committee for a 'Grand Girdle Railway and Boulevard under Glass'. The railway would circle London for 12 miles and would be built above ground and within a glass arcade incorporating shops and houses. Linking all the main railway termini, 'The Great Victorian Way', as Paxton suggested the development should be called, would soar above the filth and smoke of nineteenth-century London. For those living in the houses under glass, the atmosphere would be 'almost equal to going to a foreign climate and would prevent many infirm persons being obliged to go into foreign countries in the winter'. Sadly, the cost of Paxton's visionary plan would be £34 million. At a time when Brunel's entire Great Western Railway had cost only £6 million, the price of the Great Victorian Way was clearly prohibitive and the parliamentary committee, while impressed by Sir Joseph's ideas, felt unable to proceed any further.

8. **Brunel's Great Exhibition Hall**

Before Sir Joseph Paxton's design for what became known as the Crystal Palace was adopted, there were innumerable other plans put forward in 1850 and 1851 for a Great Exhibition Hall. Many were by more eminent and renowned architects and engineers than Paxton. One of those who submitted plans was Isambard Kingdom Brunel. Described by one writer who saw the blueprints as 'a vast, squat, brick warehouse four times the length and twice the width of St Paul's Cathedral', Brunel's building would have required 15 million bricks in its construction. It was to have been topped by an iron dome that, again, would have been larger than that of St Paul's.

9. **Standing Crystal Palace on its End**

Just as the Millennium Dome has proved to be a difficult structure to re-use, Paxton's Crystal Palace presented a problem when the Great Exhibition finished in 1851. What was to be done with it? Although there were those who argued that it should stay where it was, most people realised that it simply took up too much space in its original location, Hyde Park. One architect called Burton had an ingenious solution. Why not just stand the Crystal Palace on its end? Burton published drawings, showing the Crystal Palace neatly transformed into a glass tower 1000 feet high but, in the event, moving the building to Sydenham seemed an easier option.

10. **The Crystal Tower Bridge**

In the midst of World War II, an architect called WFC Holden approached the committee charged with responsibility for London's bridges with an imaginative suggestion for remodelling Tower Bridge. The bridge was to be entirely encased in glass. Thus converted, Tower Bridge would not only provide a crossing over the river but could also incorporate hundreds of thousands of square feet of airy office space. No mention was made of how the Bridge could open to allow ships passage through it and Holden's scheme was not pursued with any enthusiasm.

THE 5 TALLEST BUILDINGS IN LONDON (AS OF JANUARY 2006)

1. **One Canada Square: 50 floors, 771 feet (235m)**
   Commonly known as Canary Wharf Tower, it was designed by the Argentinian architect César Pelli and completed in 1991.

2. **8 Canada Square: 45 floors, 655 feet (200m)**
   The HSBC Building in Canary Wharf was designed by Norman Foster's architectural firm and was completed in 2002.

3. **25 Canada Square: 45 floors, 655 feet (200m)**
   The Citigroup Centre in Canary Wharf was designed, like the Canary Wharf Tower, by César Pelli and was completed in 2001.

4. **BT Tower: 43 floors, 625 feet (including the mast) (191m)**
   Built as the Post Office Tower in Cleveland Street, W1, and completed in 1965, this was London's tallest building for nearly thirty years.

5. **Tower 42: 43 floors, 600 feet (183m)**
   Originally known as the NatWest Tower, this building in Old Broad Street was designed by Richard Seifert and completed in 1980. It is the tallest building in the City of London.

6 LONDON BUILDINGS DESIGNED BY RICHARD ROGERS

Richard Rogers, Lord Rogers of Riverside, first came to prominence as an architect of world stature when he designed the Pompidou Centre in Paris in the 1970s but he has worked extensively in London. Some of his projects, most obviously the Millennium Dome, have been controversial yet his buildings have changed the cityscape of London like those of few other architects in the last century. His London buildings include:

1. Lloyds Building
2. The Millennium Dome
3. 88 Wood Street
4. Montevetro Building, Battersea Church Road
5. Channel Four TV Headquarters, Horseferry Road, Westminster
6. National Gallery extension

6 LONDON BUILDINGS DESIGNED BY NORMAN FOSTER

Born in Manchester in 1935, Norman Foster, Lord Foster of Thames Bank, has become one of the great stars of world architecture and is renowned for projects like the Reichstag redevelopment in Berlin and Hong Kong International Airport. However, the majority of his most striking buildings have been constructed in London. These include:

1. British Museum Great Court
2. HSBC Headquarters, Canary Wharf
3. Canary Wharf Tube Station
4. Swiss Re HQ (The Gherkin)
5. No 1, London Wall
6. City Hall

12 LONDON BRIDGES

1. ## London Bridge: 1176

For centuries the only bridge across the Thames in the city, the first stone bridge was begun in 1176, replacing a wooden one which had been there since Roman times. The driving force behind the building of the bridge was a churchman called Peter of Colechurch but, from the beginning, he had difficulty raising the money to go ahead with his project. Eventually Henry II stepped in, imposing a tax on wool, the proceeds of which went towards the bridge, and it was finally completed in 1209. The old London Bridge is best remembered for two things – it had houses built on it and the heads of traitors were, for many years, impaled on the turrets of the gate at its southern end as a warning to those approaching the city of the fate of those who conspired against the king. The earliest record of houses on the bridge dates from 1201, during the period of its construction. They survived for centuries. According to a writer in Stuart times, the bridge was 'adorned with sumptuous buildings and statelie and beautiful houses on either side, inhabited by wealthy citizens, and furnished with all manner of trades, comparable in itself to a little city, whose buildings are so artificially contrived, and so firmly combined as it seemed to be more than an ordinary street, for it is as one continual vault or roof'. The houses were finally removed in the 1750s. Among those whose heads have adorned the bridge have been the Scottish hero William Wallace, the medieval rebel Jack Cade and Henry VIII's minister Thomas Cromwell.

The foundation stone of a new London Bridge was laid in 1825 by the Lord Mayor, who descended 45 feet beneath the Thames in a cofferdam in order to do so. George IV had turned down the opportunity of laying the stone because of 'the injury he might sustain in his health by descending to such a depth surrounded by such an element'. Opened in 1831, this was the bridge sold to an American buyer who, according to legend, was under the impression he was buying the more distinctive Tower Bridge. It now stands in Lake Havasu City, Arizona. It was replaced by the present bridge in the late 1960s.

2. **Putney Bridge: 1729**

The first bridge to span the Thames between London Bridge and Kingston was built of timber in 1729. Putney Bridge had a toll house at either end with a bell to warn of approaching highwaymen. In 1795, Mary Wollstonecraft, the proto-feminist and mother of Mary Shelley, tried to commit suicide by throwing herself into the Thames close to the bridge after her partner, the American writer Gilbert Imlay, ran off with an actress. In 1870 the wooden bridge was severely damaged when a river barge struck it and the present bridge, designed by Sir Joseph Bazalgette, was finally opened in 1886. Since the mid-nineteenth century the bridge has been the starting point for the University Boat Race.

3. **Westminster Bridge: 1750**

The Swiss engineer Charles Labelye first submitted his designs for a bridge across the Thames at Westminster in 1738 but it was not opened until twelve years later. One of the difficulties lay in the opposition of the Archbishop of Canterbury, who owned the ferry that ran from Lambeth Palace to Horseferry Road and was concerned that the bridge would end his income from it. He was eventually given more than £20,000 to soothe his ruffled feathers. Another problem was shortage of cash, and money raised by state lottery had to be used to build the bridge. By-laws forbade dogs to cross the bridge and imposed the death penalty for anyone who defaced it. (There is no record of any graffiti artist suffering the ultimate penalty.) The bridge was the one on which Wordsworth recalled standing in his poem that declared that, 'Earth has not anything to show more fair' than the view of the city in the early morning. It was also the bridge beneath which Boswell entertained prostitutes. 'At the bottom of Haymarket I picked up a strong jolly young damsel, and taking her under the arm I conducted her to Westminster Bridge ... The whim of doing it there with the Thames rolling below us amused me much.' There had been difficulties with the foundations of the bridge's piers from the beginning – one MP, working on the assumption that, when in doubt, it's best to blame a foreigner, accused Labelye of being an 'unsolvent, ignorant, arrogating Swiss' – but it was not until the 1850s that Labelye's bridge was replaced by the present structure.

4. **Blackfriars Bridge: 1769**
Blackfriars Bridge was ready for pedestrians in 1766, for horses two years later and wheeled traffic finally crossed it in November 1769. When it was opened Boswell, according to his journals, was 'agreeably struck with its grandeur and beauty'. The bridge, designed by Robert Mylne, was intended to be known as Pitt Bridge, after the politician William Pitt the Elder, but the public refused to accept this and referred to it as Blackfriars Bridge from the start. It was originally a toll bridge but the tolls were abolished in 1785, five years after the Gordon Rioters had unilaterally decided that they were an unnecessary imposition and broken down the toll gates (*see* **9 London Riots**, pp. 142–3). The present bridge dates from 1869. In 1982 the body of the Italian banker Roberto Calvi was found hanging beneath it. Calvi, known as 'God's Banker' because of his close association with Vatican finances, is presumed to have been killed by the Mafia, who had been using his Banco Ambrosiano to launder money, but no one has ever been charged with his murder.

5. **Battersea Bridge: 1772**
Built of wood and designed by Henry Holland, who was

the architect of many of the more elegant houses in the streets around Sloane Square, Battersea Bridge replaced a ferry that ran from Chelsea to Battersea. It was rebuilt as an iron bridge by the great Victorian engineer and architect of the London sewers, Sir Joseph Bazalgette, in the late 1880s. The old bridge survives in many of Whistler's Thames paintings, which depict it looming out of the mists and shadows on the river. The climactic sequence of Guy Ritchie's movie *Lock, Stock and Two Smoking Barrels* was filmed on Battersea Bridge.

6. **Vauxhall Bridge: 1816**
Opened by the Prince Regent and originally called Regent's Bridge, this was the first iron bridge over the Thames in London. Like most other Thames bridges in the earlier part of the nineteenth century, it was a toll bridge. Pedestrians paid a penny and anyone wishing to drive a score of cattle across the bridge was obliged to fork out 6d. Tolls were finally removed in 1879. The present bridge dates from the last years of Queen Victoria's reign. In 1966 the opening sequence of *Alfie*, the movie that did much to consolidate Michael Caine's career as archetypal Londoner, was filmed on Vauxhall Bridge.

7. **Waterloo Bridge: 1817**
According to the Italian sculptor Antonio Canova, who saw it soon after it opened, Waterloo Bridge was 'the noblest bridge in the world' and 'worth a visit from the remotest corners of the earth'. Designed by the Scottish engineer John Rennie and opened on the second anniversary of Wellington's victory at the Battle of Waterloo, the bridge carried tolls for the first 60 years of it existence. The last day of the tolls, 5 October 1878, was treated as a high holiday with large crowds of pedestrians jostling one another for the honour of being the last to pay the halfpenny toll. *Waterloo Bridge* is the title of a twice-made film melodrama in which the betrayed heroine ends

her life by throwing herself off the bridge. In the 1931 version, the bridge was reconstructed in Hollywood; only in the 1940 remake, starring Vivien Leigh, are some of the shots of the real bridge. It was on Waterloo Bridge that the Bulgarian dissident Georgi Markov was stabbed by a poisoned umbrella in 1978. He died later in hospital.

8. **Hammersmith Bridge: 1827**

The first suspension bridge in London when it was originally built, the original Hammersmith Bridge was replaced by the present structure, designed by Sir Joseph Bazalgette, in the 1880s. An IRA bomb in 1996 resulted in the bridge being closed for four years and it was targeted again in 2000 almost immediately after it had re-opened. These were not the first times that Hammersmith Bridge had been subjected to bomb attack. In 1939, during an earlier campaign of militancy, the IRA left a bomb under the bridge. A pedestrian found it and, acting with admirable speed and courage, threw it into the river where it exploded.

9. **Chelsea Bridge: 1858**

Excavations undertaken at the time the bridge was first built unearthed human bones and large numbers of discarded weapons which have led archaeologists to believe that a river-crossing here was the site of a battle, probably between ancient Britons and invading Romans. The present bridge was built in the 1930s. In the 1960s the Chelsea Bridge tea stall became a well-known gathering place for Rockers.

10. **Albert Bridge: 1873**

A still-existing sign on the bridge which states that, 'All troops must break step when marching over this bridge' is an indication that, when it was built, it was close to several barracks and that the authorities were concerned that too many soldiers stamping their way across it in unison would threaten its suspension. It was in danger of being officially rather than accidentally demolished in the 1950s but a campaign was mounted to save it, led by the poet John Betjeman who wrote that, 'Shining with electric lights to show the way to Festival Gardens or grey and airy against the London sky, it is one of the beauties of the London river.'

11. **Tower Bridge: 1894**
One of the most familiar tourist sights of the city, Tower Bridge took eight years to construct and its co-designer was Sir John Wolfe-Barry, the son of the architect responsible for another very famous symbol of London, the Houses of Parliament. The upper span of the bridge, between the two towers, was originally a walkway, but it was closed in 1910 because it had become a haunt of prostitutes and thieves. It has recently been re-opened as part of the Tower Bridge Experience. When the port of London was at its busiest the bridge was raised several times a day but today, with markedly less traffic along the river, any ship wanting the bridge to lift must give 24 hours' notice. In 1952 a London bus was caught on the bridge when it was opening and the driver was forced to accelerate his vehicle across the widening gap. Just below Tower Bridge, marked by a sign, is 'Dead Man's Hole' where bodies thrown into the river from the Tower and surrounding districts were retrieved and stored in a mortuary before burial.

12. **Millennium Bridge: 2000**
Designed by Norman Foster, the pedestrian bridge linking Bankside and the City was closed within days of its opening in 2001 because of its inability to carry any more than a handful of pedestrians without wobbling alarmingly. Official statements talked of its 'pedestrian-induced vibration' and, in a flurry of mutual recrimination, architects blamed engineers and engineers

blamed architects for the fault. The bridge was closed for more than six months while structural changes were made to stop the wobbling and it re-opened in January 2002.

The Millennium Bridge

7 CITY GATES

The seven city gates, most of them built in the first instance by the Romans (although, like the Wall, they were regularly rebuilt and renovated through the centuries), were all demolished at the beginning of the 1760s. They were:

1. **Aldersgate**
    First built by the Romans but named after an otherwise unknown Saxon called Ealdred, the gate stood opposite what is now 62 Aldersgate Street and led out into Watling Street, the Roman road to Dover. It was the gate through which James I, having journeyed from Scotland, first entered his new capital city in 1603.

2. **Aldgate**
    When he was appointed Controller of the Customs for hides, skins and wools in the port of London in 1374, Geoffrey Chaucer was granted a lease on a dwelling above

Aldgate. The gate was demolished, along with the others, in the early 1760s, although it was briefly re-erected at Bethnal Green.

3. **Bishopsgate**
The gate takes its name from a seventh-century Bishop of London, Eorconweald, who had it rebuilt on its Roman foundations during his episcopacy. In the Middle Ages, the bishops of London made hinges for the gate and in return received one stick from every cart of wood that passed through it. The gate stood opposite where the NatWest Tower now stands.

4. **Cripplegate**
The derivation of its name – either from the cripples who gathered there to beg or from the fact that there was a hospital for cripples close to the site – would seem to be straightforward but scholars are not certain. It could derive from an Anglo-Saxon word 'crepel' meaning 'underground passage'. It was through Cripplegate that Elizabeth I rode into her capital for the first time as queen.

5. **Ludgate**
Traditionally supposed to have been built by the legendary King Lud in the first century BC, the gate was almost certainly, like most of the others, the work of the Romans. It stood opposite St Martin's Church on Ludgate Hill.

6. **Moorgate**
Not built until the fifteenth century, Moorgate led out of the City Wall into fields and fens beyond. Demolished in 1762, along with its older fellows, its stones were recycled and used to shore up London Bridge.

7. **Newgate**
As the name suggests, Newgate was built after the Romans had built many of the other city gates but it still

dated back to at least the ninth century and possibly even earlier. The prison, for which it is best remembered, was in existence in the area by the twelfth century.

22 TOWERS WITHIN THE TOWER OF LONDON

The Tower of London is not one single tower but a complex of buildings. The towers that make up the Tower are:

1. **Beauchamp Tower**
   Built by Edward I, the tower takes its name from a fourteenth-century prisoner, Thomas Beauchamp, Earl of Warwick. The Beauchamp Tower is home to some of the most elaborate inscriptions carved by those who were kept prisoner in Tudor times. Some show remarkably detailed heraldic symbols but one of the most moving is simply the name 'Jane', which refers to the nine-day queen, Lady Jane Grey, executed at the age of 17 in 1554, and was probably carved into the wall by her husband, Lord Guildford Dudley, who was imprisoned here before mounting the scaffold himself.

2. **Bell Tower**
   The second oldest of the towers, the Bell Tower was built in the reign of Richard the Lionheart. Sir Thomas More was imprisoned there in 1534, as was the future Elizabeth I, who was confined there during the reign of her sister Mary.

3. **Bloody Tower**
   Originally the Garden Tower, the Bloody Tower gained its more familiar name in the sixteenth century because it was the place where the young princes, sons of Edward IV, were supposed to have been done to death on the orders of their wicked uncle. The Bloody Tower has undoubtedly

seen other murders. It was the place where the Jacobean courtier and writer Sir Thomas Overbury met his end, finished off by a poisoned enema applied on the orders of a powerful noblewoman he had been foolhardy enough to cross.

4. **Bowyer Tower**
    According to tradition, the Bowyer Tower was where the Duke of Clarence, troublesome brother of Edward IV and Richard III, was drowned in a butt of malmsey wine. Shakespeare shows the murder in *Richard III*, although his setting is described simply as 'The Tower. London'.

5. **Brick Tower**
    Sir Walter Raleigh was imprisoned in the Brick Tower in 1592 after incurring Elizabeth I's displeasure by seducing one of her maids of honour, Elizabeth Throckmorton, making her pregnant and having the temerity to marry her in secret. The queen's servants were expected to seek her permission before marrying and, although Sir Walter was released from the Tower, the Raleighs were in disgrace for many years.

6. **Broad Arrow Tower**
    Part of Henry III's extensions to the Tower in the middle of the thirteenth century, the Broad Arrow Tower took its name from the motif that was stamped on goods to show they were the property of the crown.

7. **Byward Tower**
    Probably named for its proximity to the old Warders' Hall, this is the tower from which the chief warder emerges each night to perform the Ceremony of the Keys before locking the whole Tower complex for the night.

8. **Constable Tower**
    In the past, this tower has been the used as the official

accommodation of the Constable of the Tower. Today it contains a model of the Tower of London as it appeared in the Middle Ages.

9. **Cradle Tower**
    Built in the middle of the fourteenth century, the Cradle Tower owes its name not to a bed for a child but to a kind of hoist which allowed boats to be raised from the river to the level of the tower's gateway. It was from the Cradle Tower that the Jesuit priest John Gerard made his escape in 1597.

10. **Develin Tower**
    The furthest east of the towers and one not open to the public, the Develin Tower once opened onto a drawbridge which ran across the moat to the since-demolished Iron Gate.

11. **Devereux Tower**
    The tower is named after Queen Elizabeth's favourite, Robert Devereux, Earl of Essex, who was imprisoned here after his abortive coup against her in 1601. Essex had hoped that Londoners would rise to join him but most watched with indifference as he marched through the streets with a handful of men. He was captured, imprisoned in the tower that bears his name and executed on Tower Hill.

12. **Flint Tower**
    The tower is so named because of the flint stone used to build it. Like many of the towers within the complex it was largely reconstructed in Victorian times.

13. **Lanthorn Tower**
    The tower was named for the lantern that was placed at its top as a guide for boats on the Thames.

14. **Lion Tower**
    The Lion Tower, no longer in existence, stood on the site

of the present ticket office and refreshment room and it was where the Royal Menagerie was once housed. The menagerie was established during the reign of Henry III after gifts of three leopards from the Holy Roman Emperor and a polar bear from the king of Norway. With a chain around its neck to prevent it escaping, the polar bear would swim in the Thames near the Tower to catch its supper. Other animals followed, including an elephant from the king of France which is buried somewhere within the Tower of London, and the menagerie became one of the great sights of London for centuries. The animals were eventually sent to Regent's Park to the new London Zoo in the early 1830s. The tower was demolished some twenty years later, although the Lion Gate still stands.

15. **Martin Tower**

Built by Henry III, the Martin Tower was where Henry Percy, the ninth earl of Northumberland, known as the 'Wizard Earl' for his scientific and alchemical experiments, was imprisoned by James I for sixteen years on suspicion of involvement in the Gunpowder Plot. Also known as the Jewel Tower (the Crown Jewels were kept here from 1669 to 1841) this was the scene of Colonel Blood's attempt to steal the Crown Jewels. Eleven German spies faced a firing squad outside the tower in World War I.

16. **Middle Tower**

The main entrance for visitors to the Tower complex today, the Middle Tower, as the name suggests, once stood between the demolished Lion Tower and the Byward Tower.

17. **St Thomas's Tower**

Standing above Traitor's Gate, the tower takes its name from St Thomas à Becket who was Constable of the Tower in 1162. Sir Roger Casement, the former diplomat and Irish Nationalist who was accused of treason after attempting to transport arms from Germany for use in Dublin's Easter Rising, was held in this tower in 1916 before his trial and execution.

18. **Salt Tower**

The Salt Tower contains a number of elaborate carved inscriptions including one which was created by a man called Hugh Draper who was imprisoned on suspicion of witchcraft in 1561. This complicated diagram cut into the stone and intended for casting horoscopes has the words 'Hew Draper of Brystow made this sphere the 30 daye of Maye anno 1561'.

19. **Wakefield Tower**

Henry VI died in the Wakefield Tower and a ceremony in which lilies are placed on the spot where he was believed to have been murdered was instituted in 1923, paid for by Eton College as a mark of respect to the college's founder.

20. **Wardrobe Tower**

Partially demolished in the reign of Charles II, the Wardrobe Tower was originally built on the foundation of a Roman bastion and was the place where the king's clothing, armour and equipment were kept in the Middle Ages.

21. **Well Tower**

Built at the time that Edward I was expanding the Tower complex in the thirteenth century, the Well Tower contained two shafts used for drawing up water.

22. **White Tower**

The oldest part of the Tower, this was built in the reign of William the Conqueror.

See also **4 People Who Escaped from the Tower of London**, pp. 121–2.

8 DEEP-LEVEL SHELTERS

During World War II, eight deep-level shelters were built under existing tube stations to house key government workers and essential equipment during air raids. Later in the war, some were opened to the general public and one, at Goodge Street, was used by General Eisenhower and his entourage during the planning of the D-Day landings. Since the war the shelters have rarely been used, although one was converted for a time into a telephone exchange, but they all still exist and the entrances to them can still be seen at ground level. The eight are:

1. Belsize Park
2. Camden Town
3. Goodge Street
4. Chancery Lane
5. Stockwell
6. Clapham North
7. Clapham Common
8. Clapham South

Stockwell deep-level shelter entrance

9 HISTORIC LONDON HOTELS

1. **Claridge's**

   The actor Spencer Tracy once remarked: 'Not that I intend to die, but when I do, I don't want to go to heaven, I want to go to Claridge's.' William Claridge, butler to an aristocratic family, bought a small hotel in Brook Street and, in 1854, expanded his business by adding another hotel in the same street called Mivart's. 'Claridge's, late Mivart's', as it was known for several years, had a high reputation as the London haunt of Continental aristocrats and its prestige was enhanced in 1860 when Queen Victoria visited the French empress, Eugènie, who had taken up temporary residence there during her stay in England. During World War II the exiled king of Yugoslavia was living at Claridge's when his wife gave birth to a son and heir. Churchill declared the suite Yugoslav territory for a day to ensure that the child would have a right to the throne – a right that the 60-year-old prince still maintains in 2006.

2. **The Ritz**

   Although he had already retired from the Savoy following financial scandals and mental health problems, the hotel was built to the specifications of the legendary hotelier César Ritz and it became what he called 'the small house to which I am very proud to see my name attached'. Opened in 1906, the Ritz immediately became a haunt of the rich and the famous. In the years since, the Aga Khan and John Paul Getty have had suites there, minor European royalty in exile from republican regimes have haunted its corridors and Hollywood stars have fled the attentions of their fans by retiring to its rooms. In 1921, Charlie Chaplin, returning for the first time to the city he had left as an unknown music-hall performer, nearly caused a riot outside the Ritz and forty policemen had to be employed in order to escort him in safety through adoring but demanding fans. The Ritz is now owned by the famously reclusive Barclay Brothers.

3. **Brown's**

The hotel was opened by James Brown, a manservant, and his wife Sarah, who had been a maid to Lady Byron, in 1837. It was where Alexander Graham Bell made the first long-distance telephone call in England in 1876. Sitting in a room in Brown's, he called a colleague who was in a house near Ravenscourt Park. Theodore Roosevelt was married in London and he was staying at Brown's when he walked to his wedding to Edith Kermit Carow in St George's, Hanover Square. Franklin D. Roosevelt and his wife Eleanor spent their honeymoon in the hotel. During World War II the Dutch government in exile declared war on Japan from Room 36 in Brown's.

4. **The Savoy**

The Savoy was built by the impresario Richard D'Oyly Carte, who first staged the Gilbert and Sullivan operettas, and opened in 1889. Its first manager was César Ritz, its first chef Auguste Escoffier. Oscar Wilde and Lord Alfred Douglas, at the height of the affair which eventually ruined Wilde, stayed at the Savoy frequently. In his third trial in 1895 Wilde was, amongst other counts, charged and found guilty of committing acts of gross indecency with unknown male persons in Rooms 346 and 362 of the Savoy. The short road leading to the Savoy is the only thoroughfare in England where drivers drive on the right, a custom that dates back to the time of horse-drawn hansom cabs. The hotel's staff entrance is now in Fountain Court, where William Blake lived in the last years of his life.

5. **The Langham**

Opened in 1865 with a celebratory dinner for two thousand guests, including the Prince of Wales, the Langham rapidly established itself as one of London's finest hotels with an elite clientele. In a fraud case at the Old Bailey in the 1880s a witness expressed her faith in the bona fides of one of the defendants by saying, 'I knew he must be a perfect gentleman – why, he had rooms at the Langham.' The hotel was the scene of a meal which produced two of the finest short novels of the late nineteenth century. Joseph Stoddart, publisher of *Lippincott's Magazine* in America, was visiting London and staying at the Langham when he entertained Oscar Wilde and Arthur Conan Doyle to dinner. He commissioned 'The Sign of Four' from Doyle and 'The Picture of Dorian Gray' from Wilde.

6. **The Dorchester**

Built on the site of the mansion Dorchester House, the hotel was opened in 1931. Famous guests over the years have included Somerset Maugham, Elizabeth Taylor, Danny Kaye (who had performed in cabaret at the hotel in the years before his fame was such that he could afford to stay in one of its suites), Jackie Collins and General Eisenhower, who had a set of rooms in the Dorchester while he was planning the Normandy invasions. Prince Philip's stag night was celebrated in the hotel. Foyle's Literary Luncheons began at the Dorchester in the 1930s and still continue.

7. **The Connaught**

The hotel was originally known as the Coburg but German-sounding names were unlikely to improve business during World War I and it changed its name. General de Gaulle stayed in the hotel for a period when he was leader of the Free French in London during World War II. So too did the crime writer Raymond Chandler, creator of Philip Marlowe, who visited London in the 1950s, but he was asked to leave when a woman was found in his room.

8. **The Cadogan**

Built in 1887, the Cadogan is the hotel in which Oscar Wilde was arrested on charges of gross indecency. After the collapse of his libel case against the Marquess of Queensberry, who had accused him in a misspelled message of being a 'somdomite', Wilde was clearly threatened by prosecution himself and friends urged him to flee to the Continent. Apparently paralysed by indecision, Wilde remained in room 118 at the Cadogan with his lover, Queensberry's son Lord Alfred Douglas, sipping glasses of hock and seltzer until officers arrived to arrest him.

9. **The Carlton**

The Carlton stood in the Haymarket and was opened in 1899 by the experienced team of hotelier César Ritz and chef Auguste Escoffier who had had such success at the Savoy. Three years after opening, the Carlton was to be the scene of a lavish banquet to celebrate the coronation of Edward VII and preparations for it were underway when news came through that the king required an appendectomy. The coronation, and therefore the banquet, were to be postponed. The workaholic and perfectionist Ritz was so dismayed that he had a breakdown from which he never properly recovered, although he went on to open the hotel in Piccadilly that still bears his name. Bombed in World War II, the Carlton remained empty for years after the war until it was finally demolished in 1958. New Zealand House now stands on the site.

10 LONDON LANDMARKS THAT HAVE BEEN DEMOLISHED

1. **The Adelphi**

   Built by the Adam brothers in the 1760s and 1770s ('Adelphi' is the Greek for 'brothers'), this was a grand development of houses alongside the Thames. Using the ruined palace of the Roman Emperor Diocletian at Split in present-day Croatia as a model, the brothers created what they intended should be the most prestigious living accommodation in the Georgian city. The scheme was plagued by financial difficulties from the beginning and, at one point, a lottery had to be organised to raise money to continue but tenants did eventually move into the buildings. The actor David Garrick was one of the first. In later years famous tenants have included George Bernard Shaw, Thomas Hardy and the theatrical impresario Richard D'Oyly Carte. The development was largely demolished in 1936.

2. **Euston Arch**

   The original entrance to Euston station was designed by Sir Philip Hardwick and inspired by the Roman architecture he had seen on his travels in Italy. Although described by the architect AW Pugin as 'a piece of Brobdingnagian absurdity' when it was first erected in 1837, this seventy-two-foot-high Doric Arch became a much-loved landmark and there was uproar when British Rail, claiming that it stood in the way of progress and new platforms, announced that it would be demolished. Despite a campaign to save the Euston Arch, led by the poet John Betjeman, it was knocked down in 1962.

3. **St James Theatre**

   Built in King Street, SW1, in 1835, this was the theatre where several of Oscar Wilde's plays, including *Lady Windermere's Fan* and *The Importance of Being Earnest*, were first staged. In the early fifties it was under the management of Laurence Olivier and Vivien Leigh but it was closed in 1957 and demolished despite protests including one which involved Vivien Leigh heckling the peers in a debate in the House of Lords until she was forcibly removed.

4. **The Pantheon**

Opened in January 1772 in Oxford Street, the Pantheon was intended as an assembly rooms which would rival the pleasure gardens at Vauxhall and Ranelagh. Its main room was a vast rotunda modelled on Santa Sophia in Constantinople and, according to the writer and musicologist Charles Burney, it was 'regarded both by natives and foreigners as the most elegant structure in Europe, if not on the globe'. After initial success, visitors to the assembly rooms began to decline in numbers and the Pantheon went through several incarnations. It was a theatre until it was gutted by fire in 1792. For a short period it was the home of the grandly named but largely unsuccessful 'National Institution for Improving Manufactures of the United Kingdom and the Arts Connected Therewith'. For thirty years in the middle of the nineteenth century, it was a bazaar. In 1937 the building was bought from the wine merchants Gilbeys by Marks and Spencer who demolished it and built their Oxford Street store on the site.

5. **The Egyptian Hall**

Built in Piccadilly in 1812, with a facade that supposedly was in the form of an ancient Egyptian temple, this was an exhibition hall intended to hold 'upwards of Fifteen Thousand Natural and Foreign Curiosities, Antiques and Productions of the Fine Arts'. One of the earliest successes of the owner, William Bullock, was a display of Napoleonic relics in 1816, including the former Emperor's carriage. Throughout the nineteenth century, the hall was one of the chief venues for exhibitions and entertainments in the city. It was at the Egyptian Hall that the 25-inch tall American Charles Stratton, known as General Tom Thumb, appeared in 1844. Other sensations advertised at the hall included a 'Living Male Child, with four hands, four arms, four legs, four feet, and two bodies, born at Staleybridge, Manchester' in 1838, 'the Eureka, a machine for composing hexameter Latin verses' in 1845 and, appropriately, *Bonomi's Panorama of the Nile*, 800 feet long: representing 1720 miles distance, closing with the Pyramids and Sphinx' in 1850. The hall was demolished in 1905 and an office block, now called Egyptian House, was built on the site.

6. **Columbia Market**

Built in Bethnal Green, using money provided by the philanthropist Baroness Burdett-Coutts, Columbia Market was intended to tempt the local costermongers off the streets and into its elaborate buildings, which included a huge Gothic hall that looked more like King's College Chapel in Cambridge than it did a commercial centre. The costermongers, resolutely unimpressed, stayed in the streets and the market was a colossal failure. Let as workshops in the 1880s, the building was finally demolished in 1958.

7. **Colosseum**

The Colosseum was a large rotunda in what is now Cambridge Terrace, designed by Decimus Burton and built between 1823 and 1826. It contained a vast panorama of London based on drawings made by Thomas Hornor from a wooden observatory erected above the ball and cross on the top of St Paul's dome. Hornor and his backer ran up huge debts and promptly absconded to avoid their creditors. The Colosseum also tempted visitors with a

Hall of Mirrors, a Gothic aviary and a 'Swiss chalet' with a panorama of Mont Blanc. By the 1860s the building had fallen into disrepair and it was demolished in 1875.

8.   **Astley's Amphitheatre**
Opened in the late eighteenth century by the former circus strongman and cavalry soldier Philip Astley, a man described as having 'the proportions of a Hercules and the voice of a Senator', this stood in Lambeth near Westminster Bridge and was a venue where horses performed elaborate feats and battles were re-staged. Part circus and part theatre-on-horseback, the shows at Astley's remained popular long after the death of Philip Astley in 1814. The amphitheatre was finally demolished in the 1890s.

9.   **Exeter Change**
Situated just off the Strand, Exeter Change was a kind of historic version of a shopping arcade – a large building subdivided into smaller units run by small traders and shopkeepers. In the early decades of the nineteenth century, however, it was most famous for its menagerie run by one Edward Cross. The roars of the lions and the tigers could be heard in the street outside and often frightened horses. Byron, recording a visit to the Exeter Change menagerie in 1813, wrote that 'The elephant took and gave me my money again – took off my hat – opened a door – trunked a whip – and behaved so well, that I wish he was my butler.' This elephant may well have been Chunee, the menagerie's best-known inhabitant who met an unfortunate death in 1826. After years of placidity, Chunee became unmanageable and had to be shot by soldiers specially hired for the job. More than 150 bullets were fired at the beast and even then it had to be finished off by its keeper wielding a spear. When improvements were made to the Strand in 1829, Exeter Change was demolished.

10. **Northumberland House**

The town house of the Dukes of Northumberland, this Jacobean mansion stood at the western end of the Strand from the early part of the seventeenth century to the 1870s. In the 1860s approaches were made to the fifth duke offering to purchase the house and gardens with a view to creating a better access from Trafalgar Square to the Victoria Embankment. The Duke refused the offers and it was only after he died that his successor, the sixth duke, sold it for the then colossal sum of £500,000. It was destroyed in 1874 to create Northumberland Avenue. Other less architecturally distinguished buildings, including one that housed Coles's Truss Manufactory, were also lost at the same time.

7 LESSER-KNOWN FACTS ABOUT NELSON'S COLUMN

1. **Not the First**

The column was not erected until 1843, nearly forty years after Nelson's death at Trafalgar. By that time there were already a number of other Nelson's Columns in existence, including one in Dublin, erected in 1807, and one in Great Yarmouth, erected in 1819.

2. **Landseer's Lions**

The sculpted lions at the foot of the column, not put in place until 1867, were the work of Sir Edwin Landseer. He used a dead lion as a model for the sculptures but the beast became so decomposed and smelly that it was almost impossible for him to work in his studio and neighbours called the police to investigate the source of the stench.

3. **Hitler's Desire**

After his troops had conquered Britain, Hitler planned

to ship Nelson's Column back to Berlin. A plan drawn up by the SS noted that 'the Nelson Column represents for England a symbol of British Naval might and world domination. It would be an impressive way of underlining the German Victory if the Nelson Column were to be transferred to Berlin'.

4. **The Czar's Contribution**
   The Czar of Russia, Nicholas I, donated £500 to the fund established for the building of the column.

5. **Meal at the Top**
   On 23 October 1843 fourteen of the stonemasons who had been working on the construction of the column ate a meal on the platform at its top just before the statue of Nelson was placed on it.

6. **Parachute Drop**
   A professional stuntman protesting against Chinese policy towards Tibet parachuted off the top of the column in May 2003.

7. **Trafalgar Day**
   In the past, Trafalgar Day was marked by the hoisting on Nelson's Column of flags which spelled out Nelson's signal – 'England expects that every man will do his duty'. The ceremony has not been carried out for many years.

6 OVERLOOKED MEMORIALS IN LONDON

1. **Chilianwalla Memorial**
   Standing in the grounds of Chelsea Hospital, this memorial is dedicated 'To the memory of 255 officers, non-commissioned officers and privates of the 24th regiment who fell at Chilianwalla, 13 January 1849.' Nearly everyone apart from historians specialising in

obscure imperial military campaigns has now forgotten the Battle of Chilianwalla, which was fought in the Punjab between British forces and a Sikh army. As the memorial records, the encounter was a costly one for the British and the battle ended indecisively, but the Sikhs were comprehensively defeated the following month at the Battle of Gujarat.

2. **Imperial Camel Corps**

   Formed in early 1916 to serve in Palestine and the Middle East, the Imperial Camel Corps was only in existence for a few years, but a memorial to the 346 men of its battalions who lost their lives in World War I stands in Victoria Embankment Gardens. The statue of a cameleer mounted on a camel looks slightly incongruous in its setting near the Thames.

3. **Burton Monument**

   In the churchyard of St Mary Magdalene, Mortlake, sits the eye-catching mausoleum of Sir Richard Burton, the nineteenth-century explorer, translator of the Kama Sutra and one of the few Europeans of his time to visit Mecca. Taking the form of an Arab tent made from stone, it is an unusual sight in a suburban burial ground.

4. **Speke Memorial**

   Every day thousands see the Speke Memorial, a large obelisk in Kensington Gardens, but few will know that it is so called or who Speke was. Another Victorian explorer, he was first a companion and friend of Sir Richard Burton (see above) and then a bitter enemy after they fell out over the vexed question of whether or not Speke had discovered the source of the Nile on his travels. Speke died in mysterious circumstances (either a hunting accident or suicide) in September 1864, just hours before he was due to debate the issue publicly with Burton. The obelisk was erected soon after his death.

5. **Heminge and Condell Memorial**

In the gardens created from the churchyard of the vanished St Mary Aldermanbury, a bust of Shakespeare on a memorial might suggest it commemorates the playwright but it actually recognises the achievements of John Heminge and Henry Condell. They were fellow actors of Shakespeare who supervised the publication of the First Folio of his works. As it says on the memorial, 'To their disinterested affection, the world owes all that it calls Shakespeare. They alone collected his dramatic writings, regardless of pecuniary loss and without the hope of any profit, gave them to the world. They thus merited the gratitude of mankind.'

6. **Jehangir's Fountain**

Situated in the north of Regent's Park, this fountain, which was unveiled in the 1860s, was erected by the splendidly named Metropolitan Drinking Fountain and Cattle Trough Association, using money provided by a wealthy Bombay trader called Sir Cowasjee Jehangir. He intended the fountain as a token of gratitude to the people of London for the protection he and his fellow Parsees enjoyed under British rule in India.

5 BEASTLY SITES IN LONDON

1. **The Pets' Cemetery in Hyde Park**

Behind the old gatekeeper's cottage at Victoria Gate, Hyde Park, is a nineteenth-century pets' cemetery that began when the Duchess of Cambridge needed somewhere to give a beloved pet a decent burial. Close to 300 little memorials survive from the years in which it was open to receive the bodies of dear departed pets. Many carry epitaphs which record the circumstances of death or express such sentiments as 'Not One of Them is Forgotten Before God'.

2. **Gravestone of German Ambassador's Dog**

In what was formerly the garden of 9 Carlton House Terrace, the German Embassy in the 1930s, there is a small memorial which reads 'Giro: ein treuer Begleiter!' ('Giro: a true companion!'). Giro, who died in 1934 when he bit into an exposed electrical wire, was an Alsatian which belonged to Leopold von Hoesch, ambassador from 1932–36. The memorial is still clearly visible in what is now a small space next to the Duke of York steps.

3. **Jamrach's**

At the north entrance to Tobacco Dock, near to the headquarters of News International, there is a statue of a small boy in front of a tiger. This records an incident in the mid-nineteenth century when a fully grown Bengal tiger escaped from Jamrach's, an emporium run by an importer of animals for zoos and circuses, and began to make its way down the Commercial Road. According to a plaque near the statue, 'Everybody scattered except an eight year old boy, who, having never seen such a large cat, went up to it with the intent of stroking his nose. A tap of the great soft paw stunned the boy and, picking him up by his jacket, the tiger walked down a side alley. Mr Jamrach, having discovered the empty box, came running up and, thrusting his bare hands into the tiger's throat, forced the beast to let his captive go. The little boy was unscathed and the subdued tiger was led back to his cage.'

4. **Charles Cruft's Grave**

Charles Cruft was born in Bloomsbury in 1846 and he began his career as a teenager selling pet food at James Spratt's shop in Holborn. In 1886 he held his first 'Great Terrier Show' at the Royal Aquarium, a palace of Victorian entertainment which once stood where the Methodist Central Hall now stands, opposite Westminster Abbey. It attracted 500 entries. The show became an annual event and grew in fame as the years went by. When Cruft died at the age of ninety-one in 1938 and was buried in Highgate Cemetery they were renowned throughout the world. Ironically, it is said that Cruft himself did not much care for dogs and greatly preferred cats.

5. ## The Savoy Cat

Created in the 1920s by the sculptor Basil Ionides, Kaspar the Savoy Cat is a three-foot-high, black wooden cat which is used in the dining rooms of the hotel when thirteen people sit down to a meal. The unlucky number is brought up to fourteen by Kaspar who is placed at the table, with a napkin around his neck, and provided with each of the dishes in turn. Hotel legend has it that the tradition of avoiding a dinner party of thirteen in the Savoy began in 1898 when the host of such a dinner was fatally shot soon after giving it. At first numbers were made up by a member of the Savoy staff but Kaspar, once he had been sculpted, became a better choice because he ate none of the food and could not gossip about anything he heard at the table.

12 LONDON RUNS IN THE KNOWLEDGE

'The Knowledge' is the name given to the course of study any prospective licensed London taxi driver has to take before he or she can gain the driver's licence and badge. 'The Knowledge' is tested by the official body in charge of cabs, the Public Carriage Office, and takes the shape of hundreds of London 'runs' which the candidate must memorise together with all the places of interest (museums, hospitals, government buildings, hotels etc.) along the routes. Here are just a dozen of these runs:

1. Manor House Station N4 to Gibson Square N1
2. Thornhill Square N1 to Queen Square WC1
3. Chancery Lane Station WC1 to Rolls Road SE1
4. Pages Walk SE1 to St Martins Lane WC2
5. Australian High Commission WC2 to Paddington Station W2
6. Lancaster Gate W2 to Royal Free Hospital NW3
7. Fitzjohns Avenue NW3 to Fitzhardinge Street W1
8. Ritz Hotel W1 to Battersea Park Station SW8
9. Ponton Road SW8 to Camberwell Grove SE5
10. Knatchbull Road SE5 to Surrey Quays Station SE16
11. Timber Pond Road SE16 to Grocers Hall Court EC2
12. Barbican EC2 to Mile End Station E3

London cab

THE 14 CHURCHES AND WHAT THEIR BELLS SAY IN THE SONG 'ORANGES AND LEMONS'

There have been a number of explanations of the verses, including the theory that they allude to a man's journey from prison to scaffold and to the bells of London ringing to mark the stages of that journey. Wherever the origins of the rhyme lie, it is clear that it is rooted in the everyday life of London in the centuries before the Great Fire and reflects the major role the bells of the city played in the lives of its citizens.

Gay go up and gay go down/To ring the bells of London town

1. **Bull's eyes and targets/Say the bells of St Marg'ret's**
   St Margaret's stands in Lothbury and the reference in the rhyme is to the archery practice held in fields near the church.

2. **Brickbats and tiles/Say the bells of St Giles**
   St Giles Cripplegate in Wood Street was the church in which Cromwell was married. The reference is to the builders that worked nearby.

3. **Oranges and Lemons/Say the bells of St Clements**
   The church is St Clement in Eastcheap. The wharf where ships carrying citrus fruit from the Mediterranean were unloaded was close to the church, hence the reference to oranges and lemons. The song has no original connection to St Clement Danes in The Strand but a vicar of the church laid claim to it in the 1920s and not only do the bells now ring out the tune three times a day but an Oranges and Lemons service is held there each year.

4. **Pancake and fritters/Say the bells of St Peter's**

   St Peter upon Cornhill is reputed to be the oldest place of Christian worship in London. The pancakes and fritters were probably the food provided for workers in the area.

5. **Two sticks and an apple/Say the bells at Whitechapel**

   The church is probably St Mary, Whitechapel High Street although the rhyme may refer to the Whitechapel Bell Foundry which has been in existence since the sixteenth century.

6. **Old Father Baldpate/Say the slow bells at Aldgate**

   The church is almost certainly St Botolph, Aldgate High Street and the 'old father baldpate' is St Botolph himself who, in common with many other male saints, is often depicted as bald.

7. **Maids in white aprons/Say the bells at St Catherine's**

   The church is St Katherine Cree in Leadenhall Street. 'Maids in white aprons' is a reference to the women who sold goods in the nearby Leadenhall Market and the costume they traditionally wore.

8. **Pokers and tongs/Say the bells of St John's**

   The reference is probably to St John's Chapel in the Tower and the pokers and tongs are the instruments of torture used on those imprisoned in the Tower.

9. **Kettles and pans/Say the bells of St Anne's**

   St Anne and St Agnes is a church in Gresham Street. The kettles and pans refer to the utensils made by coppersmiths who worked in the area.

10. **You owe me five farthings/Say the bells of St Martin's**

    The church is St Martin Ongar in Martin Lane and moneylenders traded nearby.

11. **When will you pay me?/Say the bells at Old Bailey**

    The bells of Old Bailey would have been those of St Sepulchre-without-Newgate and the question would have been one asked of the debtors who were kept in the prison.

12. **When I grow rich/Say the bells at Shoreditch**

    St Leonard's in Shoreditch High Street was at the heart of one of the poorest areas of the city and the statement of the bells was unlikely to come true for most of the local inhabitants.

13. **Pray, when will that be?/Say the bells of Stepney**

    The church is St Dunstan and All Saints in Stepney High Street.

14. **I'm sure I don't know/Says the great bell at Bow**

    The great bell at Bow is a reference to the bells of St Mary-le-Bow within hearing distance of which, according to tradition, true cockneys must be born.

    Here comes a candle to light you to bed/Here comes a chopper to chop off your head

2

PEOPLE

11 Unlikely Londoners

6 Well-Known Americans (1 Inanimate) Who Were Actually Londoners

6 Exotic Visitors to London

7 Visitors to the British Museum Reading Room in Fact and Fiction

10 People (2 Fictional) Whose Names have been Used in Cockney Rhyming Slang

12 Fictional Londoners

6 London Lord Mayors

10 Famous People Who Have Spoken at Speakers' Corner

7 Inmates of Bedlam

4 Mummified Londoners

6 Men Who Founded London Hospitals

10 Men Who Founded Famous London Stores

6 London Chefs Past and Present

6 London Cross-Dressers

5 Famous Londoners Who Have a Blue Plaque (Or Several)

5 Londoners Who Should Have a Blue Plaque But Don't

11 UNLIKELY LONDONERS

The following famous people are not primarily associated with London but they all spent long or significant periods of their lives in the city:

1. **Voltaire**
   The French *philosophe* lived in London for nearly three years in the 1720s, after being exiled from France following a bitter quarrel with a powerful nobleman. He admired both the English and their system of government, although the feeling was not always reciprocated. On one occasion, it is said that he was chased through the streets of London by a mob enraged by the fact that he was so obviously French. Cornered, he saved himself by his eloquence. 'Brave Englishmen,' he said, 'am I not already unfortunate enough not to have been born among you?' The brave Englishmen were so impressed by this admission of their superiority to the French that they carried him in triumph back to his lodgings. If the story is true, the lodgings may have been those in Maiden Lane, where he lived in 1727–28, now marked by a plaque.

2. & 3. **Arthur Rimbaud and Paul Verlaine**
   The two poets left France together for England in September 1872, seeking an anonymity in which to conduct their intense affair which Paris could not provide. Rimbaud ended by spending more of his life in London than he did in Paris. Lodging in Howland Street and then in Great College Street, Camden, they advertised themselves as teachers of French but it seems unlikely they had any pupils. Most of their time was spent drinking and quarrelling in assorted dives in Soho. Rimbaud liked London and wrote parts of his most famous works, *Illuminations* and *A Season in Hell* in the city. Verlaine was less impressed, particularly by English food. Oxtail

soup appalled him. 'Fie on such a horror!' he wrote, 'A man's sock with a rotten clitoris floating in it.'

4. **Edgar Allan Poe**

Born in Boston, Massachusetts, Poe nonetheless lived in London as a boy and went to Manor House School in Stoke Newington, which he described in later life as 'a misty looking village of England, where there were a vast number of gigantic and gnarled trees'.

5. **Ho Chi Minh**

Ho Chi Minh

The future President of North Vietnam worked as a vegetable cook at the Carlton Hotel (destroyed in the Blitz and now the site of New Zealand House) in 1914. The restaurant in the hotel was a favourite haunt of Churchill at the time and the vegetables he ate may well have been prepared by the man who later founded the Vietnamese Communist Party.

6. **Mahatma Gandhi**

Gandhi arrived in London as a law student in the late 1880s and lived for a period in Baron's Court Road. He returned to the city in 1931 as the spiritual leader of Indian nationalism. 'The little man with no proper clothes on', as George V once described him, was even received at Buckingham Palace.

7. **Vincent Van Gogh**

As a young man, Van Gogh spent some time in London. He arrived first in June 1873 and stayed for more than a year, working as an assistant at the art dealers Goupil and Co. in Bedford Street, Covent Garden. During this period he lived at 87 Hackford Road, SW9, lodging with a woman called Mrs Loyer. After only weeks the emotionally volatile Van Gogh had decided that he had fallen in love with his landlady's daughter, a girl called Eugenie. She rejected his proposal. Van Gogh's second stay in London was in the summer and autumn of 1876 when he lived and worked in Isleworth. A local clergyman was impressed by the young Dutchman's religious fervour and employed him as a part-time preacher in his church.

8. **Sigmund Freud**

The city with which Freud is inescapably associated is Vienna. He arrived there with his family from the small Moravian town of Freiburg (now Pribor in the Czech Republic) when he was four years old and he lived there until he was an old man of eighty-two. However Freud was also, briefly, a Londoner. When the Nazis overran Austria in 1938 his life was in danger, since he was not only a Jew but a Jew who had advanced supposedly decadent and demoralising theories about human nature. Strenuous efforts were made by well-wishers and supporters to get him and his family out of Vienna. He came to London in 1938, briefly living in Primrose Hill, and then moved to 20 Maresfield Gardens, Hampstead, where he spent the last year of his life, writing *Moses and Monotheism*, his last significant work, and suffering from cancer of the jaw, which claimed his life on 23 September 1939. The house in Maresfield Gardens is now a museum devoted to Freud's life and work where visitors can see one of the famous couches on which the psychoanalyst's patients reclined.

9. **Alois Hitler**

In June 1910, Adolf Hitler's older half-brother married an Irishwoman, Bridget Dowling, in London where he was working as a waiter and they lived briefly in Percy Street, Fitzrovia. The story that his half-brother visited them there that year is as unlikely to be true as the better-known claim, the basis for Beryl Bainbridge's novel *Young Adolf*, that the future German dictator spent time in Liverpool, where Alois moved in 1911. Alois returned to Germany in the summer before World War I began and remained there for the rest of his life. During the Third Reich he ran a restaurant in Berlin popular with SS troops but he had little, if any, contact with his younger half-brother. He died in 1956.

10. **Jean-Paul Marat**
The French revolutionary, famously murdered in his bath by Charlotte Corday, settled in London in the 1770s, working as a physician, and, in 1776, he published a book on diseases of the eye which he dedicated to the Royal Society.

11. **Peter the Great**
The Russian Tsar toured Europe in the late 1690s in order to study Western technology, especially shipbuilding. Staying in England for four months, he rented a house called Sayes Court in Deptford from the diarist John Evelyn. The Tsar proved a tenant from hell, destroying Evelyn's carefully tended gardens and taking delight in being pushed through the hedges on a wheelbarrow by his servants. Sayes Court Park stands on the site of the garden Peter ruined, and a statue of the Tsar was erected in 2001 in Deptford to commemorate the visit.

6 WELL-KNOWN AMERICANS (1 INANIMATE) WHO WERE ACTUALLY LONDONERS

1. **John Harvard**
The man who gave his name to one of America's most prestigious universities only spent a little over a year in America. He was born in Southwark, the son of a butcher, in November 1607 and was baptised in St Saviour's

Church, now Southwark Cathedral. After graduating from Cambridge, Harvard, a man of Puritan beliefs, emigrated to the new settlements in America but died there of consumption in 1638. He left £780, half his estate, and his library to a college that had been founded in Cambridge, Massachusetts, two years earlier. The college is now Harvard University.

2. **William Penn**

Born in London in 1644, the man who founded Pennsylvania and named it, not after himself, but his deceased father, was baptised in All Hallows, Barking. Pepys knew and worked with the older Penn, who was an admiral, and, with his eye for women, described Penn's wife as a 'well-looked, fat, short old Dutch woman, but one who hath been heretofore pretty handsome'. The younger Penn was able to establish his colony in the New World because his father had loaned Charles II £16,000 during the years the king was in impoverished exile. Twenty years after the Restoration Charles eventually discharged his debt to the elder Penn, by that time long dead, by granting land in America to his son.

3. **Samuel Gompers**

One of the most significant figures in the American labour movement and President of the American Federation of Labor for nearly forty years, Gompers has parks, schools and even a naval vessel in the US named after him but he was born in Tenter Street, Spitalfields in 1850. Briefly schooled at the Jews' Free School in Bell Lane, he went to work for an East End shoemaker at the age of ten and emigrated to America with his family three years later.

4. **Abe Sapperstein**

The Harlem Globetrotters have been one of the most famous black sports teams in American history but their founder was neither black nor American. Abe Sapperstein, a Jewish businessman, was born in Flower and Dean Street (now Lolesworth Close) in London's East End in 1900. Emigrating to the States when young, he created and coached the Globetrotters, then known as the Savoy Big Five, in Chicago in the 1920s.

5. **Bob Hope**

An American institution when he died at the age of 100, Hope was born in Craigton Road, Eltham in 1903. According to Hope himself, in a much-repeated joke, 'I left England at the age of four when I found out I couldn't be king.' His family left London in 1907 and emigrated to Cleveland, Ohio where, as a teenage dancer, he was to join the vaudeville circuit and launch himself on an eighty-year career on stage and screen.

6. **Liberty Bell**

The bell which rang in Philadelphia in July 1776 to summon citizens to hear the reading of the Declaration of Independence is now a cherished, if cracked, symbol of American liberties but it was not made in America. It was cast at the Whitechapel Bell Foundry in Whitechapel Road, London in 1752 and prophetic instructions were given to inscribe the biblical verse 'Proclaim liberty throughout all the land unto all the inhabitants thereof' on the side of it. The Whitechapel Bell Foundry, listed in the Guinness Book of Records as Britain's oldest manufacturing company was established in 1570 and is still in business now. In 1858 it also cast Big Ben, the bell in the clock tower at the Palace of Westminster.

6 EXOTIC VISITORS TO LONDON

1. **Pocahontas**

    The story of Pocahontas and how she saved the life of Captain John Smith when he was held captive by her father Powhatan, a chief of the Algonquian Indians, is one of the best-known events in America's early colonial history and has been much embellished and mythologised over the years. Less well known is the fact that Pocahontas later married an Englishman, John Rolfe, and travelled to London in 1616. She was presented at court and, while she was

    1616 engraving of Pocahontas by Simon van de Passe, the only portrait made within her lifetime

    staying in a house in Brentford, she met Captain Smith once more. The arrival of an Indian princess caused a stir in London. Pocahontas sat for a portrait (which survives only as an engraving used to illustrate a 1624 book on the colony in Virginia) and she is supposed to have met the playwright Ben Jonson who writes, in a play called *The Staple of News* of 'blessed Pokahontas ... great king's daughter of Virginia'. When John Rolfe decided to return to America Pocahontas was to accompany him, but by this time she was seriously ill, possibly with tuberculosis. She died at Gravesend in March 1617, aged about twenty-two, and is buried in the churchyard there.

2. **Cherokee Indian Chiefs**

    Seven Cherokee Indians were taken to England in 1730 by a British army officer called Sir Alexander Cuming.

Acting largely on his own initiative, Cuming had travelled through Cherokee territory in America, persuading the Indians that they would be better off allied to the British than to the French. Taking a delegation of Cherokees across the Atlantic to meet George II was the last stage in his campaign to get the Indians to accept British sovereignty. It is not clear whether or not the men who arrived in London were actually chieftains rather than simply the most adventurous members of the tribe, nor whether they fully understood the ceremonies in which Cuming involved them, but they made a big impression on Londoners who saw them. 'On Wednesday the Indian Chiefs were carried from their lodgings in King-street, Covent Garden, to the Plantation Office at Whitehall, guarded by two Files of Musqueteers,' one writer recorded. 'When they were brought up to the Lords Commissioners, they sang four or five songs in their country language; after which the interpreter was ordered to let them know, that they were sent for there to join in peace with King George and his people ...'

3. **Omai**

The first Polynesian to visit Britain, Omai arrived in London in 1774, having travelled from his native Tahiti on Captain Cook's ship, the *Adventure*. Introduced to George III and Queen Charlotte at Kew Palace, Omai is supposed to have demonstrated his command of English by greeting the king with the words, 'How do, King Tosh'. Seen as a living example of the Romantic ideal of the 'noble savage', Omai was fêted wherever he went. He met Dr Johnson, among many others, who wrote to a friend describing the encounter: 'Lord Mulgrave and he dined one day at Streatham; they sat with their backs to the light fronting me, so that I could not see distinctly; and there was so little of the savage in Omai, that I was afraid to speak to either, lest I should mistake one for the other'. He returned to the South Seas in 1777 but his visit was remembered for many years afterwards. One of the great stage successes of 1785 was a play, *Omai or A Trip Round the World*, based (very loosely) on his life, and performed at the Theatre Royal, Covent Garden.

4. The Hottentot Venus

Saarjite Baartman, known as the Hottentot Venus, was brought from South Africa to London in 1810 by a ship's surgeon who put her on display as a medical and anthropological curiosity. Exhibited, sometimes naked, in a cage in a hall in Piccadilly, the Hottentot Venus became an object of prurient fascination. Her enlarged buttocks and elongated labia proved particularly entrancing to the visitors. Attempts by anti-slavery societies to end the exhibitions were thwarted when Baartman signed depositions stating that she was a willing participant in them, presumably because she was sharing, in some way, in the profits. Her sponsor took her on to Paris where she died in 1815. For many years, her preserved brain and sexual parts were on display at the Musée de l'Homme in the French capital and were only returned to South Africa in 2002.

5. The Shah of Persia

In 1873 London was treated to a dazzling spectacle of oriental splendour when the Shah of Persia, Nasr-ed-Din, visited the country. Dressed, according to one observer, in 'an astrakhan cap and a long coat embroidered with gold' and wearing 'as many diamonds and precious stones as his apparel would bear', the Shah fitted perfectly with 'the preconceived notions people had formed of an Eastern potentate'. His visit was one of the nine-day wonders of the 1870s. 'Have you seen the Shah?' became a popular catchphrase, endlessly repeated in everyday conversation and in songs performed on the music-hall stages. During the visit Buckingham Palace, deserted because Victoria spent most of her time at Windsor, was briefly put at the Shah's disposal. While he was there, he was, allegedly, so angered by the incompetence of one of the servants he had brought with him that he had the man strangled and cremated in the palace garden.

6. **Cetewayo**

In 1879, warriors loyal to the Zulu king Cetewayo inflicted one of the most embarrassing defeats in imperial history on British forces at the Battle of Isandhlwana. In response the British government poured men and resources into South Africa, columns of soldiers marched on Cetewayo's capital at Ulundi, his armies were slaughtered and, eventually, he was captured and deposed. In 1882, secure in the knowledge that Cetewayo was defeated and his kingdom dismantled, the British allowed the Zulu king to travel to London, where he met Prime Minister Gladstone in Downing Street, and to journey on to Osborne House on the Isle of Wight where he had an audience with Queen Victoria. Cetewayo was, briefly, the talk of the town. Music-hall songs celebrated his visit and his potential to flutter female hearts. 'White young dandies get away, O!/You are now 'neath beauty's ban/Clear the field for Cetewayo/He alone's the ladies' man'. Photographs taken on the visit of the twenty-stone-plus ex-monarch, uncomfortably squeezed into frock coat and trousers, suggest that he was, in fact, an unlikely ladies' man.

7 VISITORS TO THE BRITISH MUSEUM READING ROOM IN FACT AND FICTION

1. **Karl Marx**

In exile in London, Karl Marx spent long hours and long years working in the British Museum Reading Room, acquiring his first ticket of entry in 1850. Much of the research and writing for *Das Kapital* was done there. As Mikhail Gorbachev once remarked, 'If people don't like Marxism, they should blame the British Museum'.

2. **Enoch Soames**

Max Beerbohm wrote a short story about a poet called Enoch Soames, sadly neglected in his own day, who makes a pact with the devil in order to visit the British Museum Reading Room for a few hours in 1997 (a hundred years later) in the confident expectation that posterity will have recognised his merits and his books will be prominently on display. He finds that the only mention of him is as an imaginary character in a work by Max Beerbohm. On 3 June 1997, the day mentioned by Beerbohm, a party was organised to visit the Reading Room and see if Soames showed up. He didn't.

3. **Jonathan Harker**

In Bram Stoker's *Dracula*, the narrator Jonathan Harker visits the Reading Room in order to 'search among the books and maps of the library regarding Transylvania'.

4. **George Bernard Shaw**

As a young man, Shaw spent many hours in the British Museum Reading Room, reading widely in politics, literature and economics and writing a sequence of novels, all of which met with rejection by publishers. In great old age, Shaw remained grateful to the Reading Room for the education with which it provided him and it was one of a handful of institutions (RADA was another) to be granted money from his royalties in his will.

5. **Sherlock Holmes**

In 'The Adventure of Wisteria Lodge' Holmes visits the Reading Room to consult Eckermann's *Voodooism and the Negroid Religions* in the hope that it will shed light on the mystery he is investigating.

6. **Colin Wilson**

   As a young man, disdainful of bourgeois ambitions and proprieties, Wilson spent his nights sleeping in a waterproof sleeping bag on Hampstead Heath and his days working in the Reading Room on a novel about the Jack the Ripper murders and a philosophico-literary study of alienated intellectuals which eventually became the sensational bestseller of the 1950s, *The Outsider*.

7. **The Jackal**

   In the film version of *The Day of the Jackal*, the hit man (Edward Fox) who has been hired to assassinate de Gaulle is shown doing research in the Reading Room.

10 PEOPLE (2 FICTIONAL) WHOSE NAMES HAVE BEEN USED IN COCKNEY RHYMING SLANG

Cockney rhyming slang dates back to the middle of the nineteenth century, when it was developed as a secret language which initiates could use to communicate without the police or other figures of authority understanding them. A definition in an 1859 dictionary of slang is still apposite today: 'The cant … is known in Seven Dials and elsewhere as the Rhyming Slang, or the substitution of words and sentences which rhyme with other words intended to be kept secret.' Secrecy was often assisted by dropping the word which actually rhymed, a fact which continues to puzzle many tourists. Thus 'barnet' for 'hair' and 'whistle' for 'suit' become doubly baffling if you don't realise that they are abbreviations of 'Barnet Fair' and 'whistle and flute' respectively. In the twenty-first century, new rhyming slang ('Britneys' i.e. 'Britney Spears' for 'beers' or 'queers', for example) continues to be invented but the argot has long since ceased to be anything much more than either an expression of nostalgia for a lost London of cheery costermongers and pearly kings and queens, or an easily used means of identifying oneself as a particular type of Londoner. Some of the words genuinely used in rhyming slang in the past do, however, reveal odd and curious snippets about London's social history. Here are ten people, many of whose names mean little today, which were or are remembered in rhyming slang.

1. **Oscar Asche**
   Oscar Asche's name was used as rhyming slang for 'cash', particularly in the first few decades of the twentieth century. An Australian-born actor in Shakespearean roles, he was later the writer of the immensely successful musical *Chu Chin Chow* which ran from 1916 to 1921 at His Majesty's Theatre, Haymarket. 'I must have drawn well over £200,000 in royalties from *Chu*. And everyone connected with *Chu* made a fortune. Some kept it. I didn't.'

2. **Joe Baksi**
   Bearing in mind the limited number of words that rhyme with 'taxi', users of rhyming slang must have greeted the arrival of Joe Baksi on the boxing scene of the 1940s with great delight. The American heavyweight was, briefly, thought to be a contender for the world championship and he fought several times in Britain, where his name now lives on in rhyming slang.

3. **Sexton Blake**
   The poor man's Sherlock Holmes, Sexton Blake first appeared in a story called 'The Missing Millionaire' in the Halfpenny Marvel magazine of 15 December 1893. In the century and more since, he has been the hero of more than 3000 cases, chronicled by more than 200 writers, including, at various times, Michael Moorcock, John Creasey and Jack Trevor Story. He was also the lead

character in a long-running BBC radio series of the 1940s and 1950s. His name has long been used as rhyming slang for 'fake'.

4. **Gertie Gitana**

A music-hall performer known as 'the star that never fails to shine', Gertie Gitana (1887–1957) made her London debut at the age of thirteen and was originally a child-member of a group called Tomlinson's Royal Gipsy Children. Her most famous song was the tear-jerkingly sentimental 'Nellie Dean', and the Nellie Dean pub in Dean Street had a gallery of signed photos of Gitana on the wall of the bar until very recently. Her name was used as rhyming slang for 'banana', particularly in the first half of the twentieth century.

5. **Ruby Murray**

The use of Ruby Murray's name as rhyming slang for 'curry' helps date the beginning of the national taste for curries. She was a Belfast-born singer who, in 1955, had five singles in the top twenty at the same time. Although she continued to perform until her death in 1996, her heyday was the late 1950s and early 1960s, when Britain was learning to appreciate Indian food.

6. **Harry Randall**

Harry Randall (1860–1932) was a popular music-hall and stage comedian who specialised in dame roles. His name was used as rhyming slang for candle, particularly in the first half of the twentieth century.

7. **J Arthur Rank**

Owner of a flour mill in the north of England, Rank, a devout Methodist, first entered the film industry when he formed the Religious Film Society in the early 1930s. In less than a decade he became the most important figure in the British film industry, head of his own Rank Organisation and owner of both Pinewood Studios and the Odeon cinema chain. The god-fearing and prudish producer would be particularly distressed that his name has long been used as rhyming slang for 'wank'.

8. **Tod Sloan**

Born in America in 1874, James Todhunter Sloan was a jockey who arrived in Britain in 1896 to ride for the then Prince of Wales, later Edward VII. A flamboyant and aggressive personality, Sloan was also a brilliant jockey who pioneered the 'monkey crouch' style of riding (head almost on the horse's neck, bottom in the air) now used by almost every rider. Richly rewarded and forever in the newspapers, he became a popular figure with the London working class. 'On your Tod Sloan' was adopted as rhyming slang for 'on your own' and then usually abbreviated to 'on your tod'. Ironically, Sloan squandered most of the money he earned, fell out with the racing authorities and ended his life very much 'on his tod'. He died alone in a Los Angeles boarding house in 1933.

9. **Sweeney Todd**

Sweeney Todd, the barber who killed his customers and delivered their bodies to Mrs Lovett's Pie Shop to be transformed into meat pies, is one of England's great bogeymen. Despite claims that he was a real person, he was a fictional character and owes his fame to a minor nineteenth-century playwright, George Dibdin-Pitt, author of a blood-and-thunder melodrama called *The String of Pearls, or The Fiend of Fleet Street*. His name is used as rhyming slang for a branch of Scotland Yard. Formed just after World War I, the Mobile Patrol became known as the Flying Squad, because of the power it had to operate or 'fly' across the boundaries of the city's police divisions, and then as 'the Sweeney'. Hence the title of the TV series of the 1970s.

10. **Harry Wragg**

Harry Wragg was a British jockey who, in the course of a career lasting nearly three decades, won more than a dozen classics, including the Derby three times. After retiring, he became a successful trainer. His name is used in rhyming slang for a 'fag' or cigarette.

12 FICTIONAL LONDONERS

1. **Charles Pooter in George & Weedon Grossmith's *The Diary of a Nobody* (1892)**

The Grossmith brothers were both connected with the London stage in the late nineteenth century (George was a leading player in the original productions of Gilbert and Sullivan operas) but their jointly produced comic novel is what has ensured their ticket to posterity. This is the story of Charles Pooter, a lowly clerk who lives with his wife and family in Holloway and who decides to follow in the footsteps of Pepys and John Evelyn and keep a diary. A bemused and accident-prone victim of class prejudice and his own aspirations, Pooter is at his most hilarious when recording the seemingly mundane aspects of his life at home or at work, but the book is also an accurate look into the world of the tens of thousands of clerks like him in Victorian London.

2. **Liza in W. Somerset Maugham's *Liza of Lambeth* (1897)**

The novel which launched Maugham's career is a tale of life (and death) in the slums of south London. Partly autobiographical, since its author was a medical student at nearby St Thomas's Hospital, the book records the struggles of Liza, a young woman who slaves in a factory, then returns home to look after her alcoholic mother. Lively and popular, Liza attracts the attentions of Jim, a married man, whose charms provide a welcome relief from her drudgery, although the way is inevitably paved for tragedy. In a preface to a later edition, Maugham wrote of the book, 'I exercised little invention. I put down what I had seen and heard as plainly as I could.'

3. **Auberon Quin in GK Chesterton's *The Napoleon of Notting Hill* (1904)**

Chesterton's political fantasy was published in 1904 and set in 1984, a popular year for dystopian novelists. In this futuristic London, there is no conventional monarchy and the ruler is chosen from a rota of civil servants. Lowly bureaucrat Auberon Quin is duly crowned king and then the fun begins. A roly-poly fellow with a babyish face, Quin is also a poet, publishing verse under the name of Daisy Daydream. His love of pageantry leads him, on a whim, to re-establish city-states for five West London boroughs. When legislation threatens a little street in Notting Hill, war breaks out and Quin's reign descends into chaos.

4. **George Harvey Bone in Patrick Hamilton's *Hangover Square* (1941)**

Set in 1939, *Hangover Square* minutely observes the seedy, dissolute world of Earl's Court pubs as the citizens steadfastly drink to distract themselves from the imminent threat of war. Against this bibulous backdrop, George Harvey Bone worships the cruel beauty, Nettie, hoping that one day she will yield to his pitiful advances. Plagued by blackouts, when he loses track of time and reality, the hapless George is barely tolerated by Nettie who uses him to fund her incessant drinking. After she finally spurns him, Georges loses his frail grip on sanity and his hopeless desire spirals into madness and murder.

5. **Harry Fabian in Gerald Kersh's *Night and the City* (1946)**

Gerald Kersh wrote a number of novels with London

settings, but the *noir*-esque thriller, *Night and the City* was his most successful and Harry Fabian, a dreamer and a victim who drifts around the fringes of the capital's fight racket, always on the lookout for that elusive big score, is his most memorable character.

6. **Vaughan in JG Ballard's *Crash* (1973)**

    Published in 1973, following Ballard's own car accident, *Crash* is narrated by a man who wakes up in hospital following a pile-up in which a doctor's husband dies. Compelled to return to the scene of the accident, he meets the doctor and they begin a torrid affair, having strange sex in cars and on London's motorways. Even stranger is the narrator's friend, Vaughan, a 'TV scientist', who is obsessed with dying in a collision with the actress Elizabeth Taylor, a destiny that he almost achieves. Ballard's vision of death, sex and the city's obsession with the car brings fresh meaning to the term 'auto-erotic'.

7. **Keith Talent in Martin Amis's *London Fields* (1989)**

    Amis's mesmerising and often hilarious tale of murder and mystery is set in a vividly-drawn west London with its elegant Georgian houses and grim high-rises. Chief among a cast of surreal and exotically named characters, like the beautiful and fated Nicola Six and the handsome, wealthy Guy Clinch, is the appalling but curiously charismatic thief and darts fanatic Keith Talent. A yob supreme, Keith is a classic Amis protagonist: a gross, inarticulate petty crook and adulterer, who, despite his array of grotesqueries, remains human and even engaging.

8. **Robinson in Christopher Petit's *Robinson* (1993)**

    The eponymous protagonist of Petit's novel is a mythical figure in a dark suit and well-shined brogues, haunting the pubs of Soho. Charming, mysterious and somewhat sinister, Robinson befriends the narrator, enticing him into the city's nocturnal netherworld before promptly vanishing, only to re-emerge later in the book as a maker of porn films.

9. **Rob Fleming in Nick Hornby's *High Fidelity* (1995)**

    Rob Fleming is the trainspotter-ish owner of a vintage record shop in London, and a dreamer whose life is ruled by an almost religious adherence to 'top five' lists. When his girlfriend, Laura, leaves him for another man, he hangs out with the other geeks who work in the shop, burying his sorrows with more lists and more compulsive consumption of pop culture. He also trawls the city, tracking down old flames and warming himself by having a fling with a pretty American singer. It's really Laura whom he wants though, so all he has to do is compile the top five ways of winning your girlfriend back ... and keeping her.

10. **Bridget Jones in Helen Fielding's *Bridget Jones's Diary* (1996)**

    Ms Jones made her debut in a series of columns in the *Independent* and then became a massive best-seller when a novel appeared. Slaving away at a publishing company, obsessive about her weight, her consumption of cigarettes and Chardonnay and her woeful existence as a 'singleton', Bridget gads about London in search of Mr Right, whilst having a fling with her cad of a boss.

11. **Harry Starks in Jake Arnott's *The Long Firm* (1999)**

    Arnott's first novel is set in the Swinging London of the 1960s, when gangsters rubbed shoulders (and more) with celebrities and politicians. Ruling the roost is East Ender Harry Starks, racketeer, nightclub owner, pornographer, intellectual and homosexual, whose story is told by five different narrators. An intriguingly complex character, equally at home with a cosh or a volume of Bertrand Russell, Harry pulls the strings that control the other people in the book (some invented, some real-life individuals like the small-time gangster and victim of the Krays, Jack 'The Hat' McVitie).

12. **Nazneen in Monica Ali's *Brick Lane* (2003)**
Forced into an arranged marriage with a man twenty years her senior, Nazneen leaves her home in Bangladesh to live in London, in an East End tower block. Speaking no English, she has to rely on her ineffectual husband, but her resourcefulness and determination win through, as she befriends another Asian girl, who helps her to find a place in the multi-racial city.

6 LONDON LORD MAYORS

1. **Henry Fitzailwyn**
The very first Mayor of London was a wealthy merchant, probably a draper, who lived in a house by the long-vanished River Walbrook (*see* **6 Lost London Rivers**, p. 161). Variously recorded as having become mayor in 1189 or 1192, he still held the post in 1215. In 1193 Fitzailwyn was one of those active in raising money in the city to ransom Richard the Lionheart who was being held captive by the Holy Roman Emperor. Fitzailwyn and his fellow subscribers may not have been so keen to release their king had they heard the remark attributed to Richard by one chronicler that, in order to pursue his ambitions in the Holy Land, 'If I could have found a buyer, I would have sold London itself.'

2. **Sir William Walworth**
Walworth was Mayor at the time of the Peasants' Revolt in 1381, and it was he who killed the peasant leader Wat Tyler in Smithfield. According to an anonymous

contemporary chronicle, it was all done in self-defence. 'Wat stabbed the Mayor with his dagger in the stomach in great wrath. But, as it pleased God, the Mayor was wearing armour and took no harm, but like a hardy and vigorous man drew his cutlass, and struck back at the said Wat, and gave him a deep cut on the neck, and then a great cut on the head.' The wounded Tyler attempted to take refuge in the church of St Bartholomew the Great but was dragged out and finished off. The dagger with which Walworth is supposed to have stabbed Tyler is now in the possession of the Fishmongers' Company.

3. **Dick Whittington**

The real Richard Whittington was a wealthy merchant who was mayor of London four times (1397, 1398, 1406 and 1419). During his lifetime and after his death in 1423, Whittington was a great benefactor to the city. Among many other gifts to the city he had a large public lavatory built at his own expense which could seat more than a hundred and became known as Whittington's Longhouse. The story of Dick Whittington and his cat, now familiar from pantomime, first appeared in print in the early seventeenth century, although it must have been circulating orally before then. Some scholars have suggested linguistic confusion between 'cat' and the French word 'achat', meaning 'trade', as the reason for the cat's appearance in the story. Others have speculated that the cat was not an animal but a boat. A 'cat' was a type of sailing ship with a narrow stern and deep waist, the kind of vessel on which Whittington's trade goods might have travelled.

4. **Sir Thomas Bludworth**

Bludworth was Lord Mayor in 1666, the year of the Great Fire. Awoken in the early hours of 2 September to be told of the fire, Bludworth was contemptuous of all the fuss. 'Pish! A woman might piss it out!', he is supposed to have said before returning to bed and to sleep. By the time Pepys came across him later in the day the Lord Mayor had changed his tune. According to Pepys, he was 'like a fainting woman' and said, 'Lord, what can I do? I am spent, people will not obey me. I have been pulling down houses but the fire overtakes us faster than we can do it.'

5. **John Wilkes**

Engraving of John Wilkes, by William Hogarth

John Wilkes, who was Lord Mayor in 1774, is the subject of the only cross-eyed statue in London, which stands at the point where Fetter Lane and New Fetter Lane converge. The statue is true to life. Wilkes *was* cross-eyed, as can be seen clearly in a famous engraving of him by Hogarth. Despite these unconventional looks, he was a legendary and eloquent womaniser who once said that, when meeting an attractive woman, it took him only ten minutes to talk away his face. It was Wilkes who, when told by the Earl of Sandwich that he would die either of pox or on the gallows, immediately replied, 'That depends, my lord, whether I embrace your mistress or your principles'.

6. **David Salomons**

A banker and financier, Salomons became the first Jewish Lord Mayor in 1855. He had previously stood for parliament, won a seat and then refused to take the oath 'on the true faith of a Christian' which was required of MPs at the time. His electors in Greenwich kept returning him in election after election and eventually he was able to take his place in the House when the requirements of the oath were changed. One of the long overdue acts of Salomons's mayoralty was the removal from the Monument of the inscription which had, for nearly 200 years, placed the blame for the Great Fire squarely on the shoulders of mysterious Roman Catholic arsonists.

10 FAMOUS PEOPLE WHO HAVE SPOKEN AT SPEAKERS' CORNER

Although some writers have claimed that the tradition of open-air public speaking in the north-east corner of the park has its origin in the final speeches of condemned men at nearby Tyburn, it really dates from 1872, when the Royal Parks and Gardens Act delegated tricky decisions about allowing large-scale meetings in Hyde Park to the park authorities rather than the government. One result, not necessarily anticipated by parliament, was that the park authorities were relatively relaxed about people gathering to speak and protest in certain areas of the park. Speakers' Corner, as it became known, rapidly developed into an open-air forum for the exchange of ideas and opinions and it continues to be so today. Those with strong views on religion, politics and the issues of the day stand up to make them known, to brave heckling from the audience and to entertain passing tourists. Those who have spoken there include the following:

1. **Tony Benn**
   The veteran Labour politician is a great enthusiast for the freedom of speech represented by Speakers' Corner and has spoken there on many occasions throughout his long political career.

2. **Friedrich Engels**
   The co-author, with Karl Marx, of *The Communist*

Manifesto, spoke at meetings in Hyde Park in the 1850s, close to the place that was later to be designated Speakers' Corner.

3. **Marcus Garvey**

The black nationalist and champion of the 'Back to Africa' movement lived in London during the late 1930s. Although he was suffering from severe illness during much of the period, and he died in London in 1940, he spoke frequently at Speakers' Corner.

4. **Vladimir Lenin**

The Soviet leader lived in London briefly during the first years of the twentieth century when he was nothing more than the head of a tiny revolutionary party in exile. He was fascinated by Speakers' Corner and attempted to speak there at least once. However, Lenin's English was not fluent and, because he lodged with an Irish family, he spoke it with a noticeably Irish accent. Probably, few who heard him understood him.

5. **CLR James**

The West Indian writer, politician, polymath and cricket enthusiast lived in London in the 1930s and spoke at Speakers' Corner when he was one of the leading figures in a small Trotskyist party later known as the Revolutionary Socialist League.

6. **Karl Marx**

Marx assumed, wrongly, that riots in Hyde Park in the 1850s marked the beginning of the revolution in Great Britain and spoke to the crowds assembled at the spot which, in the 1870s, would first become known as Speakers' Corner.

7. **William Morris**

The poet, artist and craftsman was a member of several revolutionary socialist parties in the last decades of the nineteenth century and spoke at Speakers' Corner on several occasions. Of one meeting in June 1886, he wrote to his daughter, 'I was quite nervous about it, I don't know why: because when I was speaking at Stratford I was not nervous at all, though I expected the police to attack us. At Hyde Park we had a very quiet and rather good audience ... '

8. **George Orwell**
    The reserved and taciturn Orwell was not a natural public speaker but he did once address an audience at Speakers' Corner on the subject of the Spanish Civil War, in which he himself had fought and been seriously wounded.

9. **Christabel Pankhurst**
    The suffragette leader spoke in favour of women getting the vote at Speakers' Corner on a number of occasions in the years before World War I.

10. **Lord Soper**
    Methodist minister and left-wing campaigner for all kinds of causes, Soper was a regular orator at Speakers' Corner. He gave his last speech there in 1998, a few weeks before his death at the age of ninety-five.

7 INMATES OF BEDLAM

Founded in the thirteenth century as a priory dedicated to St Mary of Bethlehem, the Bethlem Royal Hospital has for centuries been dedicated to the care of the mentally ill and its name, corrupted to 'Bedlam', has come to mean both an asylum in general and a scene of confusion or uproar. Located first in Bishopsgate, close to where Liverpool Street Station now stands, the hospital moved to Moorfields in 1676, Southwark in 1815 (the building is now the Imperial War Museum) and Beckenham, where it still exists, in 1930. Over the centuries many patients have passed through Bedlam. The following are just a few of the more famous:

1. **Nathaniel Lee**

   Lee was a seventeenth-century playwright who was committed to Bedlam in the 1680s. 'They called me mad, and I called them mad,' he wrote, 'and damn them, they outvoted me.' He was released from Bedlam after five years only to die when 'he drank so hard, that he dropped down in the street, and was run over by a coach.' He is buried in St Clement Danes in the Strand.

2. **James Tilly Matthews**

   One of the first ever detailed records of the delusions of a mental patient, *Illustrations of Madness*, was published in 1810. The author, John Haslam, was a doctor at Bedlam and his patient was a London merchant called James Tilly Matthews. Matthews believed that he was being persecuted by a gang of undercover Jacobin revolutionaries who were using a mysterious machine called an Air Loom to control his mind. Matthews could draw elaborate plans of the Air Loom and was eloquent on the subject of the different settings and markings on it, from 'foot-curving' and 'knee-nailing' to 'eye-screwing' and 'brain-saying', which the gang could manipulate to inflict their torments on him. According to Matthews, other Air Loom gangs were operating in the capital, influencing the minds of leading men, including the prime minister. Eventually transferred from Bedlam to a private asylum, Matthews died in 1815, still convinced of the dangers posed by the Air Loom operators.

3. **Jonathan Martin**

   In 1829, a religious fanatic called Jonathan Martin, inspired by his hatred of the worldliness of Church of England clergy and driven by a series of prophetic dreams, set fire to York Minster. He had written letters to senior churchmen, threatening that, 'Your great minsters and churches will come rattling down upon your guilty heads', but they had been ignored so Martin concealed himself in the Minster overnight and used material from the Bishop's pew to start his fire. At his trial, it was decided that Martin was of unsound mind and he was committed to Bedlam where he died nine years later.

4. **Richard Dadd**

One of the most compelling paintings in Tate Britain is *The Fairy Feller's Master-Stroke*, a strange vision of fantastic creatures at play amidst the grass and flowers of an English hedgerow. It is the work of an artist called Richard Dadd. As a young man in the 1840s, Dadd travelled to Europe and the Middle East and, during this period, he became increasingly obsessed by religious fantasies and was haunted by the belief that God had singled him out to fight the Devil in whatever form he took. Back in England, Dadd decided that one of the forms the Devil took was that of his own father and he stabbed him to death. Declared insane, he spent the rest of his life in asylums, including, briefly, Bedlam.

5. **Hannah Chaplin**

The mother of Charlie Chaplin, Hannah was a singer in the music halls who became mentally ill when her son was still a young boy. She spent periods of time in Bedlam but, when Charlie Chaplin's Hollywood success made him the most famous man in the world, he arranged for his mother to be cared for in California where she died in 1928.

6. **Louis Wain**

Well-known in the Edwardian era as a painter of anthropomorphic cats who mimic the activities of humans, Louis Wain became seriously ill in the 1920s and was committed to an asylum in Surrey before being transferred to Bedlam after a campaign by his admirers, including the then prime minister, Ramsay MacDonald, to get better care for him. He died fifteen years later in another hospital near St Albans. His pictures are still popular and an exhibition of his work was recently held in the gallery at the current Royal Bethlem Hospital in Beckenham.

7. **Antonia White**

In the early 1920s, the novelist Antonia White, author of *Frost in May,* was committed to Bedlam by her mother after a breakdown and an attempt to drown herself in the Thames. She was held at the hospital for nine months and later wrote extensively of her experiences of mental illness.

4 MUMMIFIED LONDONERS

1. **Catherine of Valois**

Henry V's queen, Catherine, died in 1437 and was buried in the Lady Chapel of Westminster Abbey. More than half a century later Henry VII, making major alterations to the Abbey, felt obliged to move her embalmed body. She was placed in a crude coffin constructed of flimsy boards and left above ground, close to the tomb of her husband. There she remained a public spectacle for more than two centuries. Vergers used to charge a shilling to take off the lid so that curious visitors could view her corpse. Samuel Pepys went one better when he visited the Abbey on his thirty-sixth birthday. He 'had the upper part of her body in my hands, and I did kiss her mouth, reflecting upon it that I did kiss a Queen, and that this was my birthday, thirty-six year old, that I did first kiss a Queen'. The body was finally removed from public view in 1776.

2. **Jeremy Bentham**

The philosopher Jeremy Bentham died in 1832 at the age of eighty-four and left most of his estate to the newly founded University of London, now University College, London.

His worldly goods were not all he left the university. He also left his body. In accordance with his belief that the dead should be useful to the living, he instructed his medical friends at the university to use it as 'the means of illustrating a series of lectures to which scientific & literary men are to be invited'. Once the lectures were over and 'all the soft parts have been disposed of', his skeleton was to be dressed in the clothes that he usually wore and placed on perpetual display. In an unpublished pamphlet written some years before his death, Bentham had put forward the idea of creating what he called 'auto-icons' of people after they died, and he was to become the first 'auto-icon'. He still sits in the college in a large case with a plate-glass front, wearing the clothes he used to put on, and with his stick in his hand. A wax head has replaced his own, which is preserved in a mummified state in a box nearby. His idea of auto-icons has not, however, caught on and his suggestions about their possible use ('If a country gentleman have rows of trees leading to his dwelling, the auto-icons of his family might alternate with the trees') have not been carried out.

3. **'Jimmy Garlick'**
London's only medieval mummy is in the church of St James Garlickhythe. Known as Jimmy Garlick, the body was discovered in 1839 by workmen excavating under the chancel. Well-preserved, although thoroughly desiccated by time, the corpse, that of a young man, was not artificially embalmed but is the result of natural mummification, a rare event in Britain.

4. **'The Preserved Lady'**
Martin van Butchell was an eccentric who lived from 1735 to 1812. In his marriage contract there was a clause stating that he could own certain articles only 'while [his wife] remained above ground'. When she died, he retained title to the property by having her embalmed, dressed in

her wedding clothes and placed in a glass-topped case in his drawing-room. 'The Preserved Lady' became a great attraction, with van Butchell always introducing her as 'my dear departed'. When he remarried, his new wife – irritated by the competition – insisted the corpse be removed. To fulfil the provision that she remain above ground, van Butchell presented her to the Royal College of Surgeons, where she remained on public view until she was cremated by a German bomb during a Luftwaffe raid in May 1941.

6 MEN WHO FOUNDED LONDON HOSPITALS

1. ## Rahere: St Bartholomew's (1123)

   A courtier, perhaps a jester, at the court of Henry I, Rahere travelled on a pilgrimage to Rome in the early 1120s. En route he is said to have caught malaria and vowed to build a hospital and church if he survived. Returning to England, he was granted land in Smithfield by his royal master, and St Bartholomew's, the oldest hospital in London, was built in 1123. Rahere also founded a priory nearby and his tomb stands in the church of St Bartholomew the Great, the only surviving part of his foundation. Members of staff at Bart's hospital over the years have included William Harvey, the man who first described the circulation of the blood; the cricketer WG Grace; Edward Wilson, who died with Captain Scott on the way back from the South Pole and the eighteenth-century physician John Abernethy, a robustly commonsensical doctor who once said to a lady suffering from depression, 'Don't come to me; go and buy a skipping-rope.' In the Conan Doyle stories Sherlock Holmes is introduced to Dr Watson at Bart's. Attempts to close the hospital in 1992 were thwarted and it still stands as a monument to nearly nine centuries of patient care.

2. **Thomas Guy: Guy's (1723)**

   Guy's Hospital was established in 1723, using £18,793 from the fortune of Thomas Guy. Guy, a bookseller, had made his money from illegally importing bibles from Holland (he was breaking a monopoly in doing so) and through careful investment in the stock of the South Sea Company before the company's bubble famously burst. Guy died at the age of eighty, the year after the foundation of his hospital, leaving further finance for it in his will and a stipulation that it should 'receive and entertain therein four hundred poor persons, or upwards, labouring under any distemper, infirmity or disorders thought capable of relief by physic or surgery'. Three doctors at Guy's have given their names to diseases. Richard Bright (Bright's Disease), Thomas Addison (Addison's Disease) and Thomas Hodgkin (Hodgkin's Disease) all worked at the hospital in the early nineteenth century.

3. **Thomas Coram: Foundling Hospital (1741)**

   The Hospital for the Maintenance and Education of Exposed and Deserted Children, soon known as the Foundling Hospital, opened in 1741. The driving force behind it was a former sea-captain, shipwright and colonial entrepreneur (he had spent many years of his life in America) called Thomas Coram. On his return to London from the American colonies, Coram had been appalled by the number of destitute children on the streets of the city and the Foundling Hospital was the result of his determination to do something to help them. One of the first governors of the hospital was the artist William Hogarth, who designed the uniform and the coat of arms, and the composer George Frederick Handel also donated his talents to the cause. Annual performances of Handel's *Messiah* provided money for the hospital for many years. In the fourteen years between 1756 and 1769, almost 15,000 babies were admitted, of whom more than 10,000 died. Even this apparently terrible mortality rate was better than that in parish workhouses. Some parts of the original hospital still survive in what is now called Coram's Fields, including the lodges where mothers unable to look after their babies left them to receive Coram's charity.

4. **Benjamin Golding: Charing Cross (1818)**

Golding was a wealthy medical student in Regency London when, in his own words, 'I opened my house … to such poor persons as desired gratuitous advice and presented myself daily for all such applicants from eight o'clock in the morning until one in the afternoon.' In 1818, he established what he called 'The West London Infirmary and Dispensary' in Suffolk Street which was later to move premises and change its name to Charing Cross Hospital.

5. **William Marsden: Royal Free (1832) and Royal Marsden (1851)**

When Marsden's first wife died from cancer, he realised that, as he wrote in a letter at the time, 'we know absolutely nothing about the disease'. He went on to create the first hospital intended solely for patients with cancer which was established in Canon Row, Westminster, in 1851. Its present buildings in Fulham Road opened in the early 1860s. This was not the first hospital Marsden had been instrumental in founding. More than twenty years earlier he had chanced upon a young woman dying on the steps of St Andrew's Church, Holborn, and had been unable to find a bed for her because all London hospitals at the time demanded a letter of recommendation from a subscriber. Outraged, Marsden had gathered together a group of like-minded colleagues and, in a meeting at the Gray's Inn Coffee House, they had committed themselves to creating a hospital which would not require either payment or a letter from a subscriber for admission. This was the beginning of what became the Royal Free Hospital.

6. **Sir Morell Mackenzie: Throat Hospital (1863)**

Morell Mackenzie was a high achiever at an early age and established the first hospital specifically for those suffering from diseases of the throat in Golden Square before he was thirty. Twenty years later a spectacular misdiagnosis was to reduce his reputation to tatters. Summoned to treat Queen Victoria's son-in-law, the German Crown Prince Frederick, for a throat condition, Mackenzie pronounced his patient's illness to be non-malignant and, bringing relief and comfort to the royal family, was knighted. The following year the condition proved only too malignant and Frederick, by now German Emperor, died. Mackenzie was in disgrace and he failed to improve his standing when, in an attempt to defend himself, he published a book in which he suggested that Frederick's death might have been due not to his throat disease but to syphilis.

10 MEN WHO FOUNDED FAMOUS LONDON STORES

1. **John Hatchard**

The oldest surviving bookshop in London was founded in 1797 by John Hatchard. Hatchard's rapidly became a meeting place for London's literati as much as a shop and early customers included Lord Byron, William Pitt and the Prince Regent. Benches were placed outside the shop so that the servants of Hatchard's aristocratic clientele could rest while their masters were inside browsing and chatting to friends. The Royal Horticultural Society was founded in a room above Hatchard's shop on 7 March 1804.

2. & 3. **William Fortnum and Hugh Mason**

William Fortnum was a footman to Queen Anne who received the used candles from the Royal Household as one of the perks of his job. Enterprisingly, Fortnum began to sell these to other members of the court and also to trade in groceries. In 1707 he went into business with his landlord, Hugh Mason, the owner of a stables near St James's Palace (there is still a Mason's Yard just off Duke Street) and the two men founded a firm in Piccadilly which continues to be grocers 'by appointment to Her Majesty the Queen'.

4. **William Whiteley**

William Whiteley first came to London from his native Yorkshire to visit the Great Exhibition in 1851 and was so impressed by the capital that he decided to move there to work as a draper's assistant. Opening his own shop in Westbourne Grove in 1863, by the 1890s he had a business empire employing 6000 people and a shop that claimed to be able to provide 'everything from a pin to an elephant'. A ruthless man, with a hidden taste for womanising, Whiteley made many enemies and, in 1907, was shot dead in his private office by a man claiming to be his illegitimate son.

5. **Gordon Selfridge**

An American who had already amassed a large fortune in his own country, Selfridge, unimpressed by the quality of British retailing, chose to invest some of his money in a superstore in Oxford Street that would show Londoners how Americans shopped. It opened in 1909 and, thanks to Selfridge's innovations in marketing and advertising, was a huge success. Allegedly, it was Selfridge who first came up with the motto that, 'The customer is always right'. Selfridge was an extravagant man, with a fondness for high living and the risks of gambling, and the depression of the 1930s and unwise investments saw his fortune disappear. He died in Putney in relative poverty in 1947.

6. **Arthur Lasenby Liberty**

Arthur Lasenby Liberty opened his shop in Regent Street in 1875, intending to sell ornaments, fabrics and *objets d'art* from the Far East. The opening coincided with a fashion for all things Japanese and Liberty's soon became *the* place for the most up-to-date interior decoration. In 1885 Liberty was hired by WS Gilbert to supply the Japanese costumes for the first performance of *The Mikado*.

7. **Charles Henry Harrod**

Now probably the most famous shop in the world, Harrod's began life in 1849 as a simple grocery shop in what was then the village of Knightsbridge. A wholesale tea merchant who had been trading in Eastcheap, Harrod passed the shop on to his son Charles Digby Harrod in 1861 and it was under the shrewd management of this second Harrod that the store grew to become a London institution.

8. **William Hamley**

A Cornishman from Bodmin, William Hamley moved to the capital in 1760 to found a toy store in Holborn which he originally called 'Noah's Ark'. The store moved to Regent Street in the nineteenth century.

9. & 10. **Bourne & Hollingsworth**

Bourne and Hollingsworth were brothers-in-law who opened a shop to compete with Whiteley's in Westbourne Grove in 1894. In 1902 they moved to a site in Oxford Street. The store closed in 1983. The Plaza Shopping Centre now stands on the site.

6 LONDON CHEFS PAST AND PRESENT

1. Domenico Negri

An Italian pastry-cook who founded a confectioner's in Berkeley Square 'making and selling all sorts of English, French and Italian wet and dry sweetmeats', Negri helped to establish a taste for continental ice-cream in Georgian London. In 1777 he took Robert Gunter into partnership and, by 1799, Gunter was in sole charge. Gunter's Tea Shop became one of the most famous and fashionable places to visit in Mayfair. The sight of Gunter's waiters dodging through the traffic carrying ices and sorbets to customers sitting or standing in the square was a familiar one to Londoners until the middle of the twentieth century.

2. Alexis Soyer

Born in 1810 at Meaux-en-Brie in France, Soyer came to London in his twenties and worked for a number of aristocratic masters before becoming chef at the Reform Club in 1837. In 1850 he took over Gore House, a mansion which stood on the site now covered by the Albert Hall, and opened a vast restaurant there which he described as 'the Vatican of Gastronomy'. Extravagantly furnished, themed rooms with names like 'La Grotte des Neiges Eternelles' and 'La Chambre Ardante D'Apollo' were intended to pull in the customers. The venture was a disaster, losing Soyer £7000 in five months, and it soon closed. During the Crimean War he wrote a letter to *The Times* in which he offered his services to the army. Surprisingly, the army took him up on the offer and he visited the Crimea to advise on cooking and provisioning for the tens of thousands of soldiers who had been sent there to fight the Russians. Soyer was also one of the first celebrity chefs to put his name to cheap and readily available cook books. *A Shilling Cookery Book for the People,* published in 1855, proved particularly popular. Soyer died in 1858 and is buried at Kensal Green cemetery.

3. **Auguste Kettner**
A former chef to Napoleon III, Kettner came to London in 1867 and founded his restaurant (which still exists) the following year. Originally Kettner's catered largely for French exiles living in Soho but its fame spread when a journalist on *The Times*, who had chanced to visit the restaurant, wrote an article praising it. The next day Kettner's was overrun by gourmets who had read the article. The restaurant became one of the most renowned in late nineteenth-century London, counting Oscar Wilde and the Prince of Wales amongst its diners. Kettner lent his name to a best-selling cookery book, *Kettner's Book of the Table*, published in 1877, which had recipes he provided accompanied by text from a journalist with the resounding name of Eneas Sweetbread Dallas.

4. **Auguste Escoffier**
Known as 'the King of Chefs and the Chef of Kings', Escoffier was born near Nice in 1846 and was already a renowned restaurateur when he moved to London to run the kitchens of the newly opened Savoy Hotel in 1890. Forming a partnership with the hotelier César Ritz, Escoffier went on to even greater glory. He is remembered today for the many dishes he created at the Savoy and, later, at the Ritz. Peach Melba was his tribute to the Australian diva Nellie Melba who stayed at the Savoy in the 1890s when she was singing at the Opera House in Covent Garden.

5. **Marco Pierre White**
Born on a council-house estate in Leeds, the son of an English father and an Italian mother, Marco Pierre White became the youngest person ever to be awarded

three Michelin stars. He is now the owner of a number of London restaurants, from the Grill Room at the Café Royal and the Belvedere in Holland Park to Quo Vadis in Soho. A joint venture with the artist Damien Hirst – the now-closed Pharmacy in Notting Hill – was not a success and the partnership disintegrated amid claims that White had replaced Hirst's paintings on the walls of Quo Vadis with imitations the chef had created himself.

6. **Gordon Ramsay**

The famously foul-mouthed Ramsay, scourge of failing restaurants and inadequate chefs around the land, nearly made his mark on the football field rather than in the kitchen. As a teenager, he signed for Glasgow Rangers and played in their reserve teams for a number of years until a knee injury ended his first career when he was nineteen. A protégé first of Marco Pierre White and then of the Roux brothers (he worked at Le Gavroche), Ramsay opened his own restaurant, Gordon Ramsay's, in Chelsea in 1998 and quickly gained the coveted three Michelin stars. He now owns several other restaurants, including one at Claridge's, and is a familiar face on TV, where he can be seen in programmes such as *Ramsay's Kitchen Nightmares*, yelling obscenities at those who have failed to meet his exacting standards.

6 LONDON CROSS-DRESSERS

1. **Chevalier D'Eon**

D'Eon was an eighteenth-century French diplomat and spy whose sexual status aroused much speculation in his native country and in London, where he lived for long periods of his life. Although he was fond of such traditionally masculine pursuits as fighting and fencing, D'Eon delighted in dressing as a woman and, on one occasion, even petitioned Louis XVI to be officially recognised as female. Perhaps caring little what sex the Chevalier was, the king agreed and D'Eon dressed as a woman at court. After the French Revolution, he returned to England, where he had served as a diplomat in the 1760s, and lived the rest of his life there, mostly in drag, dying in 1810. Londoners were intrigued by D'Eon and large sums of money were gambled on wagers about his true sex. Horace Walpole, who met D'Eon in 1786, noticed that he was heftier and more muscular than the average woman. 'Her hands and arms seem not to have participated of the change of sexes,' he wrote, 'but are fitter to carry a chair than a fan.' After his death, examination proved that he was, and always had been, a man.

2.   James Miranda Barry

Born in the 1790s, Barry entered medical school in Edinburgh as a man, graduated as a man, practised as a surgeon in the army abroad for many years as a man and retired to London as a man. It was only after death that it was discovered that Barry was, in fact, a woman. She was buried in Kensal Green cemetery in 1865. Barry was described by one contemporary, who had no idea of the doctor's true sex, as 'the most wayward of men; in appearance a beardless lad ... there was a certain effeminacy about his manner which he was always striving to overcome'.

3. & 4. Ernest Boulton and Frederick Park

Boulton and Park were two androgynous young men who delighted in donning silk and satin dresses to cruise the theatres and arcades of the Strand as 'Stella' and 'Fanny'. At their trial in 1871 they were charged with 'conspiring and inciting persons to commit an offence', one of the witnesses against Boulton describing how he had kissed 'him, she or it' under the impression he was canoodling with a woman. Both men were intimate with a young aristocrat called Lord Arthur Clinton and exchanged letters with him, in one of which Park complained that 'the weather has turned so showery that I can't go out without a dread of my back hair coming out of curl'.

5. **Vesta Tilley**

Born Matilda Powles in 1864, Vesta Tilley was one of the most famous and best-paid music-hall stars of her era. Her speciality was male impersonation. Dressed as an effete dandy, she delighted working-class audiences in the halls by poking fun at the manners and foibles of the rich. Off-stage she married a theatre manager called Walter de Frece who later became a Conservative MP and was knighted for his fund-raising activities during World War I. Lady de Frece died in Monte Carlo in 1952.

Original poster featuring
Vesta Tilley

6. **Colonel Leslie Barker**

Arrested for bankruptcy at the Regent Palace Hotel in 1925, the self-styled Colonel turned out to be an Australian woman called Lillias Barker. She had taken to dressing as a man after World War I and married as such, telling her wife that her 'impotence' was the result of war wounds. After the contretemps in the Regent Palace, she was later arrested as a member of the National Fascist Party, a tiny group of Mussolini admirers, and, in 1927, appeared in court on a charge of illegal possession of a firearm. Barker again made use of alleged war wounds as an excuse, this time claiming to be not impotent but blind and therefore unable to use a weapon. She was still masquerading as a man when she died in a Suffolk village in 1960.

5 FAMOUS LONDONERS WHO HAVE A BLUE PLAQUE (OR SEVERAL)

1. **Winston Churchill**
   There are several plaques to Churchill in London including one on a house in Eccleston Square, SW1, where he lived between 1909 and 1913, when he was Home Secretary and First Lord of the Admiralty in Asquith's Liberal Government, and one on 28 Hyde Park Gate where he lived for the last twenty years of his life and where he died on 24 January 1965.

2. **Charles Dickens**
   48 Doughty Street, now the Dickens House Museum, bears a plaque to the novelist who actually lived there for only a relatively brief period. He moved to Doughty Street in April 1837. It was, he wrote to a friend, 'a frightfully first-class Family Mansion, involving awful responsibilities'. In the two years he lived at Doughty Street, Dickens wrote *Oliver Twist* and most of *Nicholas Nickleby*. It was here that his two daughters, Mary and Kate, were born and that his sister-in-law Mary, to whom he was almost obsessively attached, died. Aged only seventeen when she died, Mary became a symbol of innocence and purity to Dickens ('I solemnly believe that so perfect a creature never breathed,' he wrote) and she can be glimpsed behind characters like Little Nell in *The Old Curiosity Shop* and Florence in *Dombey and Son*.

3. **Benjamin Disraeli**
   The nineteenth-century prime minister and novelist was born in a house on Theobalds Road which now bears a plaque. During his final illness, at the house in Curzon Street which is marked by a plaque, he turned down the idea of a visit from Queen Victoria, 'No, it is better not,' he said, 'she would only ask me to take a message to Albert.'

4. **Samuel Pepys**

The house in Salisbury Court, EC4, in which Pepys was born in 1633, has long since disappeared but a plaque on a bank marks the place where it stood. Other plaques mark the site of the Navy Office in Seething Lane where he worked when he was writing his diary and two houses in Buckingham Street, WC2, where he lived in the 1680s.

5. **Alfred Hitchcock**

Hitchcock was born in Leytonstone, where his father owned a grocer's shop, in 1899. The site, at 517 Leytonstone High Road, is now a garage. Entering the world of silent movies as a writer of film titles at a studio in Islington, he was directing by the time he was in his mid-twenties. He was soon the country's most admired movie-maker and was tempted to move to Hollywood, where his fame grew exponentially. For the last thirteen years before his move to America, Hitchcock lived with his wife Alma, a film editor, at 153 Cromwell Road, now a rather seedy hostel for refugees, which is marked by an English Heritage plaque. Many of Hitchcock's films in the 1930s are set in London and he returned to the city of his birth in his penultimate film, *Frenzy* (1972). This story of the search for a serial killer is largely set in the old Covent Garden flower, fruit and vegetable market.

5 LONDONERS WHO SHOULD HAVE A BLUE PLAQUE BUT DON'T

1. **Augustus Pugin**
   The Gothic Revival Houses of Parliament is one of the iconic buildings of London and was largely the work of two men, Sir Charles Barry and Augustus Pugin. Barry has his plaque on the house in which he lived in Clapham but there is no similar plaque to Pugin.

2. **Harry Beck**
   The designer of the Underground map, one of London's most distinctive symbols, felt he had been slighted during his lifetime and there has been little reparation after his death. There is a plaque on the wall of Finchley Station, erected a few years ago, but no Blue Plaque on his house in Courthouse Road, Finchley

3. **Lord Byron**

   Byron was the first ever person to be honoured with a blue plaque when one was placed on the house in which he was born in Holles Street, W1, but the house was later demolished and there is no current plaque to record the poet's time in the capital.

   Lord Byron

4. **George Lansbury**
   Lansbury – MP for Bromley and Bow, supporter of the suffragettes, leader of the Poplar Rates Rebellion in the 1920s and of the Labour Party in the 1930s – was an important figure in London politics for the best part of half a century but there is no plaque to record any of his East End residences. The nearest Lansbury comes to the honour is a memorial notice on the Lido Pavilion in Hyde Park which records his 1929 battle against conservative

park commissioners to allow the Serpentine to be used for mixed bathing. Lansbury's other claim to fame is that he was the grandfather of the actress Angela Lansbury.

5. **John Nash**
The creator of Regent Street and Regent's Park changed the face of London to an extent that few other developers and architects can match and yet has no plaque to his name. He lived at one time in Dover Street in Mayfair.

3

CRIME

15 CLASSIC LONDON MURDERS

1. The Murder of Sir Edmund Godfrey, 1678

The body of the London magistrate Sir Edmund Godfrey was found on Primrose Hill on 17 October 1678. He had been stabbed with his own sword. It was a time when conspiracy and paranoia thrived and a Catholic plot was suspected. Godfrey had been involved in the interrogation of Titus Oates, the fantasist who had invented the so-called Popish Plot against Charles II and James, Duke of York, the king's brother, and the magistrate was said to have been in fear of his own life. Three men named Green, Berry and Hill were executed for the crime although they were almost certainly innocent. By a spooky coincidence, one of the alternative names for Primrose Hill was Greenberry Hill.

2. The Murder of Martha Ray, 1779

Martha Ray was the long-term mistress of the Earl of Sandwich – now best known for giving his name to the world's first and still most popular convenience food but, in 1779, First Lord of the Admiralty and a leading member of the government of the day. James Hackman was an ex-soldier and newly ordained minister of the Church of England who had first met Martha in the early 1770s and conceived an overwhelming passion for her. By April of 1779 his love had become too tormenting. Stalking Martha through the streets of Covent Garden, he shot and killed her as she emerged from the Theatre Royal. He then tried to kill himself but failed. The story of the triangular love affair fascinated Londoners at the time and there was considerable, perhaps surprising, sympathy for Hackman who was seen as the victim of a passion he was simply unable to control. The murderer was indifferent to the sympathy and maintained only that he wanted to die. He got his wish. Ten days after the murder, he was hanged at Tyburn.

3.   **The Ratcliff Highway Murders, 1811**

The murders which inspired Thomas De Quincey to write
his famous, tongue-in-cheek essay, 'On Murder as One
of the Fine Arts' took place in December 1811. On the
7th of that month Timothy Marr, a draper with a shop
at 29 Ratcliff Highway, sent his maid out at midnight to
buy some oysters. When she returned, it was to a house
of horrors. Downstairs, Marr and his apprentice lay,
with their throats cut and their heads caved in. Upstairs,
Marr's wife and child were also dead. Twelve days later
a man was seen scrambling down knotted sheets from an
upstairs room of the King's Arms tavern, half-naked and
distraught, shouting, 'They are murdering the people in
the house.' Three people – the publican, his wife and a
barmaid – were found, their throats also cut and their
bodies battered. With a homicidal maniac on the loose,
the neighbourhood was thrown into a state of panic which
was ended only when the police arrested a seaman by the
name of John Williams and held him in the House of
Correction at Cold Bath Fields, Clerkenwell. The evidence
against Williams was less than watertight – he bore no
resemblance to the description of the attacker given by
the man who had escaped through the pub window – but
on the night of 26 December he was found hanged in his
cell. With Williams conveniently dead, the magistrates
decided that he was undoubtedly the murderer and the
crimes were solved. He was buried beneath the crossroads
of Cable Street and Cannon Street with a stake in his heart
and, as De Quincey wrote, 'over him drives for ever the
uproar of unresting London'.

4.   **The Italian Boy, 1831**

On 5 November 1831, three of the capital's 'resurrection
men', as body-snatchers were known, turned up at King's
College in the Strand with the body of a young boy for
sale. Richard Partridge, demonstrator of anatomy at the

college, was suspicious. The body looked remarkably fresh. Tricking the three men into waiting in the entrance hall of the college, Partridge sent for the police. Under arrest, John Bishop, James May and Thomas Williams insisted that the body of the teenager (later assumed to be an Italian street entertainer called Carlo Ferrari) had been obtained by the usual means. He'd died of natural causes, he'd been buried and they'd come along and disinterred him in order to cart him off for dissection. Nobody believed them and the three men were placed on trial at the Old Bailey for the murder of the Italian Boy. All were convicted and, although May was reprieved at the last minute (Bishop confessed after the verdict that May had been ignorant of the murder and had only been helping in the sale of the body), the other two were hanged.

5. **The Pimlico Mystery, 1886**
Edwin Bartlett was found dead at his home in Pimlico on 1 January 1886. The cause of death was chloroform poisoning and a large amount of liquid chloroform was found in his stomach. His wife, Adelaide, admitted that she had bought chloroform but there was no evidence as to how she could have administered such a large dose of it to her husband and no explanation of the fact that there were no signs of blistering in his mouth or in his throat. When she was brought to trial, Adelaide Bartlett was acquitted, although many people continued to believe that she had murdered her husband. Sir James Paget, a consultant at St Bartholomew's Hospital, is reported to have said, 'Now that it is all over, she should tell us, in the interest of science, how she did it'. She never did.

6. **The Murder of William Terriss, 1897**
At seven o'clock on the evening of 16 December 1897 William Terriss, a leading actor in the blood-and-thunder melodramas presented at the Adelphi Theatre, was approaching the stage door in Maiden Lane, WC2, when

he was accosted by another, less successful actor called Richard Prince. Taking a knife from his jacket, Prince stabbed Terriss more than a dozen times. The assailant was apprehended even as Terriss lay dying in the street and he offered no resistance. He admitted responsibility to the police, claiming that Terriss had 'kept him out of employment for ten years, and I had either to die in the street or kill him'. At his trial medical evidence proved to the jury's satisfaction that Prince was of unsound mind and not responsible for his actions. He was sentenced to lifetime imprisonment in Broadmoor, where he became a mainstay of the asylum's theatre company and orchestra. He died in Broadmoor in the 1920s. A plaque in Maiden Lane records his crime.

7. **The Stratton Brothers, 1905**
This was the first case in which fingerprints were used to secure a murder conviction. Two shopkeepers had been killed in their shop in Deptford High Street and one of the killers had left a thumb mark on an emptied cash box. When two brothers, Alfred and Albert Stratton, were brought into custody on the basis of other evidence, the thumbprint was identified as belonging to Alfred and the identification used in court. The Strattons were convicted and hanged.

8. **The Camden Town Murder, 1907**
On 12 September 1907 a young woman called Emily Dimmock was found with her throat cut at her home in St Paul's Road, Camden. In the past, Emily had earned money as a prostitute but, at the time of her death, she was living as the common-law wife of a young man named Bert Shaw. Shaw worked as a chef on the night trains from St Pancras to Sheffield and, since he was at work at the time of the murder, he was not a suspect. The police did, however, have another suspect. Some days after the killing, they arrested Robert Wood, a young man

with artistic pretensions and a taste for the seedier side of London life and charged him with Emily Dimmock's murder. There was no dispute that Wood knew Dimmock and it seems likely that, returning to her old profession of prostitution, she had either entertained him or was planning to entertain him in St Paul's Road but the evidence that he had killed her was not strong. At his trial, his defence counsel made much of the inconsistencies in the case against his client and Wood was acquitted. No one else was ever charged with the murder and it remains one of the great unsolved mysteries in the history of London crime. The artist Walter Sickert (recently accused by the crime novelist Patricia Cornwell of being Jack the Ripper) was obsessed by the murder of Emily Dimmock and painted a series of dark and disturbing pictures which he called *Camden Town Murder*.

9. **The Houndsditch Murders, 1910**
    On the 16 December 1910 a police constable on the beat in Houndsditch heard unusual noises coming from a house in Exchange Buildings. His suspicions aroused by the man who answered the door when he knocked, the constable went to seek assistance from colleagues. Several police returned to the house and a sergeant called Bentley again knocked on the door. Bentley was invited into the house by the same man but, as he crossed the threshold, another man burst from a back room and shot the sergeant twice in the shoulder and the neck. The second bullet severed Bentley's spinal column. Other members of the gang, who had been attempting to tunnel into a jeweller's shop in Houndsditch, now ran from the adjoining house, firing repeatedly as they came. Three more policemen were hit but the only officer left standing, a constable named Choat, made a heroic effort to stop the fleeing anarchists. Seizing one man, later identified as George Gardstein, he wrestled with him for possession of his gun. Gardstein's

colleagues poured gunfire into Choat, who was hit at least half a dozen times. One of the bullets hit Gardstein, wounding him fatally. The gang fled, dragging their dying comrade with them. In January 1911, a number of the gang members were cornered in the East End by police and troops in the infamous Siege of Sidney Street (*see* **3 London Sieges**, p. 147).

10. **Dr Crippen, 1910**

Mild-mannered Dr Crippen is one of the great bogeymen of English criminal history and his wax likeness can still be found in Madame Tussaud's Chamber of Horrors. In February 1910 Crippen's blowsy and boisterous wife Cora, formerly an unsuccessful music-hall singer known as 'Belle Elmore', disappeared from the family home in Hilldrop Crescent, Camden. Her husband claimed that she had moved back to America, suffering from some unspecific but life-threatening illness. Mournfully he issued a series of reports to Cora's friends chronicling her failing health and, finally, her death. Friends of Cora grew suspicious, especially when Ethel Le Neve, Crippen's young secretary, appeared to have moved into Hilldrop Crescent, and eventually they took their suspicions to the police. Interviewed by a detective, Crippen changed his story. His wife had run off with another man and he had been too embarrassed to admit the truth. He might have got away with this new explanation of Cora's disappearance if the visit of the police had not panicked him. He fled with Le Neve and detectives, returning to the house and searching it, found what was left of Mrs Crippen in the cellar. Crippen and his mistress had headed for America on board the SS *Montrose* but the newspapers were now full of the story and the captain of the ship recognised them, despite the fact that Le Neve was disguised as a boy. He used the new Marconi telegraph to wire a message back to

England and detectives were waiting to arrest Crippen when the *Montrose* arrived in American waters.

11. 'The Blackout Ripper', 1942

The body of schoolteacher Margaret Hamilton was found in an air-raid shelter in Marylebone on 9 February 1942. In swift succession other victims of the 'Blackout Ripper' were discovered – Evelyn Oatley, a revue actress, in a flat in Wardour Street; Margaret Lowe in a West End flat and Doris Jouannet in a hotel in Paddington. The murderer, Gordon Cummins, was traced when he attacked a woman in a side street off Piccadilly and ran off, leaving his gas mask behind. He was executed in June 1942.

12. The Rillington Place Murders, 1943–53

John Reginald Christie moved out of his ground floor flat at 10 Rillington Place, where he had lived for fifteen years, in 1953. He left a terrible secret behind him. In a hidden cupboard in the kitchen were three bodies. When these were discovered, the police were called in and they found another three bodies, one in another room and two buried in the garden. It was not the first time that 10 Rillington Place had been in the news for murder – in 1949 two bodies found in the garden shed had proved to be those of Geraldine Evans and her baby daughter. Mrs Evans's husband, Timothy, had been executed for their murders. Now it seemed that an injustice might have been done. Christie, arrested outside the Star and Garter pub in Putney, eventually confessed not only to the murders of his wife and several other women whom he had used to satisfy his necrophiliac sexual tastes but also to the murder of Mrs Evans. He was hanged at Pentonville Prison. Evans was later posthumously pardoned. The street, once so notorious, was demolished in the 1970s. A new road of houses, named Bartle Road, was built on the site.

13. Ruth Ellis, 1955

A night-club hostess with a troubled love life, Ruth Ellis was the last woman to be hanged in Britain. On 10 April 1955, she waited outside the Magdala Tavern in Hampstead for her former boyfriend, racing driver David Blakely, to emerge and then fired six shots in his direction. Two hit Blakely, killing him, another hit a bystander and three made holes in the outside wall of the Magdala which, allegedly, can still be seen. Blakely had been attempting to end any relationship with Ellis and was seeing other women. Taken to Hampstead police station, Ruth Ellis admitted, 'I am guilty. I am rather confused.' At the end of her trial at the Old Bailey, she was sentenced to death and, despite a wave of public sympathy and widespread calls for her to be mercifully treated, she was hanged at Holloway on 13 July 1955. Her execution was nearly postponed when, minutes before she was due to hang, a woman purporting to be the private secretary of the Home Secretary phoned and said a stay of execution was on the way to the prison. The call was a hoax and the execution went ahead.

14. Cecil Court Murder, 1961

Elsie Batten, an assistant in an antiques shop in Cecil Court off Charing Cross Road, was stabbed to death in the shop on 3 March 1961. Taking evidence from the owner of the shop and his son, who had both seen a man acting suspiciously on the premises a few days earlier, the police created an identikit picture, the first ever used by Scotland Yard, which was widely circulated in the press. On Wednesday, 8 March, a police constable saw a man in Old Compton Street whom he believed matched the identikit picture and arrested him. Edwin Bush was later picked out of an identity parade and confessed to killing Mrs Batten with an antique dagger that he had been examining in the shop. Bush, who was Eurasian, claimed at his trial that, just prior to his attack on her, Mrs Batten had said to him, 'You niggers are all the same. You come in and never buy anything.' He was executed at Pentonville Prison on 6 July 1961.

15. **Lord Lucan, Belgravia, 1974**

Gambler and socialite Lord Lucan was, in 1974, estranged from his wife Veronica and their children, who were living in a house in Belgravia. On the night of 7 November that year an intruder broke into the house and the children's nanny, Sandra Rivett, was battered to death. It is assumed that Lucan, intending to kill his wife, mistook her for Veronica. Realising his mistake, he then attacked his wife when she came to investigate what had happened to the nanny but she escaped, running into the street shouting, 'Murder' at the top of her voice. In a letter to a friend Lucan wrote that, 'the circumstantial evidence against me is strong … I will lie doggo for a while'. He has been lying doggo ever since and, although there have been innumerable sightings of him in the last thirty years, he has never been found. In his absence he was found guilty of murder by a coroner's jury.

4 SUCCESSFUL LONDON ASSASSINATIONS

1. **Spencer Perceval**

Famously the only British PM yet to be assassinated, Spencer Perceval was shot on 11 May 1812, as he walked through the lobby of the House of Commons, by a deranged businessman called John Bellingham who believed that the government was to blame for the difficulties he had encountered while

The Rt Hon. Spencer Perceval

trading in Russia. After he had shot Perceval, Bellingham calmly sat on a bench in the lobby and awaited arrest. Despite the apparent madness of his actions, his sanity was never legally questioned and he was hanged a week after the shooting. Many may have sympathised with him. Even more than most politicians, Perceval was not a popular man. Decades later, one witness recalled that he had first heard the news when a man ran through his village street in the Midlands in great excitement, shouting, 'Perceval is shot! Hurrah!' The authorities in London decided that it was too dangerous to risk a public funeral, for fear of disturbances, so Perceval was buried in a private ceremony. A direct descendant of his assassin, Henry Bellingham, is currently a Conservative MP.

2. **Edward Drummond**

Daniel McNaghten was a nineteenth-century Scottish woodworker who suffered from a paranoid delusion that there was a conspiracy to destroy him, headed by the then prime minister, Sir Robert Peel. He decided that the only way to save himself was to kill Peel but, unfortunately, he did not know what the prime minister looked like and accidentally chose Peel's private secretary, Edward Drummond, as his target. Drummond was shot in the back as he walked along Downing Street and died several days later. In his trial in 1843, McNaghten's lawyers brought forward plentiful evidence that their client was insane and he was acquitted of murder but sentenced to detention for life in Bethlem Royal Hospital. McNaghten's name is now attached to the legal rules by which criminal insanity is defined.

3. **Sir Henry Wilson**

On 22 June 1922, Sir Henry Wilson, a British Field Marshal and Ulster MP, was returning to his home in Eaton Square after unveiling the War memorial inside Liverpool Street Station. As he was getting out of his taxi, two men came up behind him and shot him nine times. The men, Reginald Dunne and Joseph O'Sullivan, were both members of the IRA and it is assumed that it was Wilson's status as a prominent Unionist that had led to his being targeted. After the shooting, the gunmen fled the scene but O'Sullivan had difficulty making his escape because he had only one leg, having lost the other at the Battle of Ypres. Dunne stayed to assist him and both were captured. Tried and found guilty at the Old Bailey, both men were hanged at Wandsworth Prison in August 1922. The memorial which Wilson unveiled at Liverpool Street on the day of his assassination can still be seen and a plaque recording his death is now set beside it.

4. **Sir Michael O'Dwyer**
On 13 March 1940 a group of around 150 people gathered at Caxton Hall in Caxton Street, SW1, to hear a lecture on political conditions in Afghanistan by the colonial administrator, Sir Percy Sykes. On the platform with the lecturer were several other distinguished servants of Empire, including Sir Michael O'Dwyer, a man who, twenty years earlier, as Lieutenant-Governor of the Punjab, had given his approval to the infamous Amritsar Massacre in which British troops had fired on unarmed Indian demonstrators, killing hundreds of them. As the meeting came to an end, an Indian nationalist called Udam Singh stepped forward and fired a pistol several times at the men on the platform. O'Dwyer received wounds which proved fatal. During his trial Singh claimed that he had wished only to protest against British imperialism in India and had not intended to kill anyone but he was found guilty of murder and hanged at Pentonville Prison on 31 July 1940.

(... AND 3 FAILED)

1. **Oliver Cromwell**

   Cromwell escaped a large number of assassination attempts, many of them planned by an extreme republican called Miles Sindercombe who believed that the Lord Protector had betrayed the English Revolution by assuming dictatorial power himself. Proposed attacks on Cromwell by Sindercombe and fellow conspirators at Westminster Abbey, Hampton Court and in Hyde Park were all abandoned at the last minute when either the would-be assassins lost their nerve or Cromwell changed his daily routine. A final attempt involving an explosive device at Whitehall was foiled by Cromwell's spymaster, John Thurloe whose men arrested the plotters after a sword fight in which one of the soldiers cut off Sindercombe's nose. Sent to the Tower, Sindercombe escaped the traditional fate of the traitor by poisoning himself in February 1657.

2. **Queen Victoria**

   In 1840 eighteen-year-old Edward Oxford, a barman in a London pub, fired two shots at the queen's carriage as she and Prince Albert were being driven along Constitution Hill. Oxford had spent hours practising his shooting in Green's Shooting Gallery in Soho but still failed to hit even the carriage in which the queen was travelling. Acquitted of high treason, which carried, of course, the death penalty, he was deemed insane and committed to the Bethlem Royal hospital. Victoria was the intended victim of a number of more or less deranged assassins in the course of her reign. 1842 saw no fewer than three, including one in which John William Bean, described in a contemporary report as 'a deformed youth employed as a chemist's assistant', aimed a pistol at her on her way to the Chapel Royal in St James's Palace. Since his gun was loaded only with paper and tobacco, it would have done little harm even if it had gone off and Bean was sentenced to eighteen months' imprisonment. The last assassination attempt on Victoria took place as late as 1882 when another disturbed young man called Roderick Maclean fired a pistol near her carriage on the royal train as it stood in Windsor station.

3. **Sir Edward Henry**
In 1912 the Commissioner of the Metropolitan Police, Sir Edward Henry, was the intended victim of a half-baked assassination attempt. An Acton man, Albert Bowes, aggrieved because he had been denied a cab licence and convinced that this was somehow Sir Edward's fault, fired three shots at the Commissioner as he stood on the doorstep of his house in Sheffield Terrace, W8. Henry was wounded, but not fatally, by one of the shots. Bowes was sentenced to fifteen years in prison, a sentence that might have been longer had Sir Edward not generously pleaded for leniency. Released after ten years, Bowes emigrated to Canada in 1922, his passage paid by the man he had tried to kill.

8 LONDON HIGHWAYMEN

1. **Jack Collet**
The son of a Southwark grocer, Collet was unusual in that he carried out many of his robberies while dressed as a bishop, accompanied by four or five confederates masquerading as his servants. According to the *Newgate Calendar*, his career was interrupted when he lost the bishop's robes in which he had committed his crimes but he was able to replace them by robbing a real bishop on the road from London to Farnham. The Bishop of Winchester was reconciled to the idea of being held up for his money

but was astonished to be asked to strip off his vestments and hand them over. Collet was eventually arrested for breaking into the vestry of St Bartholomew's the Great and stealing the communion plate. He was executed at Tyburn on 5 July 1691.

2. & 3. Plunkett and MacLaine

The connoisseur and man of letters Horace Walpole described a terrifying encounter with two gentlemen of the road in his journal. 'As I was returning from Holland House by moonlight, about ten at night,' he wrote, 'I was attacked by two highwaymen in Hyde Park, and the pistol of one of them going off accidentally, grazed the skin under my eye, left some marks of shot on my face, and stunned me. The ball went through the top of the chariot, and if I had sat an inch nearer to the left side, must have gone through my head.' Only later did Walpole realise that his assailants were the two most famous highwaymen of their day, William Plunkett and James MacLaine. MacLaine's father and brother were both clergymen, but he was more interested in worldly rather than spiritual matters and, moving to London, proceeded to run through the small fortune he had. Joining forces with an apothecary called William Plunkett, he decided to get the money to live in the style to which he aspired by highway robbery. Hyde Park, where the pair confronted Walpole, was a favourite haunt. MacLaine, who was living as a gentleman and claiming that his money derived from an estate in Ireland, was eventually caught in July 1750 when he attempted to sell some expensively tailored clothing to a shopkeeper who recognised it as stolen property. In another letter of 18 October 1750, Walpole, using an alternative spelling of the highwayman's name, reports that, 'my friend Mr M'Lean is hanged' but omits to mention that MacLaine, ever the aspiring gentleman, had written him a letter some time before in which he'd apologised for holding him up in Hyde Park. Plunkett disappeared from London and was never caught. Two and a half centuries after their deaths, the two highwaymen appeared as the anti-heroes of a British film, *Plunkett and McLeane*, played by Robert Carlyle and Jonny Lee Miller.

4. **Claude Duval**
Other than Dick Turpin, no highwayman has had more legends attached to his name than Claude Duval who was born in Normandy in 1643 and died on the scaffold in 1670. Duval entered the service of an English aristocrat in exile while a teenager and came to London when his employer returned there after the Restoration of Charles II. He began his career as a gentleman of the road in 1666. Many of the stories told of Duval are later inventions by writers with a romantic imagination, but it may well be true that he once invited the wife of one of his victims to dance a coranto with him on the roadside and then charged her husband £100 for the entertainment the dancing had provided. He was captured in January 1670, drunk, in a pub called the Hole-in-the-Wall in Chandos Street, and found guilty of robbery. Despite attempts by many admirers, including some ladies at court, to persuade the king to pardon him, Duval was hanged at Tyburn. An epitaph to the highwayman is supposed to have once existed in St Paul's Covent Garden which began, 'Here lies Du Vall/Reader, if male thou art/Look to thy purse/If female, to thy heart'. (*See also* **6 London Pubs Named After People You've Never Heard Of**, p. 14.)

5. **Sixteen-String Jack**
'How should a hero sink to oblivion,' asked one nineteenth-century historian, 'who had chosen for himself so splendid a name as Sixteen-String Jack?' John Rann, who was really no more than a petty thief, seems to have been as interested in presenting the image of a bold highwayman as he was in committing the crimes that went with the job

description. The pride in his nickname, which came from his dandy's habit of wearing eight strings attached to each knee of his breeches, was matched by his eagerness to tell everyone he met of his exploits. Turning up at the pleasure garden at Bagnigge Wells one Sunday in August 1774, he proceeded to get extremely drunk and boast of how he could gain a hundred guineas from an evening's work. Other visitors rapidly wearied of his self-aggrandisement and threw him into the street. On another occasion he rode up to a toll gate on Tottenham Court Road and, informing the gatekeeper that he was 'Sixteen-String Jack, the famous highwayman', asked if the Bow Street Runners had passed by in search of him. Rann was eventually convicted of a robbery at Ealing that netted him 1s 6d, and was executed at Tyburn on 30 November 1774.

6. **Nathaniel Hawes**

An upholsterer's apprentice who turned to crime, Hawes committed a series of robberies on the road between Hackney and Shoreditch but was captured by one of his intended victims on Finchley Common and sent for trial. He refused to plead either guilty or not guilty because, he claimed, 'the person who apprehended me seized a suit of fine clothes, which I intended to have gone to the gallows in; and unless they are returned I will not plead, for no one shall say that I was hanged in a dirty shirt and ragged coat'. Pressed with weights of up to 250 pounds in order to persuade him to change his mind, Hawes eventually gave in and pleaded 'Not Guilty'. It did him no good. He was found guilty as charged and hung at Tyburn on 21 December 1721.

7. **Tom Rowland**

Rowland was a successful highwayman for nearly two decades at the end of the seventeenth century, a success that many attributed to his habit of always committing his robberies dressed as a woman and riding side-saddle.

Who, it was thought, would suspect a female of such atrocious crimes? Finally apprehended after a robbery on Hounslow Heath, Rowland remained unrepentant. According to the *Newgate Calendar*, he 'was so abominably wicked that the very morning on which he died, lying in the Press Yard, for he wanted for no money whilst under confinement, a common woman coming to visit him, he had the unparalleled audaciousness to act carnally with her, and gloried in the sin as he was going to execution'. He was hanged at Tyburn on 24 October 1699.

8. **Isaac Atkinson**

An Oxford-educated son of a Berkshire gentleman who took to crime to support an extravagant lifestyle, Atkinson was unusual in that he specialised in robbing members of the legal profession. He followed the legal circuits in their travels around the county towns and ambushed lawyers when they took to the roads between them. Atkinson was finally caught after a petty theft from a woman on Turnham Green. She escaped and brought a posse of men from Brentford to pursue him. Despite killing several of his pursuers with a pistol, Atkinson was taken and tried at the Old Bailey. Condemned to die, he attempted to evade the hangman by stabbing himself with a penknife but failed to inflict a mortal wound. He was hanged at Tyburn in 1640, his last words being, 'Gentlemen, there's nothing like a merry life, and a short one.'

Traditional image of a highwayman,
from an old print

8 LONDON WHORES

1. ## Clarice la Claterballock
    In the summer of 1340, the authorities in the City ordered
    large-scale arrests of 'evildoers and disturbers of the King's
    Peace'. Among the hundreds detained were many common
    whores, one of whom had the distinctly uncommon name
    of Clarice la Claterballock. The medieval records do not
    include details of how she had earned the name although
    imagination, perhaps, can supply them.

2. ## Sally Salisbury
    Born in the slums of St Giles in the early 1690s, Sally
    Salisbury was an accomplished performer in the brothels
    of Covent Garden before she was fifteen. At the time, the
    area was the centre for the sale of sex in the city. 'One
    would imagine that all the prostitutes of the Kingdom
    had pitched upon this blessed neighbourhood,' one writer
    recorded. 'For here are lewd women in sufficient numbers
    to people a mighty colony.' Sally went on to become one
    of the most famous courtesans of the early eighteenth
    century, with a string of aristocratic lovers. After more
    than a decade at the top of her profession, she met her
    downfall when she lost her temper in a tavern quarrel with
    her latest beau and stabbed him in the chest. He recovered
    and was prepared to forgive her but his family insisted on
    prosecuting her. Confined to Newgate, she died of a fever
    ('brought on by a debauch', according to one disapproving
    commentator) and was buried in St Andrew's, Holborn,
    in February 1724. An epigraph, published some years
    later, records that, 'Here flat on her Back, but unactive at
    last/Poor Sally lies under grim Death'.

3. ## Kitty Fisher
    A well-known nursery rhyme begins with the lines, 'Lucy
    Locket lost her pocket/Kitty Fisher found it'. The words
    help to date the rhyme to the 1760s, as Kitty Fisher was

a famous eighteenth-century courtesan whom Casanova met when he was living in London. 'She was magnificently dressed, and it is no exaggeration to say that she had on diamonds worth five thousand francs', the Venetian womaniser wrote. 'Goudar told me that if I liked I might have her then and there for ten guineas. I did not care to do so, however, for, though charming, she could only speak English, and I liked to have all my senses, including that of hearing, gratified. When she had gone, Mrs Wells told us that Kitty had eaten a bank-note for a thousand guineas, on a slice of bread and butter, that very day. The note was a present from Sir Akins, brother of the fair Mrs Pitt.' Mrs Wells seems to have exaggerated. According to another version of the story, the banknote was only worth £50 and Fisher chose it as a breakfast dish because she was offended that anyone should prize her charms so little as to give her such a miserable sum. Renowned for her beauty, she was painted several times by Sir Joshua Reynolds. One portrait of her as Cleopatra can be seen at Kenwood House, Hampstead. She died at the age of twenty-nine in 1767, supposedly from the effects of lead poisoning from the cosmetics she used.

4. **Anne**

The early nineteenth-century writer Thomas De Quincey arrived in London from Manchester in 1802 at the age of seventeen. Like so many others, before and since, he found the streets were not paved with gold. Starving and homeless, he befriended a prostitute called Anne who was even younger than he was. According to De Quincey, her care and kindness saved his life when he collapsed, faint with hunger, on the steps of a house in Soho Square. Some weeks later, he left the city for a while and arranged to meet Anne three nights later at the corner of Titchfield Street. In his book, *Confessions of an English Opium Eater*, published many years later, De Quincey describes what happened: 'According to our agreement I sought her daily, and waited for her every night, so long as I stayed in London, at the corner of Titchfield Street; and during the last hours of my stay in London, I put into activity every means of tracing her that my knowledge of London suggested and the limited extent of my power made possible ... All was in vain. To this hour, I have never heard a syllable about her.'

5. Harriette Wilson

Down on her luck, Wilson attempted to raise cash by writing her memoirs. Understandably impressed by how much achieving best-seller status depended on luck, she decided that a surer way of getting money for them was by using them to blackmail her high-born former lovers. She despatched copies of the manuscript to them, complete with unflattering references to themselves, together with hints that, on payment of a mere £200, these could be removed from the final book. The Duke of Wellington, approached in this way, is said to have returned the manuscript with the message, 'Publish and be damned.' In the event, Harriette Wilson's published memoirs contain nothing too dreadful about the duke, although she is less than complimentary about him. 'Wellington was now my constant visitor,' she wrote, 'a most unentertaining one, Heaven knows! And in the evening, when he wore his broad red ribbon, he looked very like a rat-catcher.'

6. Laura Bell

Bell was an Irishwoman who arrived in London in 1850 when she was in her early twenties and rapidly became one of the most glamorous and financially successful courtesans of the Victorian era, with a house in Wilton Crescent and a string of wealthy lovers from Indian princes to English aristocrats. Her later career was not one that anyone might have predicted in 1850. She married a Captain Thistlethwayte and became an evangelical preacher. On 9 August 1887 her husband was found shot dead in the bedroom of his house in Grosvenor Square. Thistlethwayte kept a revolver by his bed and the unlikely story was that, seized with a fainting fit, he fell and knocked over the table. The revolver went off and, by a terrible mischance, Thistlethwayte was in the way of the bullet.

7. & 8. Christine Keeler and Mandy Rice-Davies

Keeler and Rice-Davies were the two society call girls who were at the heart of the Profumo scandal in the early 1960s. Introduced at a party at Lord Astor's country house, Cliveden, to John Profumo, a government minister, and Yevgeny Ivanov, a naval attaché at the Soviet Embassy, Keeler had affairs with both men. These were possibly compromising relationships (what pillow talk might go via Keeler from Profumo to Ivanov?) and when news of them was leaked to the papers, the minister denied having had an affair. He was lying and, when he was found to be lying, the fallout from his admissions nearly brought down the Macmillan government. Stephen Ward, a well-connected osteopath who was half-pimp and half-friend to Keeler, and had performed the introductions at Cliveden, was charged with living off immoral earnings and brought to trial. Rice-Davies, another friend of Keeler's who had earlier been involved with the racketeer Peter Rachman, was one of those who gave evidence in the case. When told in court that Lord Astor had denied knowing her, Rice-Davies famously replied, 'Well, he would, wouldn't he?'

4 PEOPLE WHO ESCAPED FROM THE TOWER OF LONDON

1. **Ranulf Flambard**

   The Tower's first prisoner was also its first escapee. Ranulf Flambard, Bishop of Durham and political right-hand man to William Rufus (King of England 1087–1100), was arrested when Henry I succeeded Rufus and imprisoned in the newly completed keep of the Tower. He plied his guards with drink, rendering them unconscious, and escaped by letting a rope down from a window.

2. **Sir John Oldcastle**

   A leader of the Lollards, the followers of the religious reformer John Wyclif, Oldcastle escaped from the Tower in 1413. Once free, he put himself at the head of a Lollard uprising against Henry V, whose friend he had once been, but the king had been forewarned and the Lollards who gathered in St Giles's Fields were easily dispersed. Oldcastle escaped once again. On the run for nearly four years, he was eventually recaptured in Wales in 1417. Brought back to London, he was executed in St Giles's Field on 14 December. Shakespeare almost certainly based the character of Falstaff on him and it has been argued that Oldcastle's actual name was used in performances of *Henry IV* until his descendants protested and Falstaff's was substituted.

3. **Father John Gerard**

   A Jesuit priest who was imprisoned and tortured in the Tower in 1597, Father Gerard nonetheless managed to escape with the help of Catholic friends on the outside. Using orange juice as a kind of invisible ink, he was able to communicate secretly with them and succeeded in gaining the sympathy and assistance of one of his warders. On the night of 4 October a rope was strung across the moat between the Cradle Tower in which Gerard was held and

Tower Wharf. Although Gerard's hands were still disabled from the torture he had endured, he managed to use the rope to leave his prison and he was transported by boat along the Thames to safety. One of those who harboured the runaway was the future Gunpowder Plotter, Robert Catesby, and Gerard himself was implicated in that conspiracy. Despite all the trials and tribulations of his life, Gerard survived until 1637, dying in Rome at the age of seventy-two.

4. **Lord Nithsdale**

A Jacobite who was imprisoned in the Tower in 1716, he was helped by his wife to escape from the King's House, dressed as her maid, on the night before his execution. Lady Nithsdale later wrote of how 'the guards opened the door, and I went downstairs with him, still conjuring him to make all possible dispatch. As soon as he had cleared the door I made him walk before me, for fear the sentinel should take notice of his walk ...' When her husband had left the King's House, Lady Nithsdale returned to his prison cell and, in order to fool the guards in the adjoining room and give him time to get well away, continued to hold an imaginary conversation with him. Finally, she reported, 'I opened the door and stood half in it, that those in the outward chamber might hear what I said, but held it so close that they could not look in. I bade my lord formal farewell ...' Nithsdale made good his escape. His wife was arrested but soon pardoned and followed him abroad. The two lived the rest of their lives together (some thirty years) in Italy.

See also **22 Towers within the Tower of London**, pp. 29–33

8 LONDON EXECUTIONS

1. Richard Rose, 1532

All London executions were gruesome events but some were more gruesome than others. Richard Rose was a poisoner who, in 1532, was boiled alive at Smithfield. Placed in a cauldron beneath which a fire was lit, he took two hours to die. As a contemporary chronicler recorded, 'The 5th of Aprill one Richard Rose, a cooke, was boiled in Smithfielde, for poisoning of divers persons, to the number of sixteen or more, at ye Bishop of Rochester's place ... hee intended to have poisoned the bishop himselfe, but hee eate no potage that day, whereby hee escaped.'

2. Duke of Monmouth, 1685

The illegitimate son of Charles II, Monmouth attempted to take the throne from his uncle, James II. After his forces were defeated at the Battle of Sedgemoor, he was captured and, despite his desperate pleas for mercy, condemned to die at Tower Hill for treason. The executioner Jack Ketch, who was notorious for botching his executions, failed to despatch Monmouth with several blows of his axe (some reports say as many as eight) and was reduced to sawing off the duke's head with a knife. The story that, after the execution, it was suddenly realised that no official portrait of the duke existed and that his head was temporarily sewn back on to his body so that a painter could record his likeness for posterity is, sadly, extremely unlikely to be true. The portrait of a man asleep in the National Portrait Gallery, which was once thought to be the duke dead, is now catalogued as 'Portrait of an Unknown Man'.

3. Captain Kidd, 1701

Execution Dock once stood between Wapping New Stairs and King Henry's Stairs and was the place on the river where, in the seventeenth and eighteenth centuries, pirates were hanged and their bodies left in chains until three tides had washed over them. The most famous pirate to die at Execution Dock was Captain Kidd, who was led to the gallows there on 23 May 1701. The execution proved a fiasco. Kidd was so drunk he could barely stand. When the cart on which he was swaying was moved from the scaffold, he was supposed to plunge to his death but, instead, the rope around his neck

Captain Kidd
hanging in chains

broke and he was thrown to the ground. Still tipsy, and now covered in Thames mud, he was manhandled back on to the cart and eventually despatched.

4. **Earl Ferrers, 1760**
    Earl Ferrers was the only peer to be hanged for murder, having killed his steward, a man named Johnson, who obediently knelt in front of his master when told to do so and was shot. Tried by the House of Lords, Ferrers was found guilty and sentenced to hang despite attempts to claim that he was insane. When he went to meet his death on 5 May 1760, there were unseemly scenes on the scaffold when a struggle broke out between the hangman's assistant, to whom the earl had mistakenly presented 5 guineas, and the hangman, who believed the money should be his. Further trouble ensued when the hangman, who was drunk, became convinced that there were other people due to die and attempted to put a noose around the neck of the parson who was accompanying Ferrers. Only after another struggle between the hangman and the parson was Ferrers despatched. The story that Ferrers was hanged with a silk rope, befitting his status, is a myth, but he was the first person to be executed using a trapdoor.

5. **Colonel Despard, 1803**

A soldier who had served with the young Nelson in a joint military and naval expedition in the West Indies, Colonel Edward Marcus Despard was on half-pay and apparently in disgrace with the army when he drifted into the underworld of radical politics. He was arrested with dozens of others at the Oakley Arms pub in Lambeth where, according to government spies, he had been plotting the murder of the king and the overthrow of the government. Nelson, although he had not seen Despard in twenty years, appeared as a character witness at his trial but even the backing of England's naval hero was not enough to save the colonel. He was found guilty of treason and sentenced to be hanged, drawn and quartered, the traditional punishment for a traitor. The drawing and quartering part of the sentence was eventually deemed to be too medieval and did not take place but Despard was executed at Horsemonger Lane Gaol. As he mounted the scaffold, the colonel was in philosophical mood. When one of his comrades spoke of the terrible situation in which they found themselves, he said only, 'There are many better, and a few that are much worse.' His last recorded words were on the weather. Looking up to the grey London sky, he predicted rain to come, a prediction he was not around to see fulfilled.

6. **Haggerty and Holloway, 1807**

Owen Haggerty and John Holloway were sentenced to death in February 1807 for a murder committed five years earlier on Hounslow Heath. On the 22nd of the month large crowds began to gather outside Newgate to witness their execution. People were so closely pressed against one another that a panic ensued and more than thirty people were trampled to death. The worst death toll was amongst a group that had surrounded two piemen selling their wares. According to the *Newgate Calendar*, 'One of them having had his basket overthrown, which stood upon a sort of stool with four legs, some of the mob, not being aware of what had happened, and at the same time being severely pressed, fell over the basket and the man at the moment he was picking it up, together with its contents. Those who once fell were never more suffered to rise, such was the violence of the mob.'

7. **The Cato Street Conspirators, 1820**

In 1820, a group of men led by a soldier turned radical agitator called Arthur Thistlewood planned to assassinate the entire British Cabinet and launch a revolution. Gathering in a stable loft in Cato Street, just off the Edgware Road, the conspirators intended to march to Grosvenor Square and the house of Lord Harrowby where the Cabinet members were dining. The group had already been infiltrated by government spies and the loft was raided by Bow Street Runners before the revolutionaries could set out for Lord Harrowby's. In the confusion, Thistlewood killed one of the Bow Street Runners and escaped but he was captured the following day. He and four others were hung at Newgate. All died bravely, although Thistlewood, aggravated by one of his comrades' boisterous singing of 'Death or Liberty' on the scaffold, is supposed to have said, 'Be quiet, Ings; we can die without all this noise.' After the hangings, the men, as traitors, were beheaded. The executioner held up each head but dropped one, whereupon some members of the crowd cried out, 'Butterfingers!' The beheadings were the last that took place in London.

8. **The Mannings, 1849**

Mrs Manning was Swiss and had come to England to work as a maid for an English noblewoman. Together with her husband, she was found guilty of killing her Irish lover, Patrick O'Connor and the couple were executed on 13

November 1849 on the roof of Horsemonger Lane Gaol in Southwark. One of the largest crowds ever to attend a public hanging in London gathered to see the Mannings die. Among them was Charles Dickens and he was deeply shocked, not so much by the execution itself, but by the crowd's behaviour. In a letter to the press, he wrote: 'I believe that a sight so inconceivably awful as the wickedness and levity of the immense crowd collected at that execution this morning could be imagined by no man, and could be presented in no heathen land under the sun. The horrors of the gibbet and of the crime which brought the wretched murderers to it faded in my mind before the atrocious bearing, looks, and language of the assembled spectators.'

6 CANDIDATES FOR JACK THE RIPPER

Although more than a century has passed since the murders, the most notorious serial killer in London's history remains the unknown individual, nicknamed Jack the Ripper, who terrorised the East End in the second half of 1888 and killed at least five prostitutes in Whitechapel. In all likelihood, the true identity of Jack the Ripper will never be known for certain but this has not prevented the rise of an entire Ripper industry. Hundreds of books, articles, films and TV programmes have been devoted to investigating the murders. Dozens and dozens of candidates for the Ripper have been suggested. Here are just six:

1. **Lewis Carroll**
    An American researcher called Richard Wallace once 'proved' that elaborate analysis of the works of Lewis Carroll, otherwise known as the Oxford mathematics don Charles Lutwidge Dodgson, showed him to be the

real Jack the Ripper. Wallace took passages from Carroll's writings and deconstructed them to reveal anagrammatic messages in which Dodgson confessed to details of the murders and how, in company with a fellow don called Thomas Vere Bayne, he committed them. Unfortunately Wallace's anagrams aren't very precise – letters are missed out if they prove inconvenient – and Dodgson's messages seem alarmingly ungrammatical for an Oxford don.

Lewis Carroll
(photograph taken by
himself)

Even in the overheated world of Ripperology, Wallace's claim was not received with any great enthusiasm.

2. **George Chapman (Severin Klosowski)**
Klosowski, who changed his name to George Chapman, was a Pole who arrived in Whitechapel in 1888 and worked as a barber in the neighbourhood. The reasons for suspecting Chapman are that, just as it was claimed of the Ripper, he had some medical training (he had been apprenticed to a surgeon in his native Poland) and that he was later convicted of killing women. Unfortunately for anyone wishing to claim Chapman as the Ripper, his undisputed victims were poisoned. Chapman had become a pub landlord in the 1890s and, in 1902, was arrested for the murder of his barmaid and lover, Maud Marsh, whom he had despatched with a large dose of antimony. Police investigations revealed that two previous barmaids had died in unexplained circumstances. Chapman was tried, found guilty and executed the following year for the murder of Maud Marsh.

3. **Neill Cream**
One theory claims that the Whitechapel murderer was Dr Thomas Neill Cream, a deranged abortionist and poisoner

who was executed in 1892 for administering strychnine to two prostitutes in south London. Cream is alleged to have been attempting a last-minute confession on the gallows when the executioner pulled the lever and he dropped through the trap. He got as far as, 'I am Jack –' before he fell. The difficulty with this story is that, at the time of the Whitechapel murders, records show that Cream was several thousand miles away and behind bars, serving a sentence in Joliet Penitentiary in Illinois. Some researchers, unwilling to relinquish a good story, have got round this apparently conclusive fact by arguing that it was possible that he paid a double to serve his sentence. The most generous assessment of this theory is that it seems unlikely.

4.   **Montague John Druitt**
Druitt was an Oxford-educated barrister and schoolmaster with a family history of mental illness, whose body was fished out of the Thames on 31 December 1888. There is very little concrete evidence against Druitt beyond a statement, some time after the murders, by Sir Melville Macnaghten, assistant commissioner at Scotland Yard, who wrote that, 'From private information I have little doubt that his own family suspected this man of being the Whitechapel murderer; it was alleged that he was sexually insane.' On the contrary, there is plenty of evidence that suggests Druitt was not the murderer. A keen sportsman, he had played in a cricket match at Blackheath on 8 September a mere six hours after the murder of Annie Chapman. Although it is not inconceivable, it seems unlikely that he could have been stalking the streets of Whitechapel with a blood-drenched knife at 5 a.m. and practising his off spin at Blackheath at 11.

5.   **Prince Eddy**
The most notorious theory about Jack the Ripper is the claim, entertainingly advanced by Stephen Knight in his 1978 book *Jack the Ripper: The Final Solution*, that the

murders were part of a conspiracy to cover up the fact that Prince Albert Victor Christian Edward ('Eddy' to his friends), third in line to the throne, had fathered a love-child. The mother was not only a poor girl from the East End but, even worse, a Roman Catholic. Several prostitutes in the Whitechapel area knew of the child's existence and who the father was. To make sure they remained silent, they were all killed and the blame placed on a phantom serial killer. The murders were actually the work of a loyal syndicate, consisting of the queen's physician Sir William Gull, a coachman named John Netley who had ferried the prince to his assignations and Robert Anderson, a very senior officer in the CID.

6. **Jill the Ripper**
    There are those who believe that the Whitechapel murderer was not a man but a woman. Jack the Ripper was actually Jill the Ripper. Immediately after the last killing, a woman testified to the police that she had seen the victim leaving her lodgings some time after she must, according to medical evidence, have been dead. The police considered the idea that the witness had actually seen the murderer, a woman, dressed in the victim's clothing but soon dismissed it. Half a century later, a researcher returned to the theory and argued that the killer was a deranged midwife. He even gave a possible name to the midwife, claiming there were similarities between the *modus operandi* in the Ripper killings and Mary Pearcey's murders of her lover's wife and child in 1890. Mary Pearcey was hanged on 23 December of that year, unaware of the fact that her name was, decades later, to be linked with the Whitechapel murders. The whole idea that Jack the Ripper was a woman seems highly improbable, although Sherlock Holmes's creator, Sir Arthur Conan Doyle, was of the opinion that the killer disguised himself as a woman to prowl the streets of the East End.

Others suspected of the murders have included the painter Walter Sickert, the poet Francis Thompson, a cousin of Virginia Woolf called James Kenneth Stephen, a mysterious Norwegian sailor called Fogelma and a Liverpool cotton merchant named James Maybrick whose wife was accused of murdering him when he died in May 1889. Nonetheless, the case remains unsolved.

11 LONDON GANGSTERS

1. **Jonathan Wild**

   In another era Jonathan Wild's entrepreneurial skills would probably have made him a captain of industry but, in the early eighteenth century, his opportunity to make his fortune came through crime. Working as a fence, Wild hit upon the brilliant idea that it was easier and less risky to sell the stolen property he received back to its owners rather than try to get rid of it on the open market. From there it was only a short step to commissioning thieves to steal goods to order which he could then return, for a price, to those who had been robbed. Soon he controlled a vast, London-wide organisation of thieves who worked by his rules. Any villain who stepped out of line was instantly shopped to the authorities for a reward. Meanwhile Wild could pose as a virtuous citizen, the 'Thief-Taker General' who caught criminals and returned stolen property. However, his monopoly on crime in the capital could not last. He made too many enemies on both sides of the law. In 1725, he was imprisoned for attempting to spring one of his supporters from Newgate. Sensing that his time was up, many of his associates turned against him and, convicted on their evidence, he was hanged at Tyburn. After his death his body was sold for dissection and his skeleton can still be seen in the museum of the Royal College of Surgeons in Lincoln's Inn Fields.

2. **Joseph Merceron**

In the early nineteenth century Joseph Merceron ruled the roost in Bethnal Green. Outwardly a respectable JP, Merceron was spectacularly corrupt. He courted popularity by keeping the pubs open and providing entertainment in the form of dog-fights and bull-baiting but, meanwhile, he was busy feathering his own nest and finding his own uses for parish money. Merceron was eventually prosecuted for pocketing public funds in 1818 but he received only an eighteen-month prison sentence and, emerging from jail, resumed most of his activities in the East End. He died, full of years, in 1839. Merceron Street, E1, is named after him.

3. **Adam Worth**

Known as the 'Napoleon of Crime', Adam Worth is said to have been the model for the master criminal Professor Moriarty in the Sherlock Holmes stories. A German whose family emigrated to America, Worth fought in the American Civil War, began his criminal career in New York and arrived in London in the 1870s. Financed by the proceeds from a string of robberies, he was soon living in style in a flat in Piccadilly and, in 1876, he carried out his most daring theft, removing Gainsborough's famous painting of the Duchess of Devonshire from a gallery in Bond Street. Worth was infatuated by the portrait and never attempted to sell it. Imprisoned in the 1890s, after an associate betrayed him, he died in 1902 and was buried in Highgate Cemetery under a tombstone bearing the name of one of his aliases, Henry J. Raymond.

4. **Ikey Bogard**

A gangster of the Edwardian era, Bogard dressed as a cowboy and openly carried a gun. Although he was Jewish, not black, he was also known as Darky the Coon, presumably because he had a particularly dark complexion. Rivalry between his gang and the 'Harding

Gang' culminated in violent confrontations at the Bluecoat Boy pub in Bishopsgate and outside the Old Street Magistrates' Court, where a pitched battle was fought until police, emerging from the courtroom, intervened. In World War I, Bogard was forced to leave the East End for the battlefields of Flanders and was decorated for bravery.

5. **Charles 'Darby' Sabini**

The model for the gangster Colleoni in Graham Greene's novel *Brighton Rock*, Darby Sabini was born in Saffron Hill in 1889 in an area known as Little Italy and, in the 1920s and 1930s, he and his brothers became leaders of one of the most vicious of the gangs that travelled out from London to the racecourses of southern England. Criminals like the Sabinis were known in the press as 'razor gangs' but were not averse to using other means of persuasion if necessary. One senior police officer recalled that, when they were at the racecourses, 'Darby Sabini and his thugs used to stand sideways to let the bookmakers see the hammers in their pockets.' During one court appearance, the judge, seeking to impress onlookers with his skills as a linguist, addressed Sabini in Italian. Sabini, who travelled outside London only to intimidate people at racecourses and had never left Britain, merely looked baffled. Interned or imprisoned during World War II, the Sabinis lost control of their gangster empire and other, younger men like Jack Spot and Billy Hill took over their territory.

6. **Jack 'Spot' Comer**

Born in Whitechapel in 1912, Jack Spot (as he was usually known) became a local hero in the East End because of his willingness to confront Oswald Mosley's fascist Blackshirts in the 1930s, but he was also a vicious gangster who took control of many of the racecourse protection rackets when the Sabini family was interned during the war. Spot's rivalry with Billy Hill (see below) came to a head in 1956 when he was attacked outside his flat at Hyde Park Mansions by a band of Hill's men, including a shillelagh-wielding 'Mad' Frankie Fraser. Beaten and scarred by razors from the attack, Jack Spot announced his retirement from thuggery and moved to Ireland. He returned to London as an old man and died in 1996.

7. **Billy Hill**

Jack Spot's great rival was born in Seven Dials in 1911. Beginning his criminal career as a teenage burglar, he went on to become both the mastermind behind a series of spectacular robberies and post office raids and a major racketeer, running many of the gambling joints and shady nightclubs of the West End. He died in 1984 when, according to Jack Spot, he became 'the richest man in the graveyard'.

8. & 9. **Charlie and Eddie Richardson**

While the Kray Twins were terrorising the East End, another pair of brothers was doing the same south of the river. Scrap-metal dealers, who moved into the management of drinking clubs and the perpetration of insurance frauds, the Richardson brothers were just as prepared to use violence to get their own way as the more infamous Krays. 'I was a businessman who had to protect his interests', Charlie Richardson once reminisced but not every businessman felt that this self-protection should include running an electric current through the genitals of those who crossed him. On 30 July 1966, both brothers and several members of their gang were arrested, thus preventing them from watching England's World Cup final with West Germany which took place later that day. In the ensuing trial, the torture employed by the Richardsons to enforce their rule was clearly revealed and both brothers were sentenced to long periods in jail.

10 & 11. Ronnie and Reggie Kray

The most famous of all London gangsters were born in Shoreditch in 1933. The family moved to Bethnal Green six years later and 178 Vallance Road, E1, was their de facto headquarters for much of their criminal career. Promising amateur boxers in their youth, the twins decided that the protection racket offered greater opportunities than the ring and, by the early sixties, they had built up a small empire of nightclubs and other properties, financed by their criminal activities. They became East End celebrities, photographed by David Bailey and hobnobbing with people as diverse as Barbara Windsor and Lord Boothby, but the violence on which their reputation was built was escalating. On 9 March 1966 Ronnie Kray walked into The Blind Beggar pub in Whitechapel High Street and shot a man named George Cornell in the face. Not only was Cornell associated with the rival gangster family the Richardsons, he had also made the fatal mistake of calling Ronnie 'a fat poof'. (For the ex-boxer, perhaps the description of him as 'fat' rankled as much as the comment on his sexuality.) The murder of George Cornell marked the beginning of the end for the Krays, although it took the police another two years to bring them to trial. During that time, Reggie committed his own murder, stabbing a small-time crook named Jack 'The Hat' McVitie repeatedly at a basement flat in Stoke Newington. The twins were arrested in 1968, tried, convicted and sentenced to life imprisonment. Ronnie died in custody in 1995; Reggie, suffering from inoperable cancer, was released on compassionate grounds in 2000 but died soon afterwards. The funeral services of both twins were held at St Matthew's Church, Bethnal Green Road. Ronnie's funeral procession, said to be London's biggest since the death of Churchill, consisted of a horse-drawn hearse, followed by a thirty-car cortège and watched by tens of thousands of people. Outside the church gangs of young men gathered who, in the memorable words of the journalist Duncan Campbell, 'looked uncertain whether they were auditioning for *Pulp Fiction* or *The Lavender Hill Mob*'.

10 LONDON
CRIME STATISTICS

The following figures are taken from the official Metropolitan Police Services statistics for the financial year 2004/2005.

1. 182 – Number of Murders
2. 201,926 – Number of Acts of Violence Against the Person
3. 2,446 – Number of Rapes
4. 8,418 – Number of other Sexual Offences
5. 39,033 – Number of Robberies
6. 101,474 – Number of Burglaries
7. 412,264 – Number of Thefts
8. 70,144 – Number of Frauds and Forgeries
9. 135,684 – Number of Acts of Criminal Damage
10. 33,011 – Number of Drugs Offences

6 ESPIONAGE SITES IN LONDON

1. **MI6 Building, Vauxhall Cross**

   Ironically, one of the most distinctive and noticeable buildings on the whole Thames riverfront is the headquarters of a secretive and security-conscious organisation. Variously known as 'Babylon-on-Thames' and 'Legoland', the post-modern MI6 HQ at Vauxhall

   Cross, designed by the architect Terry Farrell, was also seen on cinema screens across the world when it was used as a backdrop to an opening chase sequence in the James Bond movie, *The World Is Not Enough*.

   The MI6 building, seen from Vauxhall Bridge

2. **49 Moorgate**

   In the 1920s, this was the address of the All-Russian Co-operative Society (ARCOS), supposedly an innocuous trade mission but actually the headquarters of a Soviet spy ring. Dozens of London police officers, travelling by tube rather than in marked vehicles to avoid arousing suspicion, descended on the building to search it in May 1927. Despite frenzied, last-minute attempts by ARCOS staff to destroy them, more than a quarter of a million documents were seized. Few proved as incriminating as the British authorities hoped but the raid resulted in a rupture in Anglo–Soviet relations.

3. **Brompton Oratory**

   According to the memoirs of several Soviet defectors, the church, next door to the Victoria and Albert Museum, was used by the KGB during the Cold War as a 'dead letter box', a place where agents could leave sensitive material to be collected later by other agents. A small space behind two pillars, close to a Pietà statue, was the favoured position in which to leave microfilms and cassettes of secret documents and information.

4. **2 Whitehall Court**

The offices of MI6 were at this address from 1911 to 1923, the years when it was under the command of its first chief, Mansfield Smith-Cumming, the original 'C' of the service. Cumming sat in his office ('Office all day – no one appeared', he wrote in his diary), awaiting visitors who were unable to call because its location was a secret. Working almost alone, and often paying for essentials such as typewriters and writing paper out of his own pocket, he struggled to undertake the tasks he believed he had been given. Agents were duly recruited. Most proved amateurish. In 1910, two army officers called Trench and Brandon, nominally under Cumming's control, set off on a walking-holiday-cum-spying-mission along Germany's Baltic coast. Their collars were felt by the German authorities within a few days of leaving Britain and the information they had gathered was found under the mattress in Trench's hotel bedroom. The two men went on trial and were sentenced to several years' detention in German prisons. Endeavouring to meet all his agents in the field, Cumming faced a number of surprises. One, who had filed reports as Mademoiselle Espiesse, turned out to be a large and truculent man from Belgium who was chiefly interested in rooking more money out of Cumming. Another was a semi-deranged fantasist, keen on plugging his alleged invention of a camera that could fit into a gentleman's tie-pin.

5. **10 Clifford Chambers, New Bond Street**

This was the last London address of the flamboyant Soviet agent, drunk and gay lecher, Guy Burgess, and it was from Clifford Chambers that he departed on a journey that ended with his defection to Russia, together with Donald Maclean, in 1951. One of those deputed to search Burgess's flat was Anthony Blunt, an unwise choice since he was a Soviet spy himself.

6. **31 Pembroke Gardens, W8**

Ernest Oldham was a Foreign Office clerk living in Pembroke Gardens in the 1930s when he decided to supplement his income by selling secret documents to the Soviets. After a false start as an agent, when Soviet officials refused to believe he had access to anything valuable, he regularly provided the Russians with information but he resigned from the Foreign Office in 1933, racked by guilt over his role as a traitor. The KGB, anxious that he should not confess his treachery to the British security services and compromise other agents in London, entered the flat in Pembroke Gardens and murdered him later in the same year.

4

LONDON PAST

8 London Riots

3 London Sieges

13 London Disasters

10 London Duels

15 Causes of Death in Eighteenth-Century London

6 Memorable London Fires (other than the Great Fire of 1666)

6 Lost London Rivers (including 1 that may never have existed)

6 Surviving Remnants of Roman London (And 1 That Isn't)

8 London Foods Past and Present

9 London Coffee-Houses

10 Historic Documents in the National Archives, Kew

8 LONDON RIOTS

1. **Evil May Day, 1517**

    Fuelled by resentment of foreign merchants and craftsmen who had settled in London and were supposedly preventing native citizens from gaining the jobs and financial rewards they deserved, a mob of apprentices and minor clerics, led by a man called John Lincoln, roamed through the city's streets, attacking and burning houses and workshops belonging to traders from Flanders, Italy, France and the Baltic. Troops, led by the earls of Suffolk and Surrey, were rapidly deployed and four hundred prisoners were taken. Some of the leaders in the rioting, including Lincoln, were hanged, drawn and quartered. Other prisoners were brought before the king, Henry VIII, at Westminster Hall where Catherine of Aragon and Thomas Wolsey successfully pleaded for mercy for them. Henry granted them their lives whereupon, according to a contemporary account, they 'took the halters from their necks and danced and sang'.

2. **Bawdy House Riots, 1668**

    On Shrove Tuesday 1668 large numbers of apprentices attacked brothels throughout the city. Apprentice high spirits were commonplace and invading the bawdy houses was a traditional expression of them but this year the riots were more serious, possibly due to the involvement of veterans from Cromwell's army, and they became an expression of disgust with the dissipation and debauchery of Charles II's court. Four apprentices were found guilty of high treason and hanged, drawn and quartered

3. **Gordon Riots, 1780**

    In 1778 the passing of a Catholic Relief Act, removing a number of restrictions on the rights of Roman Catholics to own and inherit property, provoked fantasies of imminent Catholic revolution in London. Wild rumours circulated.

An army of thousands of Jesuit priests was lurking in secret tunnels under the city awaiting word from the Pope to emerge and take over the city. Militant Protestants formed their own societies to protect what they believed were their threatened liberties. On 2 June 1780 members of one such group, the Protestant Association, led by the unstable and fanatically anti-Catholic aristocrat Lord George Gordon, marched towards the House of Commons. The demonstration rapidly descended into a series of riots all over the city. The houses of Catholics and chapels attached to foreign embassies, such as the Sardinian Chapel in Duke Street, off the Strand, were targeted by the mob and set alight. The authorities were slow to respond to the rioting. 'I must be cautious what I do lest I bring the mob to my own house', the Lord Mayor told one Catholic merchant. The rioting spiralled out of control and the city was thrown into violent chaos for days. Newgate prison was attacked and prisoners released. A house in Bloomsbury Square which belonged to Lord Chief Justice Mansfield, who had advocated tolerance of Catholics, was burned to the ground. Even the Bank of England was threatened and troops were called out to defend it. It took the government more than a week to restore order by which time as many as a thousand people may have lost their lives. One hundred and sixty of the rioters were eventually brought to trial and twenty-five were hanged. Lord George Gordon, who had been the catalyst that sparked the riots, was tried on a charge of treason but was acquitted because it was agreed that he had had no treasonable intentions in leading the mob to the House of Commons. Gordon later converted to Judaism. Imprisoned in Newgate for 'a libel upon British justice', he insisted on practising his new religion, eating kosher meat and wearing phylacteries, and died in prison of a typhoid fever in December 1793.

4. **The Old Price Riots, 1809**

After the Covent Garden Theatre burned to the ground in 1808 a new building was erected the following year and the management of the theatre took the opportunity to raise prices from six shillings to seven shillings for boxes and from three shillings and sixpence to four shillings for most other seats. Outraged by the rise, the audience at the first performance in the new theatre constantly interrupted the playing of *Macbeth* with loud shouts of 'Old Prices! Old Prices!' Soldiers were sent into the gallery to quell the disturbances but the gallery-goers, further angered by the fact that in the badly-designed new theatre they could see little more than the legs of the actors, continued to cause mayhem. In fact they continued to do so at every performance for the next three months, bringing rattles, whistles, trumpets and farmyard animals into the theatre to cause maximum disruption. Eventually the management, under the famous actor and impresario John Philip Kemble, bowed to the pressure and returned seats to the old prices. Kemble appeared on stage to make a public apology to the rioting audience.

5. **Sunday Trading Riots, 1855**

Tens of thousands gathered in Hyde Park on 24 June, and again a week later, to protest against a Sunday trading bill which would have made it almost impossible to buy and sell on a Sunday, at the time the only day most working people had free. As police attempted to move people on, claiming (falsely) that the park was the Queen's private property, running battles broke out between them and the demonstrators. Karl Marx, who was present as a reporter for a radical German newspaper, was convinced that the Hyde Park rioting was but the start of something larger. 'We were spectators from beginning to end,' he wrote, 'and do not think we are exaggerating in saying that the English Revolution began yesterday in Hyde Park.' He was exaggerating. The bill was withdrawn and, although there were further small demonstrations in the park later in the year, the revolution failed to materialise.

6. **Black Monday, 1886**

On Monday, 8 February 1886, two groups of radical socialists organised meetings in Trafalgar Square to protest about unemployment. Despite the possibility of violence, police preparations were laughably inadequate. The man given the responsibility for maintaining public order, District Superintendent Robert Walker, was in his seventies and not particularly active for his age. His main contribution to the day's proceedings was to get himself lost in the crowds and have his pocket picked. After the speeches in the square were over, the demonstrators showed little inclination to disperse. Walker's men proved little better than their commanding officer. As thousands left the square and headed off towards fashionable Piccadilly and St James's, intent on smashing windows and intimidating their social superiors, the police stayed put. Still standing close to Nelson's Column, they looked to one sarcastic journalist present as if they were 'propping it up ... lest it should topple, or keeping watch upon the lions for fear they should run away'. The day was a fiasco for the police and the Metropolitan Police Commissioner, Sir Edmund Henderson, lost his job as a result.

7. **Battle of Cable Street, 1936**

In the autumn of 1936, the leader of the British Union of Fascists, Sir Oswald Mosley, announced a march by his supporters in the East End, passing through areas where there were large Jewish populations. Despite attempts to have the provocative march banned, it went ahead on 4 October. Thousands of anti-fascist demonstrators gathered in the area, erecting makeshift roadblocks in an attempt to stop Mosley's followers. Barricades blocked the entrance to Cable Street. Running battles ensued between the police, still struggling to allow the Blackshirts to march, and the anti-fascists, determined that they would not pass. Eventually the march was abandoned and Mosley's men dispersed to other parts of the city. A large mural on the side of St George's Town Hall, painted in the 1980s, commemorates the 'battle'.

8. ## Notting Hill Riots, 1958

There had been race riots in London before Notting Hill – in Stepney, just after World War I, for example, and in Deptford in 1949 – but they were small beer compared with the sustained violence of the last weekend in August of 1958. Mostly centred on the streets around Blenheim Crescent, running battles ensued when white youths attacked almost anyone with a black skin. In Totobag's café in Blenheim Crescent customers were besieged by a white mob. The worst of the violence occurred on the Monday when a white racist called Jeffrey Hamm addressed a large crowd outside Latimer Road tube station, claiming that black people had turned Notting Hill into a 'brothel'. Gangs of whites, hundreds strong, roamed the streets, armed with broken bottles, knives and iron bars. Primitive petrol bombs were thrown into houses believed to have black residents. The rioting continued throughout the day and it was only on the Tuesday that an uneasy calm descended on the streets of Notting Hill.

3 LONDON SIEGES

1. ## Siege of Sidney Street, January 1911

In the first days of 1911 word reached police that two of the gang of anarchists wanted in connection with the Houndsditch murders of the previous month had gone to ground in a house in Sidney Street in the East End. Within a short time, No. 100 was surrounded by officers and most of the residents of nearby houses were evacuated. The Home Secretary, Winston Churchill, was impatient for instant results, and he gave orders to deploy troops to Sidney Street. The first soldiers, Scots Guards stationed at the Tower of London, arrived in the middle of the morning of 3 January 1911. Marksmen were put in position on the top floors of adjoining buildings from where they could pour fire into the building. Churchill himself arrived shortly after noon and was soon in de facto command of the assorted forces gathered in the street. More and more troops were poured into Sidney Street. As revolutionaries and soldiers exchanged bursts of gunfire, smoke was seen to billow from the top floor of No. 100 and soon the building was alight, forcing the men inside to retreat to those rooms still untouched by the fire. Eventually the house was clearly so gutted that it was impossible the men could still be alive and the authorities moved in to the shell of No. 100. The bodies of two anarchists, Svaars and Sokoloff, were found in the burnt-out remains of the house. Sokoloff had been shot in the head by one of the military marksmen as he stood near an open window. His comrade had been overcome by the smoke and fumes of the fire. A third man, supposedly in the building and known only as 'Peter the Painter', had disappeared.

2. **Spaghetti House Siege, September 1975**

The Spaghetti House is a still-existing chain of Italian restaurants in London. On 28 September, nine members of staff at the Knightsbridge branch were taken hostage by three gunmen and led down to the restaurant's basement. A tenth escaped and raised the alarm, and soon the premises were surrounded by police. For six days there was a stand-off between police and gunmen while the hostages were huddled miserably in the basement, but all were eventually released unharmed and the gunmen arrested. In all likelihood the siege was the result of a botched robbery (weekly takings from several of the restaurants were being counted in the Knightsbridge branch) but the leader of the gunmen, a Nigerian named Franklin Davies, claimed to be a member of a shadowy terrorist organisation known as the Black Liberation Army.

3. **Balcombe Street Siege, December 1975**
On 6 December 1975, John and Sheila Matthews were sitting innocently in the living room of their flat in Balcombe Street, Marylebone, when it was invaded by four gunmen who took them hostage. The men were members of the provisional IRA in flight from the Metropolitan Police. Barricaded in the Matthews' flat, the men demanded a plane to fly them to Dublin. Their request was refused and, for six days, hostages and captors were holed up in Balcombe Street, surrounded by hundreds of police and by several SAS teams, awaiting their moment to end the siege. Eventually, the IRA men, realising that their demands were unlikely to be met, surrendered peacefully and millions of viewers on TV saw them taken into custody.

13 LONDON DISASTERS

1. **The Fatal Vespers, 1623**
In the early part of the seventeenth century, the French ambassador's residence was Hunsdon House, Blackfriars. On the afternoon of 5 November 1623, more than 300 people were gathered in an upper room of the house to take part in a religious service conducted by two Jesuit priests. The floor beams, not designed to support the weight of so many, gave way and large numbers of the congregation were plunged into the room below. Ninety-five people, including the two priests, were killed and dozens more injured. The disaster, which has been variously called 'the Fatal Vespers', 'the Blackfriars Downfall' and 'the Doleful

Evensong', was assumed by many Londoners at the time to be the judgement of God on the French Catholics who had offended the Almighty with their idolatrous practices.

2. ### Execution of Lord Lovat, 1747
    The Jacobite Lord Lovat, the last man to be executed by beheading in Britain, faced his death on Tower Hill in 1747. Huge crowds had gathered to see him die and grandstands had been erected to allow spectators a better view of the executioner's block. One of these stands became so crowded that it collapsed and twenty people were killed. Lovat, waiting to approach the block, witnessed the disaster and appeared to be grimly amused by it. 'The mair mischief, the mair sport', he is reported to have said.

3. ### The London Beer Flood, 1814
    On 17 October 1814, in the Horseshoe Brewery in Tottenham Court Road, a huge vat burst its hoops, rupturing other vats, and more than a million litres of beer swept through the brewery walls and into the streets. The sea of beer carried away neighbouring houses and drowned nine people. After the disaster the brewery was brought to court but the judge, deciding that the beer flood qualified as an Act of God, refused to hold it responsible for the deaths. The site of the Horseshoe Brewery is now occupied by the Dominion Theatre.

4. ### The Sinking of the *Princess Alice*, 1878
    On the evening of 3 September 1878 the pleasure steamer the *Princess Alice* was returning from a day-trip down the Thames with more than 700 passengers aboard. Near Woolwich, a collier called the *Bywell Castle* approached the pleasure boat and the captain of the *Princess Alice* made a tragic mistake in manoeuvring his ship. He ran directly across the path of the collier. The *Princess Alice*

was almost cut in two and sank in less than five minutes. More than 640 people drowned in what was the worst ever river disaster in Britain.

5. **Hebrew Dramatic Club, 1887**
In March 1886 the Hebrew Dramatic Club, the first purpose-built Yiddish theatre in London, was opened in Princes Street (now Princelet Street), off Brick Lane. Less than a year later, disaster struck the theatre. During a performance of an operetta called *The Gypsy Princess* on 18 January 1887, a fire was mistakenly believed to have broken out. As the audience panicked and stampeded for the exits, seventeen people were crushed to death.

6. **The *Albion* Disaster, 1898**
On 21 June 1898, the Duchess of York arrived at the Thames Ironworks dockyard in Canning Town to launch the Royal Navy cruiser HMS *Albion*. Thousands of spectators had gathered to watch the launch and several hundreds, ignoring danger notices, made their way onto a temporary bridge that had been erected by the side of another ship in the dock. As the *Albion* travelled down the slipway and hit the water, its momentum created a large wave which smashed into the temporary bridge and plunged many of those standing on it into the water. Thirty-eight people died. The Scottish 'poet' William McGonagall, a connoisseur of Victorian disasters, wrote of the *Albion* tragedy in his own inimitable bad verse: 'Just as the vessel entered the water the bridge and staging gave way/Immersing some three hundred people which caused great dismay/Amongst the thousands of spectators that were standing there/And in the faces of the bystanders, were depicted despair.'

7. **The Silvertown Explosion, 1917**
A fire broke out at Brunner Mond's chemical works in Silvertown on 19 January and ignited 50 tons of TNT

that were being stored there. The resulting explosion was devastating, destroying many of the surrounding streets and killing 73 people. A memorial to those who died still stands in North Woolwich Road, E16, near the site of what was once the factory.

8. **Bombing of the Café de Paris, 1941**

One of the worst disasters of the Blitz took place on the night of 8 March 1941, when a bomb fell on the well-known and fashionable nightspot, the Café de Paris in Coventry Street, while the band, led by Ken 'Snakehips' Johnson, was playing. Eighty people, including 'Snakehips' and several members of his band, were killed.

9. **Bethnal Green Tube, 1943**

During an air raid warning on 3 March, crowds were making an orderly way into the station when they were panicked, probably by the unfamiliar noise of a new type of anti-aircraft rocket being launched in nearby Victoria Park. A woman carrying a baby lost her footing. Those behind her kept on coming and bodies began to pile up in the stairwell. One hundred and seventy-three people died, mostly from suffocation. Although the government acknowledged immediately that an accident had happened at a tube station, the name of the station was not officially released until two years after the disaster.

10. **Ronan Point, 1968**

On the morning of 16 May, a gas explosion destroyed much of a twenty-three-storey block of flats called Ronan Point which stood in Clever Road, Newham. Four people died in the disaster (another person died later from injuries sustained in the blast) and Ronan Point had enormous impact on housing policy in the city as those who objected to high-rise blocks found the perfect argument against them.

11. Moorgate Tube Crash, 1975

Just after 8.45 on the morning of 28 February the Northern Line train from Drayton Park, packed with commuters, drew into Moorgate station. Instead of coming to a halt at the platform, it seemed to accelerate and carried on into a dead-end tunnel, crashing into the brick wall at the end of it. The driver and forty-two passengers were killed. Mystery still surrounds the cause of the crash.

12. The King's Cross Fire, 1987

Thirty-one people died in the devastating fire of 18 November 1987, which began when rubbish and grease under one of the old, wooden escalators were ignited, almost certainly by a discarded match or cigarette end. Full of commuters even at 7.30 p.m., when the fire broke out, the station rapidly became a death trap as a fireball swept up the escalator and into the ticket hall. One of the victims of the fire was not identified until 2004. Alexander Fallon, a homeless, seventy-two-year-old man was so severely burned that it was impossible for forensic scientists to identify his remains until, nearly seventeen years later, new evidence emerged to link him with the fire scene.

13. The *Marchioness* Disaster, 1989

On 20 August, a collision between the dredger *Bowbelle* and the pleasure ship the *Marchioness* just upstream of Cannon Street Bridge resulted in the deaths of fifty-one people. Most of the victims were young people who were attending a party and disco on the *Marchioness*, and there has been much controversy, still unresolved today, about the exact causes of the disaster, the worst on the Thames since the *Princess Alice* sinking 111 years earlier.

10 LONDON DUELS

1. ### Sir George Wharton v. Sir James Stuart, Canonbury, 1609

   Both men were leading figures at the court of James I but both had a reputation for violence and dissipation. A quarrel between Wharton and the Earl of Pembroke over cards had nearly finished in a duel and only the intervention of the king had prevented it. In 1609, another argument at the gaming table, this time between Wharton and Sir James Stuart, resulted in a duel which the king was unable to stop. Fighting with rapier and dagger in fields at Canonbury, the two men both died. 'At the first thrust each of them killed the other,' according to a contemporary report, 'and they fell dead in each other's arms.'

2. ### The Field of the Forty Footsteps, 1685

   The name was given to an area behind the British Museum, long covered over by Montague Street. The name came from a story, probably apocryphal, of two brothers who fought a duel over a woman on the site at the time of the Duke of Monmouth's rebellion in 1685. Both were killed and the forty impressions of their feet, made on the ground as they paced away from one another before firing their pistols, remained there for many years afterwards.

3. ### Lord Mohun and Duke of Hamilton, 1712

   The fourth Baron Mohun was an inveterate dueller who had twice been charged and twice acquitted of murder but he made a fatal mistake when, aggravated by a long dispute between the two men over a property in the north of England, he challenged the Duke of Hamilton to cross swords with him. When they met in Hyde Park, the Duke ran Mohun through and then moved to his side to offer assistance. Mohun, gentlemanly to the last, stabbed him in the stomach. Both men died. There is a fictional account of the duel in Thackeray's novel, *The History of Henry Esmond*.

4. **William Byron v. William Chaworth, Star and Garter Inn, 1765**

    William Byron, 5th Baron Byron was the great-uncle of the poet and already had a reputation for violence and villainy before a tavern quarrel with his kinsman, William Chaworth, supposedly over the best way to hang game, ended in a duel. The fight took place in a back room of the Star and Garter Inn in Pall Mall and, in the dimly lit space, Byron stabbed Chaworth in the stomach. Chaworth lived on for a day, complaining only about the fact that he had been stupid enough to fight in a room where the light was too poor for him to see his opponent properly. Byron, soon to be known as the 'Wicked Lord', was tried by his peers in the House of Lords and, found guilty of manslaughter, was fined. The sword he had used to kill Chaworth was given pride of place on the wall of his bedroom at the family estate at Newstead Abbey in Nottinghamshire.

5. **Charles Edward Fox v. William Adam, 1779**

    Fox was a scathing critic of Lord North's policies in America and the duel was fought against one of North's supporters whom he had denounced. It was suggested by his second that Fox, a large man, should stand sideways to minimise the chances of being hit. Fox refused, remarking, 'I'm as thick one way as the other!'

6. **Lady Almeria Braddock v. Mrs Elphinstone, Hyde Park, 1792**

    The so-called 'petticoat duel' resulted from a heated discussion between the two women about Lady Braddock's true age. Pistol shots were exchanged, one of which blew off Lady Braddock's hat, and the two women then crossed swords and fenced until Mrs Elphinstone was wounded slightly in the arm. Wisely, she then chose to apologise to her opponent for doubting her word about her age and the duel came to an end.

7. **Humphrey Howarth MP v. Lord Barrymore, 1806**

Howarth stripped naked before the duel because, he claimed, he didn't want to run the risk that pieces of his clothing might enter any wounds he might receive and infect them. Acutely aware of the absurdity of exchanging pistol shots with a nude man, Barrymore withdrew from the encounter.

8. **Castlereagh v. Canning, Putney Heath, 1809**

One of the few occasions when two Cabinet ministers have tried to solve their differences with a pistol fight, the duel between George Canning, then Foreign Secretary, and Lord Castlereagh, Secretary of State for War and the Colonies, took place at the height of the war against Napoleon. The two men had quarrelled over the deployment of troops in Europe and Castlereagh, discovering what he believed to be a plot between Canning and the Prime Minister to oust him from office, challenged his rival to a duel. The duel took place on Putney Heath on 21 September 1809. Canning, who had never fired a pistol in his life, unsurprisingly missed his opponent. Castlereagh, more expert, shot Canning in the thigh. Both men lost office later in the same year, although not as a direct consequence of trying to kill one another.

9. **John Scott v. JH Christie, Chalk Farm, 1821**

A literary quarrel that escalated into violence, the argument between John Scott, the editor of the *London Magazine* and another journalist, JH Christie, began with debate about the merits of writers like Keats and Hazlitt and ended in a moonlit duel at Chalk Farm. Christie fired in the air, after Scott had missed, but Scott's second refused to accept that honour had been satisfied and demanded that another exchange of shots should be made. Scott again missed but Christie, firing this time towards his opponent, shot him through the hips and the intestine. Scott died ten days later.

10. **Duke of Wellington v. Lord Winchilsea, Battersea Fields, 1829**

When Wellington became prime minister, one of his first acts – although it was one that was forced on him and he was unwilling to do it – was to give Roman Catholics a greater role in public life. According to a backwoods peer called Lord Winchilsea, in allowing the Catholic Emancipation Act to pass, the duke had 'treacherously plotted the destruction of the Protestant constitution'. Wellington responded to the criticism by challenging Winchilsea to a duel. When the two men met at Battersea Fields on 21 March, they both deliberately fired to miss. Honour having been satisfied, Winchilsea apologised for his remarks. This is the last occasion in which a British PM fought a duel.

The Duke's duel: 'King's Colledge To Wit', cartoon by Thomas Jones

15 CAUSES OF DEATH IN EIGHTEENTH-CENTURY LONDON

The Bills of Mortality were officially published summaries of deaths in the city, the precursors of death certificates, which appeared from the middle of the sixteenth century until they were superseded by the 1836 Births and Deaths Registration Act. This is a selection of causes of death given in the Bills of Mortality for one year – 1758.

1.	Apoplexy	191
2.	Bloody Flux	5
3.	Choaked with Fat	1
4.	Colick, Gripes and Twisting of the Guts	50
5.	Dropsy	682
6.	French Pox	46
7.	Gout	39
8.	Grief	5
9.	Horseshoehead and Water in the Head	40
10.	Leprosy	2
11.	Lethargy	4
12.	Measles	696
13.	Rheumatism	10
14.	Rising of the Lights	1
15.	Smallpox	1273

6 MEMORABLE LONDON FIRES (OTHER THAN THE GREAT FIRE OF 1666)

1. **The Great Fire, 1212**

   A fire broke out in the city on the night of 11 July 1212 in which many people died. City dignitaries met at the Guildhall about a fortnight later and a record of their deliberations and recommendations survives. As well as bemoaning the fire which 'to our greatest dismay, utterly destroyed London Bridge and many other splendid buildings, and sent innumerable men and women to their graves', they suggested ways of preventing such conflagrations in the future. They recommended, among other things, that 'all cook-shops by the Thames should be whitewashed and plastered, inside and out' and that it would be 'advisable to place in front of each house a wooden or stone tub full of water'.

2. **Cornhill Fire, 1748**

   Caused by a maidservant who 'left a candle burning in the shed whilst she was listening to a band performing at the Swan Tavern', the fire raged for ten hours on 25 March in the streets and alleys around Cornhill. More than a hundred buildings, including many of the well-known taverns and coffee-houses in the area were destroyed and a dozen people killed.

3. **Albion Mills Fire, 1791**

   Arguably the mill Blake had in mind when he wrote of 'dark, satanic mills', Albion Mills was a corn mill built at the foot of Blackfriars Bridge by Matthew Boulton, the industrialist, entrepreneur and partner of James Watt. The largest and best-equipped mill of its time, it nonetheless went up in flames on 2 March 1791. Boulton's strong suspicion that the cause of the fire was arson, possibly by a business rival, was never proven and the Albion Mills were not rebuilt.

4. **Houses of Parliament Fire, 1834**

The fire was started when servants at the Palace of Westminster were instructed to destroy a large number of tally sticks, lengths of wood which were used in an ancient method of accounting. The practice of using the tally sticks was obsolete but thousands of them were littering the palace and it was decided they should be consigned to the furnace. Unfortunately, there were so many that the fire grew out of control, the wooden panelling of the buildings caught light and soon the entire palace was on fire. The Chancellor of the Exchequer at the time, Lord Althorp, on arriving at the scene of the fire, is said to have shouted, 'Damn the House of Commons. Let it blaze, but save the Hall'. The dramatic sight of the parliament buildings blazing attracted thousands of spectators, amongst them the artist JMW Turner, who sketched what he saw and later painted two large canvases of the fire lighting up the skies across the Thames.

5. **Tooley Street Fire, 1861**

The fire started in a riverside warehouse on 23 June and spread to other buildings along the Thames. James Braidwood, the fire chief, was killed during the blaze when a wall collapsed on him. It took two days to bring under control and the ruins continued to smoulder for a fortnight. The scale of the disaster and the vast insurance claims led to a parliamentary enquiry and the establishment of the Metropolitan Fire Brigade. A memorial plaque which records Braidwood's heroism can still be seen in Tooley Street.

6. **Crystal Palace Fire, 1936**

A small fire, possibly caused by faulty electrical wiring, was spotted by the manager of the Crystal Palace, Harry Buckland, who was out walking with his young daughter (whom he had named Chrystal) and his dog on the evening of 30 November 1936. Despite the efforts of

Buckland and two night-watchmen, the fire took hold and spread from an area in the central transept to the entire structure. The fire crews that began to arrive could do little to stop it. At the height of the fire eighty-eight fire engines and more than a thousand firemen were fighting the blaze but, by morning, the Crystal Palace was a smouldering ruin of twisted iron and melted glass. The television pioneer John Logie Baird had workshops in the South Tower of the Crystal Palace and lost much of his equipment in the fire.

6 LOST LONDON RIVERS (INCLUDING 1 THAT MAY NEVER HAVE EXISTED)

1. **The Fleet**
   Flowing from Hampstead and Highgate towards Blackfriars, the Fleet was much the most important of the Thames tributaries. It was driven underground in the eighteenth century. In the 1730s, it was arched over from Holborn Bridge to Fleet Bridge along what eventually became Farringdon Road and the stretches south to the river were covered some thirty years later. Nearly all the literary references to the Fleet emphasise its appalling pollution, much of it caused by the blood and entrails of the animals slaughtered in nearby Smithfield Market. In *The Dunciad*, Alexander Pope writes of 'where Fleet Ditch with disemboguing streams/Rolls the large tribute of dead dogs to Thames'. Bridewell, first a royal palace and then a prison, stood at the mouth of the Fleet where it emptied into the Thames, on a site now occupied by the Unilever Building.

2. **The Effra**
   Beneath the streets of South London flows the River Effra which rises near Crystal Palace, journeys through

Norwood and Brixton, runs close by the Oval and then enters the Thames near the MI6 building at Vauxhall Bridge. The Effra is now entirely underground and mostly incorporated into the city's sewage network but it must once have flowed freely. Elizabeth I is supposed to have travelled along the Effra by royal barge to visit Sir Walter Raleigh, who had a house in Brixton.

3. **The Tyburn**

Another tributary of the Thames, the Tyburn flowed from Hampstead to Westminster, giving its name to a village which eventually became the principal site of London executions during the eighteenth century. Thorney Island was an island at the mouth of the Tyburn which has long since disappeared under Westminster Abbey and the Houses of Parliament.

4. **The Walbrook**

The Walbrook divided Roman London in two, flowing from the area north of Moorgate and Liverpool Street Station to join the River Thames at Dowgate.

5. **The Westbourne**

Rising in Hampstead, the Westbourne flowed southwards through Kilburn towards Bayswater and Hyde Park, on through Knightsbridge (which takes its name from a crossing over the river), continued through Kensington and Chelsea and entered the Thames near what is now Chelsea Bridge. The river was dammed in the eighteenth century to form the Long Water and the Serpentine and disappeared underground as London developed in the second half of that century and the early part of the next. At one point, it passes through a nineteenth-century conduit pipe which can be seen crossing the tracks from the platforms at Sloane Square tube station.

6. **The Langbourne**

One of the wards of the City of London is called

Langbourn and the sixteenth-century historian of the city John Stow wrote that it took its name from a lost river that flowed nearby. Not only was Stow wrong about the derivation of the name – almost certainly it comes from a medieval version of the word 'Lombard' – but he was probably mistaken in believing that there was any river, lost or otherwise, in the vicinity.

6 SURVIVING REMNANTS OF ROMAN LONDON (AND 1 THAT ISN'T)

1. **Roman Amphitheatre, Guildhall Yard**
    Although it had been assumed for centuries that London, like other cities of its size in the Roman Empire, must have had an amphitheatre, it was not until 1988 that archaeologists carrying out excavations prior to the building of a new Guildhall art gallery discovered the first evidence of its existence. An outline of the arena is marked on the surface of Guildhall Square but little remains beyond part of the arch through which the gladiators entered, a drainage gutter and a small section of the wall. The arena was oval in shape and approximately a hundred metres long by eighty metres wide. It is estimated that the amphitheatre seated about 6000 people.

2. **Roman Wall, Tower Hill**
    One of the most substantial sections of the old city wall can be found at Tower Hill. Only the lower part of the wall is Roman. On top of it is the medieval wall. Nearby is a replica of the tombstone of Julius Classicianus, the Roman administrator who set London back on its feet after Boudicca's revolt. The original, in the

Statue at Roman Wall, Tower Hill

British Museum, is believed to be the oldest example of written language found in Britain.

3. **Temple of Mithras**

A temple to the Persian god Mithras, who had a particular appeal to soldiers and troops manning distant outposts of empire, was discovered in 1954 during excavations in preparation for the building of an office block in Walbrook Street. It has since been moved to Queen Victoria Street where its foundations can be seen. Originally it would have stood on the east bank of the River Walbrook, long vanished underground (*see* **6 Lost London Rivers**, p. 161). Artefacts from the site, including a sculpture of Mithras killing a bull, are kept at the Museum of London.

4. **An Inscribed Amphora**

Found in Clink Street, Southwark, an amphora on display in the Museum of London provides evidence of how Roman tradesmen advertised their wares. The beaker, which still contained mackerel bones when it was found, bears the words, 'Lucius Tettius Africanus supplies the finest fish sauce from Antipolis'. Antipolis, present-day Antibes in the south of France, was well known for the production of fish sauce and the London trader was clearly eager to advertise the fact that he supplied only the best in his shop.

5. **Spitalfields Sarcophagus**

The grave of a young Roman woman in her early twenties was discovered by archaeologists in Spitalfields in 1999. Some time in the fourth century AD she had been laid to rest in a lead coffin that had then been placed inside a limestone sarcophagus. DNA and the evidence from her teeth suggested that she was not a native Londoner but had grown up somewhere on the Mediterranean coast, possibly in Spain. Her head had been laid on a 'pillow' of bay leaves, and fragments of gold thread and purple silk damask found in the coffin suggest that she was a member of a very wealthy family in Roman London.

6. **Blackfriars Barge**

A second-century Romano-British sailing barge that was discovered in 1962 during construction work at the north end of Blackfriars Bridge, this ancient ship sank in the Thames while carrying a cargo of stone for use in building work. The stone was Kentish ragstone from near Maidstone and the barge's last voyage had probably been along the Medway and up the Thames Estuary.

+1. **'Roman' Bath, Strand Lane**

In Dickens's *David Copperfield*, David recalls that 'there was an old Roman bath in those days at the bottom of one of the streets out of the Strand – it may be there still – in which I have had many a cold plunge'. It is there still and, although it is just possible that it may have Roman origins, the bath that Dickens's hero used dates from much later. Now situated in the basement of a building belonging to King's College, the plunge bath, which measures about 13 feet by 6 feet, can only be glimpsed through a window.

8 LONDON FOODS
PAST AND PRESENT

1. **Jellied Eels**

Jellied eels were traditional London food for centuries, largely because they were cheap (the Thames was full of them) and extremely nutritious. They may seem now like a slightly disgusting dish from the past but there are still plenty of stalls selling them in the East End and elsewhere. Tubby Isaacs' well-known seafood stall in Whitechapel High Street, which sells jellied eels among its delicacies, has been in existence since 1919.

2. **Pie and Mash**

Another Cockney food which has survived into the twenty-first century, pie and mash is still served in the traditional way from a number of outlets around the capital. The pies are made from minced beef and come doused in 'liquor', a kind of parsley sauce. The kings of pie and mash are the Manzes. The Manze family arrived in London from Italy in 1878 and, settling in Bermondsey, began trading as ice-cream makers. In 1902, Michele Manze opened his first pie and mash shop in Tower Bridge Road and, over the next two decades, he and his brothers opened a dozen more. The business at Tower Bridge Road is the oldest pie and mash shop still operating in London.

3. **Oysters**

Although oysters are now seen as something of a delicacy, they were for centuries a staple of the diet of London's poor. According to Sam Weller in *Pickwick Papers*, 'Poverty and oysters always seem to go together'.

4. **Whitebait**

Whitebait from the Thames Estuary was long a London delicacy. The Ministerial Whitebait Dinner originated with an MP called Robert Preston at the end of the eighteenth century who invited friends, including the prime minister, Pitt the Younger, to dine with him on whitebait at his cottage in Dagenham. Transferred to Greenwich taverns, it became an annual event, attended by all the members of the Cabinet, until the tradition was eventually abandoned by Gladstone in the 1880s.

5. **Chelsea Buns**

The Chelsea Bun House flourished in the early eighteenth century (Jonathan Swift bought a penny bun there in 1711 only to find, as he complained in a letter, it was stale) and was patronised by George II and his family. It survived until the 1830s, competing against a rival establishment which also claimed to have the original recipe for the spicy, cinnamon-flavoured bun.

6. **Baked Potatoes**
These are not a modern innovation but a long-established tradition. There were baked potato vans on the streets of London in the nineteenth century. In *Sketches by Boz*, Dickens writes of 'the little block-tin temple sacred to baked potatoes' and describes how the owners of them loiter on the streets until late at night to tempt passers-by to a snack.

7. **Maids of Honour**
The tea room and restaurant in Kew Road which advertises itself as the home of Maids of Honour tarts has been in existence since the 1880s but the tarts themselves were famous long before that. One no doubt fanciful story claims that the recipe originated in the royal kitchens at Hampton Court and that Henry VIII named them after finding Anne Boleyn and her attendants treating themselves to an afternoon feast on the cakes.

8. **Chicken Tikka Masala**
There have been a multitude of explanations for the origins of chicken tikka masala but, according to one cookery writer, it is 'a dish invented in London in the '70s so that the ignorant could have gravy with their chicken tikka'.

9 LONDON COFFEE-HOUSES

Throughout the second half of the seventeenth century and the whole of the eighteenth century, the coffee-house was a characteristic London institution. 'Foreigners remarked that the coffee-house was that which especially distinguished London from all other cities,' wrote Thomas Macaulay in his *History of England*, 'that the coffee-house was the Londoner's home, and that those who wished to find a gentleman commonly asked, not whether he lived in Fleet Street or Chancery Lane, but whether he frequented the Grecian or the Rainbow'. By the time of Queen Anne's death in 1714 there were close to 500 coffee-houses in the city. The Grub Street writer and tavern-keeper Ned Ward provided a vivid portrait of a typical coffee-house in his book *The London Spy* and described its clientele, 'some going, some coming, some scribbling, some talking, some drinking, some jangling, and the whole room stinking of tobacco like a Dutch barge or a boatswain's cabin'. The following were some of the best-known of the coffee-houses:

1. **Pasqua Rosee's**
    The first coffee-house in London was opened in St Michael's Alley off Cornhill in 1652 by a native of Smyrna in Turkey called Pasqua Rosee who had arrived in London as servant to a merchant called Daniel Edwards. Bringing his coffee-making skills with him, Rosee was so successful in persuading his master of the delights of the drink that Edwards supported his servant in the establishment of his business. There is a plaque in St Michael's Alley which marks the site of Pasqua Rosee's coffee-house.

2. **Lloyd's**
    Edward Lloyd opened a coffee-house in Tower Street in the 1680s, moving to a site in Lombard Street in 1692. Insurance men became Lloyd's most regular customers and

his coffee-house became the place where they gathered to share gossip and swap information about the ships and cargoes they had insured. By the early decades of the eighteenth century the actual business of underwriting was taking place in Lloyd's and it remained there until 1771 when a society of shipping underwriters was formed and premises were sought in the Royal Exchange. The society continued to use the name of the old coffee-house and became the worldwide insurance business known as Lloyd's of London.

3. **Will's**

Founded by William Urwin in Russell Street, Covent Garden, soon after the Restoration of Charles II, Will's owed its reputation as the haunt of wits and writers to the regular presence of its most important customer, the poet John Dryden. It was from Will's that Dryden was returning to his home in Gerrard Street in December 1679 when he was attacked and badly beaten up near what is now the Lamb and Flag pub. The assault is still remembered in a sign on the ceiling of the passageway by the pub which recounts that 'hard by was enacted the notorious Rose Alley Ambuscade ... when the poet Dryden was almost done to death at the instance of Louise de Keroualle, mistress of Charles II'. It is now more often assumed that it was the Earl of Rochester, smarting from an attack on him in a satirical poem which he believed Dryden had written, who arranged for thugs to teach him a lesson in literary manners. Not everyone was impressed by the quality of wit on display in Will's. Jonathan Swift wrote that, 'The worst conversation I ever remember to have heard in my life was that at Will's Coffeehouse, where the wits (as they were called) used formerly to assemble; that is to say, five or six men who had writ plays, or at least prologues, or had share in a miscellany, came thither, and entertained one another with their trifling composures in so important an air, as if they had been the noblest efforts of human nature, or that the fate of kingdoms depended on them.'

4. **Garraway's**

Established in Exchange Alley, Cornhill, in 1669 by Thomas Garraway who was the first man to sell tea in England, Garraway's became one of the chief auction houses in the city where prize goods, captured in the assorted wars Britain waged against her imperial rivals, were put on sale. Most of the auctions were done 'by candle' – bids were allowed during the time that a small piece of candle burned down. An unusually miscellaneous lot of 'one box of chocolate, forty-six bags of snuff and an elephant's tooth' is recorded as having been sold at Garraway's in the mid-eighteenth century. The coffee-house survived well into Victoria's reign – Dickens records visits there – and was finally closed in 1866.

5. **King's**

Run by a former street seller called Tom King and his wife, Moll, King's was in Covent Garden and, according to one contemporary writer it was 'well known to all gentlemen to whom beds were unknown'. It can be seen in Hogarth's print *Morning*, looking more like a run-down shack than a coffee-house.

6. **Jonathan's**

The modern Stock Exchange owes its origins to Jonathan's which, like several other important coffee-houses, was in Exchange Alley. It was the place where brokers met in the eighteenth century to conduct business. When the original building burned down, the proprietors simply erected another which they called New Jonathan's. According to a report in *The Gentlemen's Magazine* of 15 July 1773, 'Yesterday, the brokers and others at New Jonathan's came to a resolution that instead of its being called New

Jonathan's it should be called The Stock Exchange, which is to be wrote over the door.'

7. **Button's**

Daniel Button was set up in business in Russell Street, Covent Garden, by the writer and politician Joseph Addison and Addison's custom was essential to the coffee-house's success. Addison set up a letter box in the shape of a lion's head in Button's into which would-be contributors to his journal could post their essays.

8. **Don Saltero's**

Situated in Chelsea, this coffee-house was run by James Salter, former valet to Sir Hans Sloane, the founder of the British Museum. Salter shared his ex-master's passion for collecting and Don Saltero's was famous for the curios that could be seen there. According to a contemporary magazine, these included, 'A curious piece of metal found in the ruins of Troy. A set of beads made of the bones of St Anthony of Padua. A curious flea-trap. A piece of Queen Catherine's skin. Pontius Pilate's wife's great-grandmother's hat. Manna from Canaan. A cockatrice serpent. The Pope's infallible candle. The lance of Captain How Tow Sham, King of the Darien Indians, with which he killed six Spaniards, and took a tooth out of each head, and put it in his lance as a trophy'.

9. **Tom's**

On the first floor of a building in Russell Street, this coffee-house was founded by a Captain Thomas West in 1700 and he was the proprietor for more than twenty years until, tormented beyond bearing by gout, he threw himself from one of its upper windows.

10 HISTORIC DOCUMENTS IN THE NATIONAL ARCHIVES, KEW

1. **First Page Printed in England**

   The very first item printed in England dates from 1476 and was the work of William Caxton. Caxton was an English businessman who had learned the new skill of printing while living on the Continent and set up his own printing press near Westminster Abbey when he returned to London. Although he went on to print more than 100 books, including an edition of Chaucer, Caxton's first page is much less impressive. It is an indulgence – a Latin certificate issued by the Church which granted to the person who received it a reduction in the time he or she had to spend in Purgatory to expiate the sins of a lifetime.

2. **Confession of Guy Fawkes**

   Famously, Guy Fawkes was discovered in possession of thirty-six barrels of gunpowder in a cellar under the Palace of Westminster on the night of 4/5 November 1605. He was taken off to the Tower of London to undergo interrogation and eventually revealed the details of the Gunpowder Plot. Two confessions signed by Fawkes survive in the National Archives. One was demanded of him immediately after he had undergone torture and his name, 'Guido Fawkes', appears to have been written in a very weak and shaky hand.

3. **Shakespeare's Will**

   More than fifty documents relating to Shakespeare and his family are kept in the National Archives but his will is the most intriguing and revealing. Notoriously, he makes no bequests to his wife, except, as the will says, 'I give unto my wife my second-best bed with the furniture'. The phrasing suggests to modern ears that the marriage of the Shakespeares was not one made in heaven but the bequest may not be as dismissive and paltry as it sounds. In fact, it was common practice at the time to bequeath the best items of furniture to children and the second-best to the wife so, perhaps, not too much should be read into it.

4. **Trial Record of Charles I**
This official account of Charles I's trial in Westminster Hall in January 1649 was written by a clerk in the court. Parliament accused the king of 'a wicked design totally to subject the Ancient and fundamental laws and liberties of his nation' and of waging a war in which 'the country has been miserably wasted, the public treasure exhausted, trade decayed, thousands of people murdered and infinite other miseries committed'.

5. **Indictment of Dick Turpin**
Indicted as 'John Palmer, otherwise Pawmer, otherwise Richard Turpin', the legendary highwayman was charged with stealing a black mare worth 3 pounds and a filly foal worth 20 shillings from Thomas Creasey at Welton, Yorkshire, on 1 March 1739.

6. **Logbook of HMS *Bounty***
The most famous mutiny in British naval history took place on 28 April 1789. The *Bounty* had been sent to Tahiti to gather breadfruit plants for transportation to the West Indies but six months in a Pacific paradise meant that the crew were less than keen on enduring the perils of the return voyage. The logbook describes the moment of the mutiny in Captain Bligh's own words. 'Just before sun rise Mr Christian, Mate, Charles Churchill, Ships Corporal, John Mills, Gunner's Mate and Thomas Buskitt, Seaman, came into my cabbin while I was asleep and seizing me tyed my hands, with a cord behind my back and threatened me with instant death if I spoke or made the least noise.'

7. **Jack the Ripper Postcard**

Saucy Jack postcard (1888)

Hysteria gripped both the inhabitants of the East End and the journalists and commentators of Fleet Street in the wake of the Jack the Ripper murders. This was only fuelled by communications sent to the police that supposedly came from the murderer himself. Some of these are kept at Kew, including a postcard which reads, in part, 'You'll hear about saucy Jacky's work tomorrow. Double event this time. Number one squealed a bit. Couldn't finish straight off. Had not time to get ears for police.' The postcard, and most of the other letters, are now thought to have been hoaxes.

8. **Telegram from the *Titanic***

The telegram from the *Titanic* was sent by the wireless operator, Jack Phillips, soon after the ship had struck an iceberg in the North Atlantic on 15 April 1912. It reads, 'We are sinking fast passengers being put into boats.' There were not enough boats to take the more than 2000 people on board and over 1500 men, women and children died. Jack Phillips was one of them.

9. **Adolf Hitler Fake Passport**

The passport was created by people employed by the Special Operations Executive (SOE) as a demonstration of their skills as forgers. Under 'occupation' it says 'painter'; under 'other distinguishing marks' the only distinction listed is 'small moustache'. The passport is also marked by a red J, the sign on German passports at the time for 'Jew'.

10. *Empire Windrush* **Passenger List**

The docking of the *Empire Windrush* at Tilbury on 21 June 1948 was a major moment in the history of black people in London. Nearly five hundred people, answering an advertisement for work, had sailed from the Caribbean to start new lives in Britain. The Colonial Office chose to house many of the men who arrived in a deep air-raid shelter at Clapham Common. The nearest labour exchange to the shelter was in Brixton which is one of the reasons that area became a centre of the West Indian community. The National Archives keep the passenger list, showing the names of those who arrived on the *Windrush*.

5

LONDON PRESENT

London's 10 Biggest Tourist Attractions

8 Unusual London Museums

10 Unusual Items Kept in the Museum of London

The Names of the 8 Ravens in the Tower of London

10 London Nature Reserves

8 Disused Underground Stations

5 Alternative Tube Maps

4 Islands in the Thames (and 1 that isn't)

8 Ships Moored on the Thames

25 Ethnic Communities in London

12 London Festivals and Events through the Year

LONDON'S 10 BIGGEST TOURIST ATTRACTIONS

Top Ten based on visitor numbers in 2005.

1. The British Museum
2. The National Gallery
3. Tate Modern
4. The London Eye
5. The Natural History Museum
6. The Science Museum
7. The Tower of London
8. Tate Britain
9. The Victoria and Albert (V&A) Museum
10. The National Portrait Museum

The London Eye

8 UNUSUAL LONDON MUSEUMS

1. **Fan Museum**

   Situated in two Georgian buildings in Crooms Hill, Greenwich, the only museum in the world devoted entirely to its subject has more than 3500 fans, some dating back to the eleventh century.

2. **Bramah Tea and Coffee Museum**

   This museum was founded in Southwark Street, SE1, in the early 1990s by a former tea taster called Edward Bramah. Among the exhibits is the world's largest teapot, which is capable of brewing 800 cups of tea at once.

   Original advertisement for the UK Tea Company

3. **British Optical Association Museum**

   The museum's collection, housed in the College of Optometrists in Craven Street, WC2, includes such treasures as Dr Crippen's spectacles, Ronnie Corbett's spectacles, 160 glass eyes illustrating ophthalmic diseases and a rare set of eighteenth-century porcelain eyebaths.

4. **London Canal Museum**

   Housed in a building erected by the ice-cream maker Carlo Gatti in the 1860s, this museum not only tells the story of London's inland waterways but also has exhibits illustrating the ice-cream trade in the capital. One of the more impressive sights at the canal-side museum is a huge ice well which was used to store the enormous blocks of ice that were harvested in Norway in the nineteenth century and shipped to Britain.

5. **Pollock's Toy Museum**

   Robert Louis Stevenson once recommended that, 'If you

love art, folly or the bright eyes of children, speed to Pollock's'. The Pollock's to which he was referring (in an essay of 1880) was a shop in Hoxton run by a man named Benjamin Pollock where toy theatres and theatrical prints were sold. After his death in 1937, Pollock's collection was rescued from destruction and eventually became the core of the toy museum named after him. Pollock's, in Scala Street, was forced to close in 2004, although attempts are being made to find a way of keeping the museum going elsewhere.

6. **Alexander Fleming Laboratory Museum**
This small museum is in the room where one of the most important discoveries in modern medicine, originating in a chance observation, took place. In 1928, the Scottish bacteriologist Alexander Fleming, returning to the laboratory after a holiday, noticed that a culture plate containing a particular bacterium had been exposed to contamination by yeasts and moulds. One of the moulds, Penicillum Notatum, had killed the bacteria in the area of the plate it had affected. The petri dish in which the mould had grown is on display.

7. **Soseki Museum**
Natsume Soseki (1867–1916), one of Japan's greatest novelists, was sent to London by the Japanese Education Ministry in 1900 and lived in The Chase, SW4, during his stay in the capital. He was utterly miserable in the city, suffered badly from racial taunts and homesickness and, on his return to Japan, vowed never to go back but the terraced house where he endured his exile is now a museum devoted to his life and work.

8. **The Library and Museum of Freemasonry**
Situated in Great Queen Street, WC2, the museum houses a collection of Masonic aprons, regalia belonging to the Royal Antedeluvian Order of Buffaloes, a philanthropic

organisation founded in London in the 1820s, and a Masonic pouch that once belonged to Winston Churchill.

10 UNUSUAL ITEMS KEPT IN THE MUSEUM OF LONDON

1. **Roman Bikini**

   At a Roman villa in Sicily there is a mosaic which shows a group of young girls wearing what look remarkably like bikinis. In the Museum of London there is the bottom half of the kind of bikini shown in the mosaic. Made out of leather and dating from the first century AD, the trunks, which were found in a Roman well uncovered in Queen Street, were probably worn by a female acrobat.

   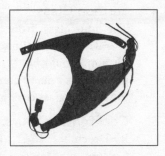

   Roman bikini bottoms

2. **Twelfth-century Ice Skates**

   Made of bone, they are polished on the undersides where they have been used on the ice. William Fitzstephen, in 1190, wrote of young people who 'equip each of their feet with an animal's shin-bone attaching it to the underside of their footwear; using hand-held poles reinforced with metal tips, which they periodically thrust against the ice, they propel themselves along as swiftly as a bird in flight or a bolt shot from a crossbow'. These skates are contemporary with his description.

3. **Oliver Cromwell's Death Mask**

   Oliver Cromwell, Lord Protector, died on 3 September 1658 and was buried in Westminster Abbey after what the

Royalist John Evelyn described as 'the joyfullest funeral that ever I saw for there was none that cried but dogs'. He was not allowed to rest there. When Charles II returned to the throne, Cromwell's body was dug up and given a posthumous execution at Tyburn. The death mask clearly shows a wart over the right eye, one of those Cromwell insisted should be visible when, allegedly, he asked the painter Sir Peter Lely to portray him 'warts and all'.

4. **Sermon Glass**
    The hour glass, from St Alban's church in Wood Street, was designed to allow a preacher to judge how long his sermon should be. When the sand had run through the glass it was time to come to an end unless he was inspired to turn the glass over and continue.

5. **Cockfighting Spurs**
    In December 1762, James Boswell visited the Royal Cockpit in St James's Park and described how 'the cocks, nicely cut and dressed and armed with silver heels, are set down and fight with amazing bitterness and resolution'. The Museum of London has a collection of cockspurs dating from the time when Boswell saw the birds fight and they give some indication of how vicious the sport was. Boswell was 'sorry for the poor cocks' but he admitted that, 'I looked round to see if any of the spectators pitied them when mangled and torn in a most cruel manner, but I could not observe the smallest relenting sign in any countenance'. Cockfighting continued quite openly in London until the 1840s.

6. **Queen Victoria's Drawers**
    The Museum of London has several items of clothing worn by Queen Victoria during her reign, including a bonnet and her accession dress, but it is safe to assume that the one she would have least liked to see on display to the public is the pair of her drawers which the museum owns.

7. **Acrobatic Flying Corset**

   These were worn by the flying dancer Azella in the 1860s. Advertising herself as 'The Female Leotard', in reference to the famous trapeze artist who gave his name to the leotard, she was a French acrobat who performed in London music halls in the 1860s.

8. **Psycho the Automaton**

   Psycho was an automaton built by the English magician John Nevil Maskelyne in the 1870s to participate in his shows at the Egyptian Hall in Piccadilly. Psycho picked up playing cards from a rack in front of it and was worked by air pressure and a hidden bellows.

9. **Stanley Green's Placards**

   For several decades until his death in 1993, Stanley Green bicycled from his home in Northolt to Oxford Street, where he walked up and down, carrying banners proclaiming his eccentric beliefs. Green was concerned that over-indulgence in protein-rich foods like meat and dairy products was resulting in a nation of lustful sex-maniacs. 'Less Passion from Less Protein' was his motto and one that appeared on his placards and home-printed pamphlets, examples of which are now preserved in the Museum.

10. **Mickey Mouse Gas Mask**

    Intended to be less sinister and distressing than the standard gas masks, Mickey Mouse gas masks bore little resemblance to Disney's cartoon character but were manufactured in bright, primary colours to encourage small children to wear them. A government advice leaflet confidently proclaimed that, 'Toddlers soon learn to put on their own masks. Let them make a game of it and they will wear their gas masks happily.'

THE NAMES OF THE 8 RAVENS IN THE TOWER OF LONDON

There have been ravens at the Tower of London for hundreds of years although no one is quite sure how the belief developed that, if they ever left, catastrophe would strike the Tower and the kingdom. Charles II took the idea seriously enough to decree that at least six of the birds should always be kept there. Today, there are eight in the Tower, their wings clipped to prevent them heading elsewhere. They are looked after by a Ravenmaster Yeoman Warder. The names of the ravens are:

1. Gwylum (male)
2. Thor (male)
3. Hugine (female)
4. Munin (female)
5. Branwen (female)
6. Bran (male)
7. Gundulf (male)
8. Baldrick (male)

10 LONDON NATURE RESERVES

1. Battersea Park Nature Reserve
2. Camley Street Natural Park
3. East Ham Nature Reserve
4. Fishponds Wood
5. Gunnersbury Triangle
6. Knight's Hill Wood
7. London Wetland Centre
8. Oakhill Wood
9. Sydenham Hill Wood
10. Totteridge Fields

8 DISUSED UNDERGROUND STATIONS

1. ## Aldwych

   Located on the Strand with an entrance on Surrey Street, Aldwych was opened in 1907 and, for many years, special trains used to run from it every night to cater for theatregoers. Because of re-routings, the station became little used and when, in 1994, it was realised that money needed to be spent in replacing the lifts, it was thought more economical simply to close it down entirely. It is now used frequently as a film set. Scenes from *The Krays* and *Patriot Games* were shot there even before the station finally closed and the video for 'Firestarter' by Prodigy was filmed in tunnels near the station. In the computer game 'Tomb Raider', one of the locations visited by Lara Croft is a tube station called Aldwych, although the designers of the game made its layout very different from the reality.

2. ## British Museum

   Situated on the north side of High Holborn, this station was closed in the 1930s but can be glimpsed when travelling on the Central Line between Tottenham Court Road and Holborn. *Death Line*, a cult horror movie of the 1970s, takes as its starting point a London myth about the station – that a gang of workers was trapped underground during its building and all attempts to rescue them failed. In the film the last descendants of the trapped workers lurk in the depths of the Tube, emerging only to capture unlucky commuters for food.

3. ## Brompton Road

   This station was opened in 1906 but was soon found to be surplus to requirements because Knightsbridge and South Kensington were so close. Many trains went straight through it and a 1928 hit play called *Passing Brompton Road* referred to the guard's cry which was a familiar sound on the Tube at the time. It closed in 1934 but was used in the war as the operations centre for the Anti-Aircraft Command.

4. **Bull and Bush**

A station that never actually opened, it was intended that it should be called North End but was christened Bull and Bush by Underground staff because of the famous pub nearby. Between Hampstead and Golders Green on the Northern Line, it can still be glimpsed from trains. Had it ever been operational, it would have been London's deepest underground station at 200 feet.

5. **Down Street**

Opened in 1903 between Green Park and Hyde Park Corner, Down Street was too close to both to be used very frequently and it closed in 1932. During the early years of World War II, the station was used by Churchill and the War Cabinet before they moved to the Cabinet War Rooms in Whitehall. Churchill's bath is still in place in a room near the end of one of the platforms.

6. **King William Street**

Built in 1890 as the northern terminus of the world's first electric underground railway, the City and South London line, King William Street had to be abandoned only ten years later when the line was extended and it was found impossible to integrate it into the new system. It was used during World War II as an air raid shelter and posters from that era still survive down there.

7. **Lord's**

Originally opened in the nineteenth century as St John's Wood, it was re-named after the cricket ground but closed in 1939. At the time of the proposed (and highly controversial) cricket tour by the white South African team in 1970, it was rumoured that demonstrators planned to use air vents from the old station as a means of access to the pitch in order to disrupt play.

8. **Wood Lane**
    Built for the Franco-British exhibition at White City in
    1908, the station was replaced by the current White City
    station which opened in 1947. When travelling east from
    White City to Shepherd's Bush it is still possible to glimpse
    the platforms of the Wood Lane station.

5 ALTERNATIVE TUBE MAPS

The Tube (or underground) map first designed by Harry Beck
in the 1930s has become an icon of the city but other designers
over the decades have felt that it lacked something and have
created their own tube maps. The following are five of them:

1. **The Geographically Accurate Tube Map**
    One of the disadvantages of Harry Beck's original map is
    that, schematic as it is, it gives little sense of real distances
    between stations. A designer called Simon Clarke has
    created a map which accurately reflects these and would
    prevent tourists from travelling from Covent Garden to
    Leicester Square on the Tube in three times the number of
    minutes it would take to walk between them.

2. **The Way Out Tube Map**
    The map shows where the exits at each station are in
    relation to the carriages so that a traveller can choose the
    carriage which will enable him to emerge directly opposite
    one and save those vital seconds wasted walking along
    the platform.

3. **The Great Bear**
    In 1992, the conceptual artist Simon Patterson created
    his own version of Harry Beck's map, which he called
    The Great Bear (after the constellation), and replaced
    the names of the stations with those of philosophers,

footballers, film actors, Italian artists and others. On the Jubilee Line you travel from Paul Gascoigne via Gordon Banks and Bobby Charlton to Gary Lineker. The Northern Line takes you through Peter Fonda, Humphrey Bogart and Kirk Douglas to Gina Lollobrigida.

4. *Have I Got News for You* Tube Map
First published in the book *Have I Got 1997 For You*, this includes stations called 'Busy', 'Full', 'Squashed' and 'Gasp, Can't Breathe'. 'Seven Sisters' is closely followed by 'Seven Brides' and 'Seven Brothers'. 'Pickpocket Central' is at the heart of the map.

5. **If England Had Lost the War Tube Map**
The tube map translated into German. On the Zentral Line you can travel from Schäfersbusch via Notting Hügel Tor and Tottenham Hof Weg to Liverpoolstrasse or join the Piccadilly at Kavaliersbrücke and journey through Hyde Park Ecke and Konventgarten to Königskreuz.

Tube mouse map

4 ISLANDS IN THE THAMES (AND 1 THAT ISN'T)

1. **Eel Pie Island**
Previously known as Twickenham Ait, it was re-named after a tavern, long demolished, which was famous for its eel pies. In Dickens's novel *Nicholas Nickleby* one of the

characters visits Eel Pie Island, 'there to make merry upon a cold collation, bottled beer, shrub, and shrimps, and to dance in the open air to the music of a locomotive band, conveyed thither for the purpose'. Described recently by Simon Hoggart as 'a strange village marooned in the middle of the river, which looks as if it might float off towards Kent at any moment', Eel Pie Island is now best known for its rock music connections. The Eel Pie Hotel played host to dozens of famous names in the 1960s. The Rolling Stones, The Who, The Yardbirds, Long John Baldry, Eric Clapton and Rod Stewart all performed on the island between 1962 and 1967.

2. **Oliver's Island, Kew**
Facing Strand-on-the-Green, the island is allegedly named after Oliver Cromwell whose daughter Mary lived nearby.

3. **Chiswick Eyot**
This is the only island on the course of the Boat Race.

4. **Trowlock Island, Teddington**
Named after a type of Thames barge called a 'trow', the island is a third of a mile long and has a small population living in the two dozen bungalows that have been built on it. Access is by a hand-wound chain ferry.

+1. **Isle of Dogs**
Actually a peninsula, the Isle of Dogs was first named as such on a late sixteenth-century map and it's speculated that it took this name because Henry VIII kennelled his hunting dogs there. Pepys visited there and had a miserable time. 'So we were fain to stay there, in the unlucky Isle of Doggs,' he wrote in his diary in July 1665, 'in a chill place, the morning cool, and wind fresh, above two if not three hours to our great discontent'. The area only became economically significant with the building of the docks in the early nineteenth century. The West India

Dock, built in 1802, was big enough to accommodate six hundred ships. The Isle of Dogs was suggested as a site for the Great Exhibition of 1851 but, probably wisely, the authorities decided that Hyde Park was a better place to stage it.

8 SHIPS
MOORED ON THE THAMES

1. ## HMS *Belfast*
   Launched in 1938, this Royal Navy cruiser served throughout World War II and played a leading role in the battle that ended with the sinking of the German battleship *Scharnhorst*. Decommissioned in the 1960s, she was opened to the public as a floating naval museum in 1971. She is moored on the south bank of the river between London Bridge and Tower Bridge.

2. ## The *Golden Hinde*
   Not the original ship in which Drake sailed around the world but a modern replica built in 1973, the *Golden Hinde* is a living history museum designed to provide a taste of what life was like for Elizabethan seamen. The ship is moored on the Thames at St Mary Overie Dock near Southwark Cathedral.

3. ## HMS *President*
   The ship, moored at St Katharine's Dock just downstream from Tower Bridge, is a shore station for the London Division of the Royal Naval Reserve.

4. ## HQS *Wellington*
   A former Royal Navy ship which served in World War II, the Wellington now serves as the livery hall of the Honourable Company of Master Mariners. During the Lord Mayor's Show, the procession stops at the ship so that his Lordship can enjoy a glass of sherry on board.

5. The *Cutty Sark*

Named from a Scottish word for a type of short chemise (one of the witches in Robert Burns's poem, 'Tam O'Shanter', wears one), the *Cutty Sark* was a nineteenth-century tea clipper and has been in dry dock in Greenwich since the 1950s.

The Cutty Sark at Greenwich

6. *Gipsy Moth IV*

The fifty-four foot long vessel on which Sir Francis Chichester made his single-handed circumnavigation of the world in 1966–67 is permanently moored alongside the *Cutty Sark*.

7. The *Queen Mary*

A former Clyde steamer which ferried passengers down the river from Glasgow, the *Queen Mary* is now moored just above Waterloo Bridge and is a floating restaurant.

8. The *Tattershall Castle*

The *Tattershall Castle* worked for more than thirty years as a ferry on the River Humber and was brought to London in 1975 to take on a new role as a floating art gallery. This venture failed, but the ship was bought by a brewing company and is now moored permanently on the Thames at Victoria Embankment as a pub.

25 ETHNIC COMMUNITIES IN LONDON

More than 300 languages are spoken in London and there are large groups of particular nationalities and ethnic origins congregated in particular areas of the city. The following are 25 of these:

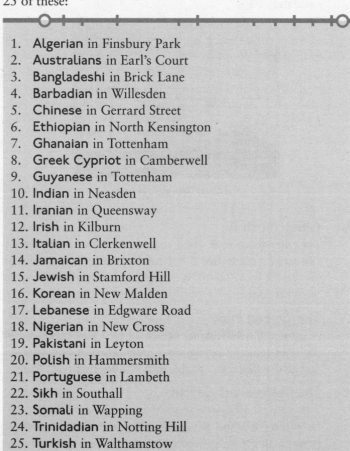

1. **Algerian** in Finsbury Park
2. **Australians** in Earl's Court
3. **Bangladeshi** in Brick Lane
4. **Barbadian** in Willesden
5. **Chinese** in Gerrard Street
6. **Ethiopian** in North Kensington
7. **Ghanaian** in Tottenham
8. **Greek Cypriot** in Camberwell
9. **Guyanese** in Tottenham
10. **Indian** in Neasden
11. **Iranian** in Queensway
12. **Irish** in Kilburn
13. **Italian** in Clerkenwell
14. **Jamaican** in Brixton
15. **Jewish** in Stamford Hill
16. **Korean** in New Malden
17. **Lebanese** in Edgware Road
18. **Nigerian** in New Cross
19. **Pakistani** in Leyton
20. **Polish** in Hammersmith
21. **Portuguese** in Lambeth
22. **Sikh** in Southall
23. **Somali** in Wapping
24. **Trinidadian** in Notting Hill
25. **Turkish** in Walthamstow

12 LONDON FESTIVALS AND EVENTS THROUGH THE YEAR

1. **New Year's Day Parade** – January
2. **Chinese New Year** – January/February
3. **University Boat Race** – March
4. **London Harness Horse Parade** – March/April (Easter Monday)
5. **Chelsea Flower Show** – May
6. **Royal Academy Summer Exhibition** – June
7. **London Mardi Gras/Pride March** – July
8. **Notting Hill Carnival** – August
9. **London Open House** – September
10. **Pearly Harvest Festival** – October
11. **Diwali** – November
12. **Spitalfields Winter Festival** – December

6

LONDON IN LITERATURE

6 Quotes Praising London

5 Quotes Damning London

6 Sayings by Dr Johnson about London

5 Shakespearean Sites

6 Dickensian Sites (and 1 that isn't)

10 Sherlockian Sites (London Locations Associated with Sherlock Holmes)

8 Novels of London in World War II

6 Novels Depicting Alternative Londons

14 Novels with London Areas in their Titles

9 Fictional Addresses in London

12 Writers' Addresses in London

8 Poets (and 1 Very Old Man) Remembered in Poets' Corner

15 Poems That have been Seen on London Underground

6 QUOTES PRAISING LONDON

1. **William Fitzstephen, 1183**

'It is happy in the healthiness of its air, in the Christian religion, in the strength of its defences, the nature of its site, the honesty of its citizens, the modesty of its matrons; pleasant in sports; fruitful of noble men.' (*Life of Becket*)

Fitzstephen thought London an almost perfect city. 'The only inconveniences of London,' he went on to claim, 'are the immoderate drinking of foolish persons, and the frequent fires.'

2. **Thomas Fuller, 1662**

'The second city in Christendom for greatness and the first for good government. There is no civilised part of the world but that it hath heard thereof, though many with this mistake, that they conceive London to be the country and England but the city therein.' (*History of the Worthies of England*)

3. **Tom Brown, 1700**

'London is a world by itself; we daily discover in it more new countries and surprising singularities than in all the universe besides. There are among the Londoners so many nations differing in manners, customs, and religions, that the inhabitants themselves don't know a quarter of 'em.' (*Amusements Serious and Comical, Calculated for the Meridian of London*)

4. **Charles Lamb, 1801**

'I have passed all my days in London, until I have formed as many and intense local attachments, as any of your Mountaineers can have done with dead nature. The Lighted shops of the Strand and Fleet Street, the unnumerable trades, tradesmen and customers, coaches, waggons, playhouses, all the bustle and wickedness round about Covent Garden, the very women of the Town, the

Watchmen, drunken scenes, rattles;—life awake, if you awake, at all hours of the night, the impossibility of being dull in Fleet Street, the crowds, the very dirt & mud, the Sun shining upon houses and pavements, the print shops, the old Book stalls, parsons cheap'ning books, coffee houses, steams of soup from kitchens, the pantomimes, London itself a pantomime and a masquerade, all these things work themselves into my mind and feed me without a power of satiating me. The wonder of these sights impells me into night walks about the crowded streets, and I often shed tears in the motley Strand from fulness of joy at so much Life.' (In a letter to Wordsworth.)

5. **Jerome K Jerome, 1909**
    'It was summer time, and London is so beautiful in summer. It lay beneath my window a fairy city veiled in golden mist, for I worked in a room high above the chimney-pots; and at night the lights shone far beneath me, so that I looked down as into an Aladdin's cave of jewels.' (In a preface to a new edition of *Three Men in a Boat.*)

6. **HG Wells, 1911**
    'London is the most interesting, beautiful and wonderful city in the world to me, delicate in her incidental and multitudinous littleness, and stupendous in her pregnant totality.' (*The New Machiavelli*)

5 QUOTES DAMNING LONDON

1. **Thomas De Quincey, 1834**
    'No man ever was left to himself for the first time in the streets, as yet unknown, of London, but he must have been saddened and mortified, perhaps terrified, by the sense of desertion and utter loneliness which belong to his situation. No loneliness can be like that which weighs upon the heart in the centre of faces never-ending, without

voice or utterance for him; eyes innumerable, that have no speculation in their orbs which he can understand; and hurrying figures of men and women weaving to and fro, with no apparent purposes intelligible to a stranger, seeming like a mask of maniacs, or, oftentimes, like a pageant of phantoms.' (*Autobiographical Sketches*)

2. **Hippolyte Taine, 1872**
'A wet Sunday in London: shops closed, streets almost empty; the aspect of a vast and well-kept graveyard. The few people in this desert of squares and streets, hurrying beneath their umbrellas, look like unquiet ghosts; it is horrible. A thick yellow fog fills the air ... after an hour's walking one can understand suicide.' (*Notes sur l'Angleterre*)

3. **Arthur Morrison, 1894**
'The East End is ... an evil plexus of slums that hide human creeping things; where filthy men and women live on gin, where collars and clean shirts are decencies unknown, where every citizen wears a black eye, and none ever combs his hair.' (*Tales of Mean Streets*)

4. **Karel Capek, 1925**
'The horrible thing in East London is not what can be seen and smelt, but its unbounded and unredeemable extent ... miles and miles of grimy houses, hopeless streets, Jewish shops, a superfluity of children, gin palaces, and Christian shelters ... everything equally dull, grimy, bare and unending, intersected by dirty channels of deafening traffic and the whole way equally cheerless ...' (*Letters from England*)

5. **George Orwell, 1933**
'I had been in London innumerable times, and yet till that day I had never noticed one of the worst things about London – the fact that it costs money even to sit down.' (*Down and Out in Paris and London*)

6 SAYINGS BY DR JOHNSON ABOUT LONDON

Dr Johnson was not originally a Londoner. Like so many of the city's most famous citizens, he became one. He arrived in London in 1737, aged twenty-eight, accompanied by David Garrick, in flight from failure as a schoolmaster and in pursuit of literary glory. He was slow to find it. It was not until the publication of his *A Dictionary of the English Language* in 1755 that he escaped the perils of Grub Street and hack writing. In 1763 he met James Boswell in a Covent Garden bookshop and the process by which Johnson was transformed into the legendary figure of Boswell's biography was begun. The biography, published in 1791, seven years after Johnson's death, includes many of his sayings about life in London. Here are six of them:

1. 'Sir, if you wish to have a just notion of the magnitude of this city, you must not be satisfied with seeing its great streets and squares, but must survey the innumerable little lanes and courts. It is not in the showy evolutions of buildings, but in the multiplicity of human habitations which are crowded together, that the wonderful immensity of London consists.'

2. 'The happiness of London is not to be conceived but by those who have been in it. I will venture to say, there is more learning and science within the circumference of ten miles from where we now sit, than in all the rest of the world.'

3. 'A country gentleman should bring his lady to visit London as soon as he can, that they may have agreeable topics for conversation when they are by themselves.'

4. 'Why, Sir, you find no man, at all intellectual, who is willing to leave London.

'No, Sir, when a man is tired of London, he is tired of life; for there is in London all that life can afford.'

5. 'By seeing London, I have seen as much of life as the world can shew.'

6. 'No wise man will go to live in the country, unless he has something to do which can be better done in the country. For instance, if he is to shut himself up for a year to study science, it is better to look out to the fields, than to an opposite wall. Then, if a man walks out in the country, there is nobody to keep him from walking in again: but if a man walks out in London, he is not sure when he will walk in again. A great city is, to be sure, the school for studying life.'

5 SHAKESPEAREAN SITES

1. **The Globe Theatre**
Shakespeare's Globe was built in Southwark in 1599 and constructed from timbers transported across the Thames from Richard Burbage's theatre in Shoreditch. The actors dismantled the old theatre overnight when the landlord was giving them trouble and moved it across the river to escape him. It was the principal theatre of the Lord Chamberlain's Men (later the King's Men), the theatrical company in which Shakespeare was a major shareholder. The original Globe burned down in 1613 during a performance of *Henry VIII* when cannons being used as stage props set the thatch alight. According to a contemporary account, 'nothing did perish but wood and straw, and a few forsaken cloaks; only one man had his breeches set on fire, that would perhaps have broiled him, if he had not, by the benefit of a provident wit, put it out with bottle ale'.

2. **White Hart Yard**

    One of the great coaching inns of London, this was the place where the medieval rebel Jack Cade set up his headquarters in 1450. Cade is a character in Shakespeare's *Henry VI Part Two* and, when his peasant army threatens to desert him, he rallies them with the rhetorical question, 'Hath my sword therefore broke through London gates, that you should leave me at the White Hart in Southwark?' Cade also refers to London Stone when he is contemplating the glories of the new regime he is about to institute. 'Here sitting upon London Stone', he says, 'I charge and command that, of the city's cost, the Pissing Conduit run nothing but claret wine this first year of our reign.' The inn also qualifies as a Dickensian site since it is in the White Hart that Mr Pickwick first meets Sam Weller in *The Pickwick Papers*. It was finally demolished in 1889.

3. **Ireland Yard**

    Shakespeare bought a property in Ireland Yard, Blackfriars, for £140 in 1613, conveniently close to the Playhouse which is now remembered in the nearby street name of Playhouse Yard. Ben Jonson had lived in the neighbourhood a few years later and some twenty years after Shakespeare's death, the painter Van Dyck also owned property in Ireland Yard.

4. **Ely House**

    Ely Place in Holborn marks the site of what was once the Bishop of Ely's town house. In earlier centuries the gardens of the house were renowned for their fruits, a fact to which Shakespeare refers in *Richard III* when Richard remarks to the Bishop, 'When I was last in Holborn/I saw good strawberries in your garden there/I do beseech you send for some of them.'

5. **The Boar's Head Tavern, Eastcheap**

Act Two, Scene Four of *Henry IV Part One* is set in the Boar's Head where Falstaff, Prince Hal and others make merry. First mentioned in the Middle Ages, the original tavern where they disported was destroyed in the Great Fire but was rebuilt two years later. It finally ceased to be a tavern at some point in the late eighteenth century. When the American writer Washington Irving visited London, he says he decided to 'make a pilgrimage to Eastcheap, and see if the old Boar's Head tavern still exists. It didn't but Irving claimed to have seen the tombstone of a teetotal 'drawer' at the tavern in the graveyard of St Michael's church who may have been a contemporary of Shakespeare. The man's epitaph read, 'Bacchus, to give the toping world surprise/Produced one sober son, and here he lies/Though rear'd among full hogsheads, he defied/The charms of wine, and every one beside.'

6 DICKENSIAN SITES (AND 1 THAT ISN'T)

1. **George and Vulture Inn**

'Trinity term commenced. On the expiration of its first week, Mr Pickwick and his friends returned to London; and the former gentleman, attended of course by Sam, straightway repaired to his old quarters at the George and Vulture.' (*Pickwick Papers*)

The pub still exists and is situated in Castle Court, EC3.

2. **Smithfield Market**

'It was market-morning. The ground was covered, nearly ankle-deep, with filth and mire; a thick steam, perpetually rising from the reeking bodies of the cattle, and mingling with the fog, which seemed to rest upon the chimney-tops, hung heavily above. All the pens in the centre of the large area, and as many temporary pens as could be crowded into the vacant space, were filled with sheep; tied up to posts by the gutter side were long lines of beasts and oxen, three or four deep.' (*Oliver Twist*)

Such sights as Dickens describes in the novel were familiar in the City until the slaughtering of the animals was moved out of Smithfield to Copenhagen Fields in Islington in the 1860s.

3. **Staple Inn**

'Behind the most ancient part of Holborn, London, where certain gabled houses some centuries of age still stand looking on the public way, as if disconsolately looking for the Old Bourne that has long run dry, is a little nook composed of two irregular quadrangles, called Staple Inn. It is one of those nooks, the turning into which out of the clashing street, imparts to the relieved pedestrian the sensation of having put cotton in his ears, and velvet soles on his boots.' (*Edwin Drood*)

4. **Clerkenwell Green**

'They were just emerging from a narrow court not far from the open square in Clerkenwell, which is yet called, by some strange perversion of terms, "The Green" when the Dodger made a sudden stop; and, laying his finger on his lip, drew his companions back again, with the greatest caution and circumspection.' (*Oliver Twist*)

5. **Hungerford Stairs**

'Both Mr Micawber and his eldest son wore their sleeves loosely turned back at the wrists, as being ready to lend a hand in any direction, and to "tumble up," or sing out, "Yeo—Heave—Yeo!" on the shortest notice. Thus Traddles and I found them at nightfall, assembled on the wooden steps, at that time known as Hungerford Stairs, watching the departure of a boat with some of their property on board.' (*David Copperfield*)

Hungerford Stairs was the site of Warren's Blacking Factory where Dickens, together with a workmate called Bob Fagin, toiled so miserably as a boy.

6. ### Jacob's Island

'In Jacob's Island, the warehouses are roofless and empty; the walls are crumbling down; the windows are windows no more; the doors are falling into the streets; the chimneys are blackened, but they yield no smoke. Thirty or forty years ago, before losses and chancery suits came upon it, it was a thriving place; but now it is a desolate island indeed.' (*Oliver Twist*)

Jacob's Island was in Bermondsey and is remembered in the name of Jacob Street.

+1. ### The Old Curiosity Shop, Portsmouth Street

Despite what is claimed on the awning above it, the shop, in a street close to Lincoln's Inn Fields, has nothing to do with the novel of the same name. The shop would have been known to Dickens, since it dates back several centuries, but it is clear from the book that Little Nell's home is nowhere near Portsmouth Street. Indeed, at the end of the novel, Dickens says that his Old Curiosity Shop has been demolished. The shop in Portsmouth Street was only renamed the Old Curiosity Shop in 1868, nearly thirty years after Dickens's novel was first serialised in his weekly periodical *Master Humphrey's Clock*.

10 SHERLOCKIAN SITES (LONDON LOCATIONS ASSOCIATED WITH SHERLOCK HOLMES)

Sherlock Homes and Dr Watson,
by Sidney Paget

London as a world city is at the heart of Conan Doyle's Sherlock Holmes stories. Although cases do take Holmes and Watson outside London, the capital is where the two men are at home. The city of Doyle's stories has also become a mythological one. The meditative calm of Baker Street, disturbed by the approaching footsteps of a new client. The breathless cab journeys through fog-enshrouded streets towards some den of crime and infamy. In the same way that Holmes and Watson have become archetypal figures, escaping the boundaries of the original fiction, the London they inhabit has become more real than the reality. Yet Doyle is careful to place his characters in the real London of the late nineteenth century, and it is still possible to track them through its streets. Here are 10 Sherlockian locations where the spirit of the great detective and his faithful companion can be strongly felt.

1. **221B Baker Street**
    'We met next day as he had arranged, and inspected the rooms at No. 221b, Baker Street, of which he had spoken at our meeting. They consisted of a couple of

comfortable bedrooms and a single large airy sitting-room, cheerfully furnished, and illuminated by two broad windows. So desirable in every way were the apartments, and so moderate did the terms seem when divided between us, that the bargain was concluded.' (*A Study in Scarlet*)

2. **Bart's Hospital**
'As he spoke, we turned down a narrow lane and passed through a small side-door, which opened into a wing of the great hospital. It was familiar ground to me, and I needed no guiding as we ascended the bleak stone staircase and made our way down the long corridor with its vista of whitewashed wall and dun-coloured doors. Near the farther end a low arched passage branched away from it and led to the chemical laboratory. This was a lofty chamber, lined and littered with countless bottles. Broad, low tables were scattered about, which bristled with retorts, test-tubes, and little Bunsen lamps, with their blue flickering flames. There was only one student in the room, who was bending over a distant table absorbed in his work. At the sound of our steps he glanced round and sprang to his feet with a cry of pleasure. "I've found it! I've found it," he shouted to my companion, running towards us with a test-tube in his hand.' (*A Study in Scarlet*)

This is the first meeting between Watson and Holmes. A plaque to mark the historic encounter has been placed on the wall outside one of the pathology laboratories at Bart's.

3. **Montague Street**
'When I first came up to London I had rooms in Montague Street, just round the corner from the British Museum, and there I waited, filling in my too abundant leisure time by studying all those branches of science which might make me more efficient.' ('The Musgrave Ritual')

4. **The Criterion Bar**

    'I was standing at the Criterion Bar, when some one tapped me on the shoulder, and turning round I recognized young Stamford, who had been a dresser under me at Bart's. The sight of a friendly face in the great wilderness of London is a pleasant thing indeed to a lonely man.' (*A Study in Scarlet*)

5. **Simpson's-in-the-Strand**

    'Thank you, Watson, you must help me on with my coat. When we have finished at the police station I can think that something nutritious at Simpson's would not be out of place.' ('The Adventure of the Dying Detective')

6. **Lowther Arcade**

    'You will drive to the Strand end of the Lowther Arcade, handing the address to the cabman upon a slip of paper, with a request that he will not throw it away. Have your fare ready, and the instant that your cab stops, dash through the Arcade, timing yourself to reach the other side at a quarter-past nine. You will find a small brougham waiting close to the curb, driven by a fellow with a heavy black cloak tipped at the collar with red. Into this you will step, and you will reach Victoria in time for the Continental express.' ('The Final Problem')

    In the late nineteenth century Lowther Arcade was a short arcade running off the Strand which was particularly famous for its toy shops. It was demolished in 1904 to make way for a bank, less than fifteen years after Holmes had given Watson the above instructions to help him avoid the attentions of Professor Moriarty.

7. **The Lyceum Theatre**

    'At the Lyceum Theatre the crowds were already thick at the side-entrances. In front a continuous stream of hansoms and four-wheelers were rattling up, discharging their cargoes of shirt-fronted men and beshawled, bediamonded women. We had hardly reached the third pillar, which was our rendezvous, before a small, dark, brisk man in the dress of a coachman accosted us.' (*The Sign of Four*)

The Lyceum Theatre is on Wellington Street, WC2. In Holmes's day it was home to the theatrical company managed by the legendary actor-manager Sir Henry Irving.

8. **The Diogenes Club**
'Mycroft lodges in Pall Mall, and he walks round the corner into Whitehall every morning and back every evening. From year's end to year's end he takes no other exercise, and is seen nowhere else, except only in the Diogenes Club, which is just opposite his rooms.' ('The Greek Interpreter')

The Diogenes Club is clearly one of the many gentlemen's clubs which are or were situated on Pall Mall but no amount of research by Sherlockian scholars has been able to pinpoint its exact location.

9. **Charing Cross Station**
'It was between the Grand Hotel and Charing Cross Station, where a one-legged news-vendor displayed his evening papers. The date was just two days after the last conversation. There, black upon yellow, was the terrible news-sheet: MURDEROUS ATTACK UPON SHERLOCK HOLMES. I think I stood stunned for some moments. Then I have a confused recollection of snatching at a paper, of the remonstrance of the man, whom I had not paid, and, finally, of standing in the doorway of a chemist's shop while I turned up the fateful paragraph.' ('The Adventure of the Illustrious Client')

10. **The Northumberland Hotel**
'Well, it was evident from what we have heard that Baskerville has been very closely shadowed by someone since he has been in town. How else could it be known so

quickly that it was the Northumberland Hotel which he had chosen?' (*The Hound of the Baskervilles*)

The Northumberland Hotel stood on the corner of Northumberland Avenue near Trafalgar Square. The Sherlock Holmes pub now stands on the same site.

8 NOVELS OF LONDON IN WORLD WAR II

1. ## Nigel Balchin's *Darkness Falls from the Air*
   Balchin's book skilfully portrays life and death in the city during the war. Bill Sarratt is filling in as a civil servant and trying to do his best, but is besieged by all manner of obstacles, including a faithless wife and the intrusion of petty bureaucrats at the Ministry. The horrors of the Blitz are powerfully described. Bill and his wife casually sidestep burning rubble as they mull over alternative nightspots, their first choice having just been destroyed. The conflict's arbitrary distribution of death or survival is chillingly evoked and behind the urban insouciance of the characters lurks a keen sense of dread and expectation of doom.

2. ## Elizabeth Bowen's *The Heat of the Day*
   Set precisely between 'the first Sunday of September 1942' and two years later, Bowen's novel is the story of a woman thrown into the male world of espionage and its dangers. Her life already dismantled by the constant threat of death and the city's bombardment, Stella seeks solace with her lover, Robert. In the impermanent, shadowy world of wartime London, however, Robert is suspected of selling information to the enemy. Harrison, who has discovered this when trailing him, decides to strike a bargain with Stella, but the cost of his silence is dear, since his price is that she must sleep with him.

3. **Francis Cottam's** *The Fire Fighter*

Cottam's novel tells the story of Jack Finlay, a man with a rather shady past, who is withdrawn from the African Front so that his talents as a fire fighter can be used. Jack's mission is to protect from the bombing raids five buildings, strategically situated in the heart of London. Alone in his underground bunker, he waits for the call to action, while the muffled sounds of destruction reverberate around him. The constant threat of spies and the dangers of fire fighting are contrasted with Jack's love affair with Rebecca Lange, the German-born daughter of one of the building's architects.

4. **Henry Green's** *Caught*

Published in 1943, five years after its author had volunteered for the Auxiliary Fire Service, Green's only war novel is a brilliant account of the horrors of the Blitz. Wreathed in smoke and unleashing giant phantasms of flame, the city's burning buildings take on a surreal, though hellish, effulgence. The strained relationship between the narrator and the fire officer unfolds as London is incinerated by deadly fire-bombs, and the contrast between their gradual discovery of a past event that links their respective lives and the awesome conflagration around them fuels Green's plot.

5. **Graham Greene's** *The Ministry of Fear*

One of Greene's 'entertainments', this tells the story of Arthur Rowe, a man consumed with guilt over the merciful killing of his terminally ill wife and seeking to escape, even briefly, the horrors of the Blitz. A chance visit to a local fete promises to be a pleasant distraction from his problems, but it soon turns into a nightmare as he is plunged into a deadly conspiracy. Before long, he realises that he is the quarry in a bizarre but deadly chase through the war-torn city, his fight for survival hampered by amnesia as he struggles to elude the foreign agents intent on killing him.

6. **Anthony Powell's *The Military Philosophers***

The last in the 'Autumn' sequence of Powell's twelve-novel masterpiece, *A Dance to the Music of Time*, this takes place in the final months of the War, with narrator Nicholas Jenkins back in London and fighting the good fight from the bowels of Whitehall. The city is constantly changing as air raids destroy parts of it but Powell also describes the more genial impact of various international refugees, whose presence means that rather drab areas like Bayswater now 'look like the back streets of a Mediterranean port'.

7. **Muriel Spark's *The Girls of Slender Means***

Set in 1945 in 'The May of Teck', a Kensington hostel for young, single ladies, Spark's slender novel is a poignant portrait of war-weary London and the women left behind there. Polite and from good families, giddy with a sense of potential but sharpened by wartime privations, the girls struggle to survive with the barest minimum of those two scarce but crucial commodities: men and money. Varying in looks, attitudes and abilities, the girls are united by this strange life of compromises and 'making do' and, partially, by their friendship with a young man, Nicholas Farringdon. Although damaged, the building has never been directly hit, but the war is not yet over, and when tragedy strikes, the girls' constrained, but cosy, world is shattered.

8. **Evelyn Waugh's *Put Out More Flags***

Published in 1942, Waugh's novel finds some of the characters from his earlier books adjusting to life during wartime. Scoundrel Basil Seal, last seen in *Black Mischief*, is still misbehaving in Mayfair but, like everybody, waits out the rather absurd 'phoney war', where a combination of bureaucratic incompetence and general uncertainty leaves people caught between restless tedium and agonising suspense. Busying himself as a billeting officer for refugees, he uses the Connolly children, a dreadful brood of London urchins whose terrible antics he encourages, foisting them on unsuspecting households and then taking them back, but for a price. He also gets up to some scandalous shenanigans when he joins Whitehall's Ministry of Information, framing his old pal, Ambrose Silk, by fingering him as a collaborator.

6 NOVELS DEPICTING ALTERNATIVE LONDONS

1. *After London* (Richard Jefferies)
   Jefferies was a journalist and naturalist, who wrote several books on the countryside before publishing, in 1885, this powerful but bitter novel about the future. With its full title, *After London, or Wild England*, this is a highly descriptive depiction of London and the rest of England, after some unspecified disaster has occurred and the country has reverted back to its natural state of fields and forests. The city is now a vast swamp, with any relics of our culture and industrial civilisation buried, forgotten, under shrubbery and bushes.

2. *News from Nowhere* (William Morris)
   First published in separate volumes in 1891, Morris' view of London is an idyllic fantasy, fuelled by his fervently held socialist beliefs and his loathing of industrial production and its alienating effect on the worker. Asleep in his house in Hammersmith, the narrator wakes up in twentieth-century London, an Eden-like place where freedom reigns and people lead contented lives, their work now fulfilling and dignified. Later, he discovers that the miraculous revolution that ushered in this utopia occurred 1952. Blessedly free of slums, sweatshops and factories, the city evoked by Morris

has radically altered, or rather evolved, and he fondly records its new wonders.

3. ### *Brave New World* (Aldous Huxley)

    Huxley wrote this dazzling anti-utopian satire in 1932, and in its scientifically wrought future world family and history have been abolished, reproduction takes place in laboratory bottles and there is no God, since Henry Ford, the father of mass production, is the new deity, and the cross is replaced by the letter 'T' (as in Model T Ford). Thus the London we see has such buildings as the Charing T Tower and, in the novel's powerful opening section, the Central London Hatchery and Conditioning Centre, a kind of futuristic combination of hospital, nursery and school.

4. ### *Nineteen Eighty-Four* (George Orwell)

    Written in 1948, Orwell's famous dystopian novel is set in London, named Airstrip One, the largest population centre of Oceania, one of three super-powers and constantly at war with the other two, Eurasia and Eastasia. The protagonist, Winston Smith, works for the Ministry of Truth and, like everybody, leads a restricted life under constant surveillance by the party's figurehead, known as Big Brother, and is force-fed a barrage of propaganda, some of which he helps create. He rebels by keeping a secret diary and by having an illicit love affair with Julia, a young woman also working for the Ministry.

5. ### *The Drowned World* (JG Ballard)

    This was Ballard's first novel and appeared in 1962. Set in a London of the future that's been ravaged by a flood of Biblical proportions, the novel is partially based on Ballard's recollections of his childhood in Shanghai, where, in the rainy season, the city would be deluged. Global warming has melted the polar ice caps, turning the now tropical metropolis into a steamy swampland. Replete with unforgettable images, such as a hunt for buried riches that involves draining Leicester Square, this is a powerful work and one that also seems uncomfortably prescient.

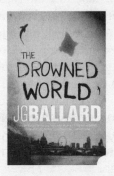

Book cover:
JG Ballard's *The Drowned World*

6. ## *The League of Extraordinary Gentlemen* (Alan Moore/Kevin O'Neill)

The League of Extraordinary Gentlemen is a graphic novel, the first issue of which appeared in 1999. Writer Moore and artist O'Neill introduce characters from *Dracula, King Solomon's Mines, The Invisible Man, Dr Jekyll and Mr Hyde* and *20,000 Leagues Under the Sea* into their vision of nineteenth-century London. Famous London landmarks, both past and present, are well to the fore. In one scene in the book the British Intelligence headquarters (situated at Vauxhall, just like its contemporary counterpart, the MI6 building) is surrounded by cranes and dirigibles, one of which bears the legend 'OXO'.

14 NOVELS WITH LONDON AREAS IN THEIR TITLES

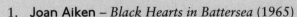

1. **Joan Aiken** – *Black Hearts in Battersea* (1965)
2. **Monica Ali** – *Brick Lane* (2003)
3. **Anthony Burgess** – *A Dead Man in Deptford* (1993)
4. **GK Chesterton** – *The Napoleon of Notting Hill* (1904)
5. **Lionel Davidson** – *The Chelsea Murders* (1978)
6. **Jenny Eclair** – *Camberwell Beauty* (2000)
7. **Graeme Gordon** – *Bayswater Bodycount* (1995)
8. **Somerset Maugham** – *Liza of Lambeth* (1897)
9. **Robert Rankin** – *The Brentford Chainstore Massacre* (1997)
10. **Iain Sinclair** – *White Chappell, Scarlet Tracings* (1987)
11. **Muriel Spark** – *The Ballad of Peckham Rye* (1960)
12. **Leslie Thomas** – *Kensington Heights* (1996)
13. **AN Wilson** – *The Sweets of Pimlico* (1977)
14. **Colin Wilson** – *Adrift in Soho* (1961)

9 FICTIONAL ADDRESSES IN LONDON

1. **The Laurels, Brickfield Terrace, Holloway**
   The address of Mr and Mrs Pooter in George and Weedon Grossmith's satirical portrait of lower-middle-class suburbia, *The Diary of a Nobody*, this is 'a nice six-roomed residence, not counting basement, with a front breakfast-parlour'. The Pooters are very proud of The Laurels, although 'we were rather afraid of the noise of the

trains at first, but the landlord said we should not notice them after a bit, and took two pounds off the rent. He was certainly right; and beyond the cracking of the garden wall at the bottom, we have suffered no inconvenience'. Although the house and Brickfield Terrace were invented by the Grossmith brothers, they are entirely typical of the developments in places like Holloway which were created to house the armies of clerks who worked in the nineteenth-century City.

2. **23 Railway Cuttings, East Cheam**
The home of Anthony Aloysius St John Hancock, 23 Railway Cuttings, East Cheam, became one of the most famous addresses in England during the 1950s when *Hancock's Half Hour* was regularly broadcast by BBC Radio. According to sleeve notes for a record version of two of the shows, written by the Hancock scriptwriters Ray Galton and Alan Simpson, the residence 'is situated in the Borough of East Cheam, pop. 73,684 (1931). Rates in the pound, three and nine. Alt. 2 feet above swamp level, three hundred feet below smog level. Subsoil, clay with vast deposits of builders' rubble. Schools, none. Churches, 1. Pubs, 267. Main industries, taking in washing, street betting, and hanging about on street corners. Hancock Towers, 23 Railway Cuttings, is a masterpiece of Victorian bad taste, which is also a good description of its owner. The house appears to be in some need of repair, which is also a good description of its owner.'

3. **Fowler's End**
In the novel of the same name by Gerald Kersh, first published in 1957, Fowler's End is a grubby, run-down corner of the city which you find by 'going northward, step by step, into the neighbourhoods that most strongly repel you'. Not entirely dissimilar to parts of King's Cross, it is visited by the hero Daniel Laverock who finds a job

in a flea-pit cinema run by the monstrous and tyrannical Sam Yudenow.

4. **The Midnight Bell**

This is a public house off the Euston Road which is at the heart of the eponymous novel by Patrick Hamilton. The novel, the first in the trilogy known as *Twenty Thousand Streets Under the Sky*, follows the trials and tribulations of a barman at the pub who is infatuated with a prostitute. In 2005, the BBC screened a three-part TV drama adapted from the trilogy.

5. **Brookgate**

In Michael Moorcock's *King of the City*, Brookgate is a semi-autonomous enclave of old London. Reminiscent of the republic briefly established in the film *Passport to Pimlico*, Brookgate, according to the book's central character, Denny Dover, is 'controlled by her citizens (or denizens as the old journos used to call us) under the power of the Huguenot Leases which, partly because of the plague, made full ownership of the land so unclear it had been disputed in Chancery since 1670'. (*See also* **5 Films with London Place Names in the Title**, p. 233)

6. **27a Wimpole Street**

27 Wimpole Street exists and is a doctors' surgery. 27a Wimpole Street does not exist and never did, outside the imagination of George Bernard Shaw. It is the address of Henry Higgins in Shaw's play *Pygmalion* and also in the stage and film versions of the musical adaptation, *My Fair Lady*.

7. **347 Piccadilly**

In Bram Stoker's novel *Dracula*, this is a crumbling mansion in Piccadilly, 'grim and silent in its deserted condition among its more lively and spruce-looking neighbours', which is bought by a mysterious aristocrat called Count De Ville. The devilish Count De Ville is later revealed to be none other than Dracula.

8. **Riceyman Steps**
    In the Arnold Bennett novel of that name, Riceyman Steps is a small corner of Clerkenwell – 'the tiny open space (not open to vehicular traffic) which was officially included in the title "Riceyman Steps". At the south corner of this was a second-hand bookseller's shop, and at the north an abandoned and decaying mission-hall; both these abutted on King's Cross Road. Then, on either hand, farther from the thoroughfare and nearer the steps, came a few private houses with carefully curtained windows, and one other shop – a confectioner's.'

9. **165 Eaton Place**
    165 Eaton Place was the house in which masters and servants played out the dramas of their lives, large and small, in the 1970s TV series *Upstairs, Downstairs*. The interior of the house was created at London Weekend Studios but the exterior shots showed a real building in Eaton Place. The producers filmed the outside of 65 Eaton Place and, in a less than masterly attempt to disguise it, simply painted a number '1' in front of the '65'.

12 WRITERS' ADDRESSES IN LONDON

1. **Thomas Chatterton: Brooke Street, EC1**
    Chatterton's death by suicide took place in a garret in a house in Brooke Street, now replaced by a branch of Barclays Bank. The seventeen-year-old Chatterton had moved to London from Bristol to make his name as a poet. In a letter to his mother, he wrote that, 'I am quite familiar at the Chapter Coffee-house and know all the geniuses there.' The coffee-house, on the corner

of Paternoster Row, was at the heart of what was then London's publishing and bookselling quarter but the geniuses there did not know Chatterton, and his attempts to earn a living by his writing failed. In despair, he took an overdose of laudanum.

2. Lawrence Sterne: 41 Old Bond Street, W1

The author of *Tristram Shandy* died in poverty in lodgings in Old Bond Street in 1768. According to legend, the two men who laid out his corpse stole his gold cufflinks by way of payment. The story that Sterne's body was stolen from its burial place by body-snatchers and taken off for dissection, where it was only saved from complete dismemberment in the interests of science by a friend who was present and recognised it, is probably apocryphal.

3. Jane Austen: 10 Henrietta Street, WC2

Jane Austen was not a regular visitor to the capital but, in 1814, she stayed with her brother above the bank in Henrietta Street of which he was part-owner. She wrote in a letter that the building was 'all dirt and confusion, but in a very interesting way'.

4. Percy Bysshe Shelley: 11 Poland Street, W1

Expelled from Oxford for circulating a pamphlet he had written called *The Necessity of Atheism*, Shelley and his friend Thomas Hogg moved into lodgings in Poland Street in 1811. Later in the same year, Shelley eloped to Scotland with his sixteen-year-old mistress, Harriet Westbrook.

5. Sydney Smith: 14 Doughty Street, WC1

A brilliant wit and conversationalist, the Reverend Sydney Smith was a Londoner by inclination who was forced to spend long years in the country. During his time in Doughty Street he was at the heart of the Whig political circle which was centred on Holland House but, unlike most of its other members, he was obliged to earn a living and eventually left the city to become vicar of the rural parish of Foston-le-Clay in Yorkshire. For a man who thought the country was 'a kind of healthy grave' and claimed that, when he was there, he always feared that 'creation will expire before tea-time', it was a hard exile, but he stayed there more than twenty years. Perhaps he entertained himself and his parishioners with his own sermons which he once described as 'long and vigorous, like the penis of a jackass'.

6. **Bram Stoker: 27 Cheyne Walk, SW3**

The Dublin-born author of *Dracula* lived in London while he was working as business manager for the legendary actor Sir Henry Irving and writing the novel which was to make him famous. While he was at Cheyne Walk, Stoker rescued a drowning man from the Thames, carrying him into the house and placing him on the dining-room table. Unfortunately the man died. Stoker left the room and his wife, unaware of what was happening, came in to find a dead man lying on her dining-room table.

7. **Raymond Chandler: Devonshire Road, Forest Hill, SE23**

Raymond Chandler may be best known for hard-boiled crime fiction and the mean streets of Los Angeles, but he went to school in London (at Dulwich) and he lived in the city as a young man before World War I, when he was working as a freelance journalist. He went to the USA in 1912 and did not return to London until he was an old man.

8. **TS Eliot: Clarence Gate Gardens, Glentworth Street, NW1**

Eliot was living in Glentworth Street at the time of the break up of his first marriage. Some time after he left the flat, his wife placed an advert in *The Times* which read, 'will TS Eliot please return to his home, 68 Clarence Gate Gardens, which he abandoned Sept. 17th 1932'. Vivien

Eliot, never the most stable of women, also embarrassed the poet by walking up and down outside the Russell Square offices of the publisher Faber and Faber, where he worked, holding a sign which read, 'I am the wife that TS Eliot abandoned'.

9. **Graham Greene: 15 Devonshire Terrace, W2**

As a teenager, Greene suffered from severe depression and, in 1921, his family sent him to live for six months with the psychiatrist and early psychoanalyst Kenneth Richmond in Richmond's house in Devonshire Terrace. Greene's later homes in London included 141 Albert Palace Mansions, Battersea and 14 North Side, Clapham Common.

10. **George Orwell: I South End Road, NW3**

In the mid-1930s Orwell worked in a bookshop called Booklovers' Corner which stood where Pond Street and South End Road meet and for six months he also lived in a flat above the shop. During the time he was there he began the novel *Keep the Aspidistra Flying*, whose central character, Gordon Comstock, also works in a bookshop not entirely dissimilar to Booklovers' Corner, one in which 'there were highbrow, middlebrow and lowbrow books, new and second-hand all jostling together, as befitted this intellectual and social borderland'.

11. **Joe Orton: Flat 4, 25 Noel Road, N1**

Joe Orton and his lover Kenneth Halliwell moved into the flat in Noel Road in 1959 and it was there that Halliwell battered the playwright to death with a hammer and then killed himself, swallowing twenty-two Nembutal pills washed down with the juice from a tin of grapefruit. Halliwell left a note saying, 'If you read his diary all will be explained.' Orton's accounts of his sexual promiscuity may have distressed Halliwell, but he was also unable to cope with the consequences of his partner's growing fame as a writer.

12. **Kingsley Amis: 16 Buckingham Gardens, Norbury**
This was Amis's childhood home, but not one he remembered with any fondness. Norbury, he later wrote, was 'like half the places south of the river' which 'were never proper places at all, just collections of assorted buildings filling up gaps and named after railway stations and bus garages'.

8 POETS (AND 1 VERY OLD MAN) REMEMBERED IN POETS' CORNER

1. **Geoffrey Chaucer**
Chaucer's grave in the Abbey provided the nucleus for Poets' Corner but it was not because of his poetry that he was buried there. Ten months before his death in October 1400 Chaucer leased a property in the garden of the Abbey's Lady Chapel and it was almost certainly because he died so close to the Abbey and was a man of consequence beyond his literary work that he was buried in the south transept. It was only in the late sixteenth century when Edmund Spenser was buried close to Chaucer that the concept of a Poets' Corner began.

2. **Ben Jonson**
Jonson died in a house near the Abbey and was buried upright, standing on his feet, in the northern aisle of the nave. He is supposed to have told the Dean of Westminster that 'six feet long by two feet wide is too much for me: two feet by two feet will do for all I want'. The memorial in Poets' Corner was erected nearly a hundred years after his death but those who wished him to be remembered could not remember how he had usually spelled his name. He appears as 'Johnson' not 'Jonson'.

3. **William Shakespeare**
Buried in Stratford-on-Avon, Shakespeare has a memorial

in Poets' Corner that dates from 1740. He is depicted leaning, slightly awkwardly, on a pile of books with his left hand pointing to a scroll with some lines from *The Tempest* on it.

4. **Lord Byron**

According to the Dean of Westminster at the time of Byron's death, the poet's 'open profligacy' was 'an obstacle to his commemoration' and it remained an obstacle until 1969. Even in 1924, the Dean of the day was not sympathetic to an attempt to commemorate the centenary of his death with a memorial in the Abbey, writing with robust morality that 'a man who outraged the laws of our Divine Lord, and whose treatment of women violated the Christian principles of purity and honour, should not be commemorated in Westminster Abbey'.

5. **Adam Lindsay Gordon**

The only Australian poet to be honoured with a bust in Poets' Corner (one sculpted by the wife of Scott of the Antarctic), Gordon was actually born in the Azores but emigrated to Australia as a young man and all his poetry was written there. He committed suicide in Melbourne, where he is buried, in 1870.

6. **Alfred, Lord Tennyson**

Tennyson died in 1892 and was laid to rest in the Abbey, between the graves of John Dryden and Robert Browning, after a funeral attended by thousands of mourners. The bust on the pillar nearby was placed there three years later.

7. **Thomas Hardy**

Hardy died in Dorchester and was cremated there, his ashes then being brought to the Abbey to be buried in Poets' Corner. The story that Hardy's heart, which was removed to be buried separately in the village in which he was born, was stolen by a cat from a biscuit tin on his sister's kitchen table and eaten, is probably apocryphal.

8. **Dylan Thomas**

    Dylan Thomas died in 1953. The campaign to install a
    memorial to him in Poets' Corner was begun much later
    after an unlikely admirer, the former US President Jimmy
    Carter, expressed his surprise that one wasn't already
    there. The memorial was finally unveiled in 1982.

+1. **Thomas Parr**

    Not all the people buried or commemorated in Poets'
    Corner were poets. Thomas Parr, who lived through the
    reigns of ten monarchs, from Edward IV to Charles I,
    fathered a child out of wedlock at the age of 100 and is
    said to have lived to be 152, is buried there. Parr lived
    most of his many years in Shropshire but was brought to
    London as a curiosity in 1635. The shock was too much
    for him and he died a few weeks after arriving. Charles I
    ordered that he should be buried in the Abbey.

15 POEMS THAT HAVE BEEN SEEN ON LONDON UNDERGROUND

Underground poem ('Separation', by WS Merwin)

For the last twenty years travellers on tube trains, raising their
eyes from their books and newspapers, have been able to see
not only adverts for travel firms, letting agencies and cheap

telephone networks but also poems. The brainchild of the London-based American writer Judith Chernaik, the 'Poems on the Underground' scheme has been running since 1986. London Underground sponsors the scheme by donating the advertising space. The poems to appear on the trains are still chosen by Chernaik and two other writers, Cicely Herbert and Gerard Benson. Hundreds of poems have been featured over the years and a wide range of literature has been available for travellers, as this small selection of titles shows:

1. Shakespeare's Sonnet No. 29 'When in disgrace with fortune and men's eyes'
2. Edward Lear's 'There was an old man with a beard'
3. The Coming of Grendel, from 'Beowulf'
4. Lewis Carroll's 'The Lobster Quadrille'
5. Robert Burns's 'My luve is like a red, red rose'
6. Two Fragments by Sappho
7. Wilfred Owen's 'Anthem for Doomed Youth'
8. An Anglo-Saxon riddle
9. William Blake's 'Jerusalem'
10. Hugh MacDiarmid's 'The Bonnie Broukit Bairn'
11. Edwin Morgan's 'The Loch Ness Monster's Song'
12. Caedmon's Hymn
13. WB Yeats's 'The Lake Isle of Innisfree'
14. 'Sumer is icumen in' by Anon
15. An excerpt from the King James Bible translation of Ecclesiastes

7

THE ARTS

12 London Film Locations

5 Films in which London Masquerades as Somewhere Else

10 Movie Stars Born in London

5 Films with London Place Names in the Title

6 Most Unconvincing Cockney Accents in the Movies

6 TV Series Set in Imaginary Parts of London

9 Memorable London Theatrical First Nights

4 Disastrous Musicals on the London Stage

6 Pieces of Classical Music with London Place Names in the Title

10 Beatles Sites in London

9 Album Covers Photographed in London

20 Rock/Pop Songs about London

6 London Locations where Rock Stars Died

10 Punk Rock Sites in London

7 Sites Associated with the Bloomsbury Group

12 LONDON FILM LOCATIONS

1. **Acton Lane Power Station (*Aliens* directed by James Cameron, 1986)**
   The huge, disused power station was used by James Cameron for some sequences in his film. Three years later, Tim Burton, in his original *Batman* film, also used the building for the transformation scene in which Jack Nicholson's is shot by the police and plunges into a vat at the Axis Chemical Plant, only to re-emerge as the Joker.

2. **Alexandra Palace (*Nineteen Eighty-Four* directed by Michael Radford, 1984)**
   Victory Square in the movie version of Orwell's dystopian vision of what was, for him, the future, was actually Alexandra Palace.

3. **Cheney Road (*The Ladykillers* directed by Alexander Mackendrick, 1955)**
   This cobbled street behind King's Cross station has been used dozens of times by recent film-makers in search of Victorian atmosphere. It was also used to great effect in the 1950s for contemporary sets in the Ealing comedy, *The Ladykillers*, in which a heavily disguised Alec Guinness leads a gang of incompetent bank robbers who are foiled by a little old lady. *The Ladykillers* also made use of Frederica Street off the Caledonian Road, where the set builders constructed the little old lady's house, and Copenhagen Tunnel, on the railway lines just

Original film poster for
The Ladykillers

north of King's Cross, where the bodies that accumulate in the course of the movie are hurled onto passing trains. In the film *Backbeat*, which told the story of the Beatles' formative years, Cheney Road has another incarnation when it appears as a substitute for the backstreets of early '60s Liverpool.

4. **Leadenhall Market (*Harry Potter and the Philosopher's Stone* directed by Chris Columbus, 2001)**

The Leaky Cauldron which leads into the magical shopping arcade of Diagon Alley was actually an empty property in Bull's Head Passage, Leadenhall Market. In a later film, *Harry Potter and the Prisoner of Azkaban*, the Leaky Cauldron, perhaps unsurprisingly, had changed its position and was situated under a railway bridge in Borough Market. The Victorian ambience of Leadenhall has proved tempting to other film-makers in search of a London that American film audiences would immediately recognise as such. In *Lara Croft: Tomb Raider*, Angelina Jolie as Lara speeds through the market on a motorbike.

5. **Liverpool Street Station (*The Elephant Man* directed by David Lynch, 1980)**

David Lynch's movie allows a brief glimpse of how Liverpool Street station looked before its redevelopment. The scene in which the Elephant Man, the hideously deformed John Merrick, arrives back from the Continent where he has been exhibited in a freak show only to find himself greeted by an angry mob was shot in the old station. Other scenes of Victorian London in the film were shot in Shad Thames and around Borough Market.

6. **Maryon Park (*Blow-Up* directed by Michelangelo Antonioni, 1966)**

The central sequences in Antonioni's classic 1966 movie, in which a fashion photographer, played by David

Hemmings, accidentally records evidence of what might be a murder in the background of snapshots he has taken, were filmed in this park in Charlton. The obsessively perfectionist Italian director, unimpressed by the actual green of the park's grass, insisted on painting it a brighter colour.

7. **Newman's Passage (*Peeping Tom* directed by Michael Powell, 1960)**

In the murder scene that opens Powell's chilling and highly controversial movie we watch the prostitute Dora, through the viewfinder of the murderer's movie camera, as she walks into this alleyway in Fitzrovia. Powell chose it because, as he later wrote, it was (and is) 'a narrow, arched passageway that gives you goose-pimples just to look at it'. According to Julian Maclaren-Ross, in his *Memoirs of the Forties*, it was known to locals as Jekyll and Hyde Alley and it was where 'one sometimes guided girls in order to become better acquainted'.

8. **Powis Square (*Performance* directed by Nicolas Roeg and Donald Cammell, 1970)**

Roeg and Cammell co-directed the cult film in which a gangster on the run, played by James Fox, hides out in the home of a rock star whose career is in terminal decline, played by Mick Jagger, and is drawn into a dangerous world of sex and drugs and mysticism. The exterior of the house is that of 25 Powis Square, off Ledbury Road.

9. **Ruislip Lido (*A Night to Remember* directed by Roy Ward Baker, 1958)**

Most of this movie about the sinking of the *Titanic*, starring Kenneth More and Honor Blackman, was filmed at Pinewood Studios where parts of the doomed ship were reconstructed on set. However some scenes, unsurprisingly, required actors playing the passengers to thrash around in the waters of the Atlantic as the *Titanic* went down and they struggled to get into the lifeboats. It was impossible to film these either in the real ocean (too dangerous) or at Pinewood (no large water tanks available), so the producers made do with the lido in Reservoir Road, Ruislip.

10. **St Bartholomew the Great (*Shakespeare in Love* directed by John Madden, 1998)**

The scene in which Shakespeare, played by Joseph Fiennes, prays in a church after the murder of Christopher Marlowe was shot in St Bartholomew the Great in Smithfield. One of the weddings in *Four Weddings and a Funeral* (the failed one which comes to an abrupt end when the groom, played by Hugh Grant, realises that he loves Carrie, played by Andie MacDowell, rather than his prospective bride) was also filmed in the church.

11. **Thamesmead Estate (*A Clockwork Orange* directed by Stanley Kubrick, 1971)**

The scene in which the central character, Alex, played by Malcolm McDowell, together with his 'droogs', beats up a tramp was filmed in a subway behind the Tavy Bridge shopping centre.

12. **Trafalgar Square (*It Happened Here* directed by Kevin Brownlow, 1964)**

Brownlow's movie, made on a shoestring, is an exercise in alternative history. It begins with a voiceover which tells the viewers that 'the German Invasion of England took place in July 1940 after the British retreat from Dunkirk. Strongly resisted at first, the German army took many months to restore order, but the resistance movement, lacking outside support, was finally crushed. Then, in 1944, the resistance movement reappeared'. As the story unfolds we see German soldiers, in Nazi uniforms, wandering the streets of London as tourists and occupiers. A group of SS men pass in front of Big Ben. In one of the most compelling sequences in the film, a Nazi rally takes place in Trafalgar Square.

5 FILMS IN WHICH LONDON MASQUERADES AS SOMEWHERE ELSE

London has often proved an attractive location for movie-makers, but some have pretended that the city was actually somewhere else. Here are five examples of cinematic deceit:

1. *Eyes Wide Shut*, directed by Stanley Kubrick, 1999 (New York)
   Kubrick adapted Arthur Schnitzler's early twentieth-century Viennese novella of sexual temptation into a screenplay set in contemporary New York and then, hampered by his unwillingness to travel, filmed it largely in the streets of London. Parts of Soho, including Brewer Street and Eastcastle Street, as well as Hatton Garden, are supposed to be Greenwich Village and the nightclub Madame Jo-Jo's becomes a haunt of New York jazz fans.

2. *Full Metal Jacket*, directed by Stanley Kubrick, 1987 (Vietnam)
   Notoriously unwilling to travel, Kubrick was never likely to do much filming in genuine locations for his Vietnam War epic and the conflict was reconstructed in the derelict Beckton Gas Works. Palm trees and plastic foliage were imported to recreate the jungles of South East Asia. Beckton Gas Works also stood in for a Japanese internment camp in some of the scenes of Spielberg's *Empire of the Sun*, based on JG Ballard's autobiographical novel about British civilians imprisoned during World War II. The gas works and the area around it have since been redeveloped.

3. *Goldeneye*, **directed by Martin Campbell, 1995 (St Petersburg)**

The courtyard of Somerset House on the Strand is the backdrop for a scene in the 1995 Bond movie which is supposedly set in a square in St Petersburg. In a later Bond film, *Tomorrow Never Dies*, the building is seen again but this time has been transformed into the headquarters of MI6. Clearly, Somerset House is a particularly adaptable location, since, in Tim Burton's *Sleepy Hollow*, it has moved across the Atlantic and is supposedly a building in old Manhattan.

4. *Indiana Jones and the Last Crusade*, **directed by Steven Spielberg, 1989 (Berlin)**

When the heroic Indiana makes his escape from Germany in one of the scenes in the film, Berlin airport is not what it seems. It is actually the Royal Horticultural Hall in Greycoat Street, Westminster. The Hall clearly made an effective airport since it was used for the same purpose in the 1997 film of *The Saint*, starring Val Kilmer.

5. *Mission Impossible*, **directed by Brian De Palma, 1996 (Prague)**

The exterior of Tate Britain and the stairs leading up to it were transformed into an embassy in the Czech capital in De Palma's movie.

10 MOVIE STARS BORN IN LONDON

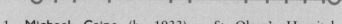

1. **Michael Caine** (b. 1933) – St Olave's Hospital, Rotherhithe, SE16

2. **Charlie Chaplin** (b. 1889) – East Street, Walworth, SE17

3. **Greer Garson** (b. 1904) – 88 First Avenue, Manor Park, E12

4. **Boris Karloff** (b. 1887) – 36 Forest Hill Road, SE23

5. **Christopher Lee** (b. 1922) – 51 Lower Belgrave Street, SW1

6. **Roger Moore** (b. 1927) – Clapham Maternity Hospital, 41 Jeffreys Road, SW4

Boris Karloff in
The Mummy

7. **David Niven** (b. 1910) – Belgrave Mansions, Grosvenor Gardens, SW1

8. **Claude Rains** (b. 1889) – 26 Tregothnan Road, Stockwell, SW9

9. **Margaret Rutherford** (b. 1892) – 15 Dornton Road, Balham, SW12

10. **Elizabeth Taylor** (b. 1932) – 8 Wildwood Road, Hampstead, NW11

5 FILMS WITH LONDON PLACE NAMES IN THE TITLE

1. ## *Limehouse Blues*, 1934

   This minor piece of 1930s Hollywood hokum plays on the long-held belief that Limehouse, London's first Chinatown, was nothing but a centre of opium-smoking, white slavery and strange, oriental vices. It stars George Raft as a half-Chinese gangster from New York who travels to London and takes over as the local crime boss. Ironically, thirty-four years later, on one of the occasions when George Raft wanted to travel to London in real life, he was banned from entry into Britain because of his Mafia connections.

2. ## *The Arsenal Stadium Mystery*, 1939

   A friendly match becomes less friendly when the team's star player is murdered and a Scotland Yard detective, played by Leslie Banks, arrives at Highbury to investigate. Members of the championship-winning Arsenal side of the period, most of them looking acutely uncomfortable, appear in the movie. The film has minor cult status and is shown from time to time at the National Film Theatre (NFT).

3. ## *Passport to Pimlico*, 1949

   The Ealing comedy, about locals declaring independence after discovering an ancient treaty proving that Pimlico is legally a part of Burgundy, not of Britain, has long been considered a classic. Most of the film was not actually shot in Pimlico but south of the river in Lambeth, where the film-makers built sets amid the bomb-damaged surrounds of Hercules Road. (*See also* **9 Fictional Addresses**, p. 215)

4. ## *We Are the Lambeth Boys*, 1958

   This documentary, directed by Karel Reisz, was part of the 'Free Cinema' movement of the 1950s, a term which was coined by Lindsay Anderson to describe a season of short films shown at the National Film Theatre. Unscripted and made outside the confines of the major studios, several of the films attempted to show everyday life in '50s London. Anderson's own movie, *Every Day Except Christmas*, was about a day and a night in the life of the old Covent Garden fruit and vegetable market, and *Momma Don't Allow* was filmed in a London jazz club. *We Are the Lambeth Boys* was shot over a period of a few weeks in the summer of 1958 at a youth club in Kennington. Morrissey makes use of some dialogue from the film in the lyrics of his song 'Spring-heeled Jim'.

5. **Notting Hill, 1999**
Much of the film was shot on location in Notting Hill. The bookshop which William Thacker (Hugh Grant) owns and where he meets the film star Anna Scott (Julia Roberts) is in Portobello Road, the couple go to the Coronet Cinema in Notting Hill Gate on their first date and their marriage reception takes place in the Zen Garden of the Hempel Hotel in Craven Hill Gardens. Most famously, the blue door on Thacker's home, which he opens to find photographers camped on his doorstep, was on a house in Westbourne Park Road, then owned by the film's writer and director, Richard Curtis.

6 MOST UNCONVINCING COCKNEY ACCENTS IN THE MOVIES

1. **Dick Van Dyke** in *Mary Poppins* (1964)
2. **Johnny Depp** in *From Hell* (2001)
3. **The Orcs** in *Lord of the Rings* (2001-2003)
4. **Richard Attenborough** in *The Guinea Pig* (1948)
5. **Cary Grant** in *None But the Lonely Heart* (1944)
6. **Johnny Depp** in *Pirates of the Caribbean* (2003)

6 TV SERIES SET IN IMAGINARY PARTS OF LONDON

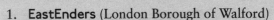

1. **EastEnders** (London Borough of Walford)
2. **The Bill** (London Borough of Canley)
3. **The Thin Blue Line** (London Borough of Gasforth)
4. **Neverwhere** ('London Below')
5. **Are You Being Served?** (Grace Brothers Department Store)
6. **Bad Girls** (Her Majesty's Prison Larkhall, South London)

9 MEMORABLE LONDON THEATRICAL FIRST NIGHTS

1. ***Twelfth Night*, Middle Temple, 1602**
   Although we cannot be certain that the performance of *Twelfth Night* by Shakespeare's company, the Lord Chamberlain's Men, which took place in Middle Temple Hall on 2 February 1602 was a premiere, it was certainly the first recorded staging of it. A diarist named John Manningham wrote that, 'At our feast we had a play called *Twelfth Night or What You Will*, much like the *Comedy of Errors*'. Manningham liked the play, singling out the sub-plot involving Malvolio for particular praise. Pepys, who saw a performance in January 1663, did not. He wrote in his diary that it was 'a silly play, and not related at all to the name or days'.

2. ***The Beggar's Opera*, 1728**
   John Gay's play opened on 29 January 1728 at Lincoln's Inn Fields Theatre and was performed 60 nights consecutively which was, for the time, an astonishing run (most plays

were only staged for a few nights). The Lincoln's Inn Fields Theatre was managed by an impresario called John Rich and *The Beggar's Opera* was said to have made 'Gay rich and Rich gay'.

3. David Garrick's *Richard III*, Goodman's Fields, 1741

Garrick worked as a wine merchant after arriving in London but his passion was the theatre and, after appearing on stage incognito as a harlequin in a pantomime, he made his full debut as Shakespeare's *Richard III* in a production at the unlicensed Goodman's Fields Theatre. Still cloaked in anonymity (he was billed as 'a gentleman who has never before appeared on stage') Garrick became the talk of the town and, although Goodman's Fields was an unfashionable venue and off the beaten track, high society began to flock to see him. In a letter to a friend, Horace Walpole reported that 'the town are gone mad after him' and that 'there are a dozen dukes of a night at Goodman's Fields, sometimes.'

4. 'Romeo' Coates, The Haymarket, 1810

Robert Coates, a wealthy amateur actor, began his career playing Romeo at the Theatre Royal in Bath. His performances were eccentric in the extreme. He appeared on stage 'in a cloak of sky-blue silk, profusely spangled, red pantaloons, a vest of white muslin, and a wig of the style of Charles II, capped by an opera hat'. The audience, already in fits of laughter, were given a further treat when 'his nether garments, being far too tight, burst in seams which could not be concealed'. Undeterred, Coates made his debut in London at the Haymarket Theatre in 1810, playing another young lover, Lothario, in a play called *The Fair Penitent*. Coates was particularly fond of death scenes (in Bath, he had responded to audience cries of 'Die again, Romeo' with not one but several encores of his death throes) and *The Fair Penitent* provided him with another opportunity to excel. While the audience cheered, he spent upwards of five minutes nosily expiring. Silence finally fell and Coates appeared to be a corpse but he had noticed that his hat had fallen off and was in danger of getting dirty on the stage. He got up, carefully spread a handkerchief on the floor and placed his hat on it. He then walked to the front of the stage to argue with members of the audience, who were hooting with derision, before eventually resuming his status as a dead man. Coates, who became a regular sight on the streets of London, driving in a carriage shaped like a seashell, was a sensation for a season but soon faded into obscurity. He died in 1848 when he was knocked down by a hansom cab.

5. **Henry Irving's *Hamlet*, Lyceum, 1874**

On 31 October 1874 the opening night of Irving's production of *Hamlet* was the theatrical event of the season but, at first, the actor's muted performance was not understood by the audience. As Ellen Terry wrote in her memoirs, 'the success on the first night at the Lyceum, in 1874, was not of that electrical, almost hysterical splendour which has greeted the momentous achievements of some actors.' Slowly those lucky enough to be there began to appreciate the subtlety and art of the interpretation and, again according to Terry, 'attention gave place to admiration, admiration to enthusiasm, enthusiasm to triumphant acclaim'. The performance established Irving, previously better known for performances in over-the-top melodramas like *The Bells*, as a Shakespearean actor.

6. ***Peter Pan*, Duke of York's Theatre, 1904**

The premiere of JM Barrie's fantasy about the boy who wouldn't grow up was originally scheduled for 22 December 1904 at the Duke of York's Theatre in St Martin's Lane, but the elaborate stage mechanics required to provide the illusion of flying were not ready and the performance was postponed until the day after Boxing

Day. Even then some of the scenes had to be omitted because the machinery was not functioning properly. The play was a success from the opening night, but its story of twee fairies and cute children was not to everyone's taste. 'Oh for an hour of Herod,' the novelist Anthony Hope remarked as he emerged from the premiere.

7. *Waiting for Godot*, Arts Theatre, 1955
The original English production of Beckett's play was directed by Peter Hall, then aged twenty-four, who recalled in later interviews how, when the lines 'Nobody comes. Nobody goes. It's awful.' were spoken, one member of the audience shouted out, 'Hear! Hear!' and pandemonium ensued as those who loved the play and those who hated it argued in the auditorium. The play transferred from the Arts Theatre, a private theatrical club, to the Criterion, a public theatre, and thus became subject to the censorship of the Lord Chamberlain who was particularly exercised by the use of the word 'erection' and demanded that it be removed. Others wanted the whole play banned. One person wrote to the Lord Chamberlain's office, claiming that, 'running through the play is the desire of two old tramps continually to relieve themselves. Such a dramatisation of lavatory necessities is offensive and against all sense of British decency.'

8. *Look Back in Anger*, Royal Court, 1956
The premiere of John Osborne's *Look Back in Anger*, often seen as a turning point in English theatrical history, took place at the Royal Court on May 8 1956. Described by one critic as nothing more than 'a self-pitying snivel', the play was championed by Kenneth Tynan who wrote in a review that, 'I doubt if I could love anyone who did not wish to see *Look Back in Anger*.' Thirty-five years later the author, John Osborne, confessed that the opening night was 'an occasion I only partly remember, but certainly with more accuracy than those who subsequently claimed

to have been present and, if they are to be believed, would have filled the theatre several times over'.

9. **Peter O'Toole's *Macbeth*, Old Vic, 1980**
Macbeth has long been considered an unlucky play, and disaster has often struck when famous actors have taken the role. At the Old Vic in 1937, Lawrence Olivier's performance was marred one night when his sword broke and part of it shot into the auditorium and hit a member of the audience, who was so startled he promptly had a heart attack. However, there has been no more disastrous *Macbeth* than the 1980 production, also at the Old Vic, which starred Peter O'Toole as the Scottish king. Variously described after the opening night as 'heroically ludicrous' and 'a milestone in the history of coarse acting', O'Toole's performance was savaged by the critics. Audiences, proving once again that there is no such thing as bad publicity, flocked to the theatre to see if it was as bad as reviewers claimed. It was. O'Toole, agreeing with the superstitions that surround the play, claimed later that it had caused his divorce and the death of a close friend.

4 DISASTROUS MUSICALS ON THE LONDON STAGE

1. *Twang!!*
Searching for a follow-up to his spectacular success with *Oliver!*, the songwriter and composer Lionel Bart chose to write a musical about Robin Hood, depicting the folk hero as a medieval con-man, and gave it the title *Twang!!* Worse even than his choice of subject and title was Bart's decision to use his own money to finance the musical and to sign away the rights to *Oliver!* to ensure that the new show was put on. The omens for the musical were not good. 'Do you know what it's like bringing this show into

London?', one producer said. 'It's like giving a crazy man £30,000 and having him flush the notes down the toilet one by one.' The sceptical producer was right. Opening in 1965, *Twang!!* was mercilessly rubbished by the critics and was a disastrous flop. Bart lost his entire investment and, it's estimated, £100 million in future earnings from *Oliver!*

2. ### *I and Albert*
    Queen Victoria would not be the first monarch to spring to mind as a potential subject for a musical and she would probably not have been amused by this attempt to depict in song her life and her love for Prince Albert. Opening at the Piccadilly Theatre in 1972, the show, written by Adams and Strouse, the creators of *Annie*, lasted only three months before disappearing from the stage. A song celebrating the achievement of building the Crystal Palace ('All Glass?') and cheery Cockney numbers such as 'I've 'Eard the Bloody 'Indoos 'As it Worse' could do nothing to save it. With hindsight the musical should probably be best remembered for thirteen-year-old Sarah Brightman, who made her West End debut as the young Victoria.

3. ### *Out of the Blue*
    Opening at the Shaftesbury Theatre on 4 November 1994, this love story set against the backdrop of the bombing of Nagasaki closed a mere seventeen days later. One critic dubbed it 'Into the Red'; another headlined his review 'A Flash in Japan'. Despite the brave assertion by one of the show's producers that *Out of the Blue* was 'always intended to have a short run', it must rank as one of the West End's least triumphant musicals.

4. ### *Leonardo*
    Leonardo da Vinci might seem an unlikely subject for a musical but even more unlikely was the source of the money which enabled the show to go on. Much of the

investment came from the tiny Pacific republic of Nauru. Political leaders in Nauru who had poured millions into the production chartered a plane to take them to the premiere. En route to Britain there were problems with the aircraft and, after several delays, the official party arrived in London only to find that the performance was over. Many people in Nauru were unhappy that their money had been used to finance a flop. 'The whole idea of going to London to sing with our cash was crazy,' one of the protesters was quoted as saying. 'They might as well sing here.'

6 PIECES OF CLASSICAL MUSIC WITH LONDON PLACE NAMES IN THE TITLE

1. ### Eric Coates – 'Knightsbridge March'
    Coates, a prolific composer of light classical music, is best known for his 'Dambusters' March' but the 'Knightsbridge March', from his *London Suite*, used as the opening tune for the immensely popular BBC Radio show *In Town Tonight*, was once just as familiar. Coates also wrote the music known as 'By the Sleepy Lagoon', which still introduces *Desert Island Discs*.

2. ### Percy Grainger – 'Handel in the Strand'
    Grainger originally intended that the piece should have the less evocative title of 'Clog Dance' but a friend who heard it suggested 'Handel in the Strand' because it sounded as if 'jovial old Handel were careening down the Strand to the strains of modern English popular music'.

3. ### Gustav Holst – *Hammersmith Suite*
    Some of the *Hammersmith Suite* was written in the Blue Anchor pub on Lower Mall, Hammersmith. Holst was music master at St Paul's Girls' School in nearby Brook Green and he also wrote a *Brook Green Suite* whilst in hospital in the year before he died. According to Holst's

daughter Imogen, the music of the *Hammersmith Suite* was 'the outcome of long years of familiarity with the changing crowds and the changing river. Those Saturday night crowds, who were always good natured even when they were being pushed off the pavement into the middle of the traffic. And the stall holders in the narrow lane behind the Broadway, with their unexpected assortment of goods lit up by brilliant flares. And the large woman at the fruit shop who always called him "dearie" when he bought oranges for his Sunday picnics ...'

4. **John Ireland – 'Chelsea Reach'**
Although he was born in Manchester in 1879, Ireland spent much of his life in London where he taught at the Royal College of Music (Benjamin Britten was one of his pupils) and was organist and choirmaster of St Luke's Church, Chelsea. 'Chelsea Reach' is a piano piece intended to evoke the atmosphere of the Thames. Ireland also wrote another piano piece called 'Soho Forenoons'.

5. **Felix Mendelssohn – 'Camberwell Green'**
Mendelssohn stayed in Camberwell in 1842 and wrote a piano piece which he called 'Camberwell Green'. His publisher disliked the title and it was re-named 'Spring Song' under which title it became one of the most popular recital pieces of the nineteenth century.

6. **Haydn Wood – 'Horse Guards, Whitehall'**
Haydn Wood, a Yorkshire-born composer of the first half of the twentieth century, is probably best known for the famous World War I song, 'Roses of Picardy', but he also wrote a number of pieces inspired by London. Taken from Wood's *London Landmarks Suite*, 'Horse Guards, Whitehall' was used as the signature tune for the BBC Radio series *Down Your Way*. The other pieces in the suite are intended to evoke Tower Hill and Nelson's Column.

10 BEATLES SITES IN LONDON

1. Abbey Road, NW8

Album cover for the
Beatles' *Abbey Road*

Following in the footsteps of Yehudi Menuhin and Edward Elgar who had recorded the latter's Violin Concerto here in 1931, the Beatles first came to Abbey Road in September 1962 when they recorded 'Love Me Do' in Studio 2 at the EMI Studios there. Subsequently, they recorded nearly all their other songs there and the Abbey Road album cover carries the famous photograph of the Fab Four on the zebra crossing in the road.

2. London Palladium, Argyll Street, W1

The Beatles appeared before 15 million viewers on ITV's Sunday Night at the London Palladium on 13 October 1963 in a performance which confirmed that Beatlemania had hit the nation.

3. Bag O'Nails Club, Kingly Street, W1

Also famous as a venue where Jimi Hendrix regularly played, the Bag O'Nails was where, in May 1967, Paul McCartney first met Linda Eastman at a gig by Georgie Fame and the Blue Flames.

4. Prince of Wales Theatre, Coventry Street, W1

This was the venue for the 1963 Royal Command Variety Performance in front of the Queen Mother and Princess Margaret. Before the band played 'Twist and Shout', John Lennon turned to the audience and said, 'For this next number we'd like to ask your help. Will the people in the cheaper seats clap your hands. The rest of you, if you'll just rattle your jewellery.'

5. **132 Charing Cross Road, WC2**

   In November 1962 the offices of Dick James Music were in Charing Cross Road and Brian Epstein came here to sign a deal for the company to publish Lennon and McCartney's songs. The company, expanding, moved to new offices in New Oxford Street in 1964.

6. **57 Wimpole Street, W1**

   This was where Paul McCartney lived in the mid-'60s (in an attic at the back of the house) and where he wrote 'Yesterday'. The house belonged to the parents of Jane Asher, who was McCartney's girlfriend at the time.

7. **Apple Boutique, Baker Street, W1**

   The boutique stood at the junction of Baker Street and Paddington Street and, at the time of its opening, Paul McCartney announced that it would be run on 'Western communism principles'. The venture was a financial disaster and within eight months there was a giveaway of all stock to passing members of the public.

8. **Apple Corporation, 3 Savile Row, W1**

   This was a house once rented by Nelson and Emma Hamilton and was the headquarters of Apple Corporation. The roof was the site of impromptu lunchtime concert on 30 January 1969 which was stopped by police after forty minutes. The last time all four Beatles met was in September 1969 in a room in the building which is now home to the Building Societies Association.

9. **165 Broadhurst Gardens, NW6**

   This is the site of the former Decca Studios where the Beatles failed an audition in January 1962 and Brian Poole and the Tremeloes were chosen as the one group Decca would sign.

10. **6 Mason's Yard, SW1**

    The art gallery Indica was in Mason's Yard and was the

site of the first meeting between John Lennon and Yoko Ono, who was staging an exhibition in the gallery. Lennon was impressed by Yoko's art, particularly one exhibit consisting of the word 'Yes' written in tiny writing which could only be seen with a magnifying glass.

9 ALBUM COVERS PHOTOGRAPHED IN LONDON

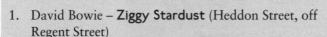

1. David Bowie – **Ziggy Stardust** (Heddon Street, off Regent Street)
2. Nick Drake – **Bryter Later** (The Westway)
3. Ian Dury and the Blockheads – **New Boots and Panties!!** (Vauxhall Bridge Road)
4. The Kinks – **The Muswell Hillbillies** (Archway Tavern, Archway Road)
5. Madness – **Absolutely** (Camden Town Underground Entrance)
6. Oasis – **What's the Story, Morning Glory** (Berwick Market)
7. Pink Floyd – **Animals** (Battersea Power Station)
8. The Rolling Stones – **Between the Buttons** (Primrose Hill)
9. Wings – **London Town** (Tower Bridge)

20 ROCK/POP SONGS ABOUT LONDON

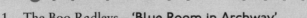

1. The Boo Radleys – 'Blue Room in Archway'
2. Carter the Unstoppable Sex Machine – 'The Only Living Boy in New Cross'
3. The Clash – 'London Calling'

Album cover for *London Calling*, by the Clash

4. Lloyd Cole and the Commotions – 'Charlotte Street'
5. Elvis Costello – 'I Don't Want to Go to Chelsea'
6. David Devant and His Spirit Wife – 'Pimlico'
7. Donovan – 'Sunny Goodge Street'
8. Nick Drake – 'Mayfair'
9. Ian Dury – 'Plaistow Patricia'
10. Eddie Grant – 'Electric Avenue'
11. The Jam – 'A Bomb in Wardour Street'
12. The Kinks – 'Waterloo Sunset'
13. Madness – 'Camden Town'
14. Kirsty McColl – 'Soho Square'
15. Morrissey – 'Piccadilly Palare'
16. The Pet Shop Boys – 'King's Cross'
17. The Pogues – 'A Rainy Night in Soho'
18. Pulp – 'Mile End'
19. Gerry Rafferty – 'Baker Street'
20. XTC – 'Towers of London'

6 LONDON LOCATIONS WHERE ROCK STARS DIED

1. **Samarkand Hotel (Jimi Hendrix)**

    Hendrix came to London in 1966 and formed the Jimi Hendrix Experience. The band had their three greatest hits the following year – 'Purple Haze', 'Hey Joe' and 'The Wind Cries Mary' – but Hendrix was still at the height of his fame and notoriety in 1970 when he died of an accidental drugs overdose. In September that year, although he was renting rooms at the Cumberland Hotel in Great Cumberland Place near Marble Arch, he was spending much of his time at the flat of his girlfriend, Monika Dannemann, in the Hotel Samarkand in Lansdowne Crescent, Notting Hill. In the early hours of the morning of the 18th, Dannemann awoke to find Hendrix apparently comatose and with vomit around his lips. Unable to rouse him, she first called Eric Burdon of The Animals for advice and then called an ambulance. Hendrix was rushed to the nearby St Mary Abbot's Hospital in Marloes Road but he was pronounced dead on arrival.

2. **Queens Ride Bridge (Marc Bolan)**

    A memorial marks the spot on the southern side of Barnes Common where, in the early hours of 16 September 1977 a purple Mini 1275 GT, driven by the soul singer Gloria Jones, left the road as it passed over a small bridge in Queen's Ride, smashed through a fence and drove into a sycamore tree. Gloria Jones was seriously injured. Her passenger and lover, the glam rock star Marc Bolan was killed. The site is still a shrine for his fans and, if it can't be recognised by the bronze bust unveiled there in 2002, it can be identified by the bouquets of flowers that are regularly left there. There is also a plaque on the house at 25 Stoke Newington Common where Bolan grew up.

3. **9 Curzon Place ('Mama' Cass Elliot and Keith Moon)**

This block of flats in Mayfair has seen the deaths of not one but two music stars. In 1974 'Mama' Cass Elliot died in a flat owned by the singer Harry Nilsson, reportedly after choking on a ham sandwich but more likely as a result of drugs and obesity. Four years later the legendary wild man, Keith Moon, the drummer with The Who, died in the night at his flat in the same block. He died of a drugs overdose but, ironically, not an overdose of any of the wide range of illegal substances he had sampled in his life. He took too much of a prescribed medicine intended to curb his raging alcoholism.

4. **Finsbury Park tube station (Graham Bond)**

Founder of the Graham Bond Organisation, a '60s group which included Jack Bruce and Ginger Baker (both later to be members of Cream), Bond spiralled into depression and paranoia after his band split up in 1967. Addicted to an assortment of drugs and convinced, after experimentation with the black arts, that demons were pursuing him around north London, he threw himself in front of a Piccadilly Line train at Finsbury Park on 8 May 1974.

5. **Overhill Road, Dulwich (Bon Scott)**

The lead singer of the Australian band AC/DC was out partying at a music club in Camden until the early hours of the morning in February 1980 and was then driven home by a friend. He fell asleep in the back of the car and could not be roused when the car reached his flat. The friend then decided to take the extremely drunk singer back to his flat in Dulwich. Scott was still out cold when the car pulled up in Overhill Road so he was left to slumber on until morning. Sadly, he choked on his own vomit in the night and was found dead the next day.

6. **Wimbledon Station (Adrian Borland)**

The singer/songwriter with the punk band The Sound killed himself in April 1999 by jumping in front of a train in the station. Borland, who had long had troubles with mental illness, had been seen in a restaurant in Kennington, complaining of voices in his head, and it seems that the voices had persuaded him to suicide.

10 PUNK ROCK SITES IN LONDON

1. **430 King's Road, SW10**

This was the site of Malcolm McLaren and Vivienne Westwood's SEX Boutique, the epicentre of the punk revolution, where the look (spiky hair, clothes ripped or held together by safety pins) was created and where the Sex Pistols were formed, initially to promote the shop. Chrissie Hynde of The Pretenders was one of several future punk stars who worked in SEX.

2. **St Martin's College of Art and Design, Charing Cross Road, WC2**

The Sex Pistols had their first gig here in November 1975, supporting a band called Bazooka Joe. (Stuart Goddard, later Adam Ant, was a member of the headlining band.) At the time, several of the Pistols were living in an attic flat in Denmark Street only a couple of hundred yards from the College so they had only a little distance to travel to the gig, an important consideration for McLaren whose earlier attempts to get all the band together at the same time had often ended in fiasco.

3. **The 100 Club, Oxford Street, W1**

This long-established music venue at 100 Oxford Street (it dates back to World War II) was the scene of a two-day punk festival, organised by Malcolm McLaren, on 20 and 21 September 1976. Many of the later-to-be-famous bands, including The Damned, The Clash, The Buzzcocks and The Sex Pistols, played during the two days. Sid Vicious, not yet a member of the Pistols, lived up to his name by attacking the music journalist Nick Kent with a bicycle chain.

4. **Thames TV, Euston Road, NW1**

London's Outrage!

Studio 5 was the scene of the December 1976 confrontation between the Sex Pistols, attended by friends like Siouxsie Sioux, and the TV presenter Bill Grundy. Goaded by Grundy and encouraged to 'say something outrageous', the band duly obliged with a volley of four-letter words of the kind not usually heard on TV in the 1970s. Grundy also made a disastrously misjudged attempt to flirt with Siouxsie Sioux and was accused of being a 'dirty old man'.

5. **181 Marylebone Road, NW1**

The Marylebone Magistrates Court at this address was where Sid Vicious and his girlfriend Nancy Spungen appeared on drugs charges in May 1978. Sid made faces at the court officers, fell asleep during the proceedings and then attacked one of the photographers waiting outside the building to snap the couple as they left.

6. **Buckingham Palace, SW1**

The short-lived signing of the Sex Pistols to A & M Records took place on a table set up outside the gates of Buckingham Palace.

7. **Lansdowne Studios, Lansdowne Road, W11**

Here was where the Sex Pistols' first single 'Anarchy in the UK' was recorded. The anarchy was not restricted to the lyrics of the song. Both EMI and Polydor were under the impression that they had booked the group to record, and representatives of both labels squabbled amongst themselves while the band members and their entourage, none of whom had any idea how to make a record, spent two weekends of studio time producing endless, unusable tape.

8. **171 North End Road, W14**
The Nashville Rooms, above a pub at this address, were the venue for numerous early punk gigs. The Stranglers, The Sex Pistols, The Damned and Joe Strummer's pre-Clash band, the 101ers, all played here. Elvis Costello made his live debut here in May 1977.

9. **Screen on the Green, Upper Street, N1**
The cinema was the venue for The Clash's first gig in August 1976.

10. **41–43 Neal Street, WC2**
Neal Street was the site of the Roxy, a punk club run by Vivienne Westwood's former accountant in the first few months of 1977. The Clash played the opening gig, The Jam and The Damned became regular attractions and Adam and the Ants made their debut at the club's closing party which took place on 23 April 1977.

7 SITES ASSOCIATED WITH THE BLOOMSBURY GROUP

1. **46 Gordon Square**
The home of Adrian, Thoby, Vanessa and Virginia Stephen between 1904 and 1907, this was where the Bloomsbury Group began. Friends gathered at informal meetings in the house, particularly on Thursday evenings, when wide-ranging discussions of art, literature, philosophy and politics took place. Many of the visitors – Clive

Bell, Leonard Woolf, Lytton Strachey and John Maynard Keynes – were Cambridge contemporaries of the Stephen brothers. The household broke up after the marriage of Vanessa to Clive Bell and the death of Thoby from typhoid fever at the age of twenty-six. Virginia later married Leonard Woolf. The house is now owned by the University of London and there is a coffee bar in the sitting room where so many of the early Bloomsbury discussions took place.

2. **Omega Workshop, 33 Fitzroy Square**
    Founded in 1913 by the art critic and painter Roger Fry, the Omega Workshop was intended to apply the principles of the finest contemporary art to design and the applied arts. Vanessa Bell and Duncan Grant, both friends of Fry, worked at Omega as did other well-known figures like Wyndham Lewis and Dora Carrington. The Omega was never a financial success and closed in 1920. The site is now occupied by the London Foot Hospital and School of Podiatric Medicine.

3. **Hogarth House, Paradise Road, Richmond**
    The house where Leonard and Virginia Woolf lived between 1915 and 1924 was also where they set up the publishing firm Hogarth Press, which began as a small private press producing books on a hand press in the couple's dining room but went on to be a major contributor to the modernist movement in England. The Hogarth Press imprint published books by Katherine Mansfield, TS Eliot, EM Forster, Robert Graves and many others and the Woolfs were the first to publish Freud's writings, in English translations by Lytton Strachey's brother James.

4. **52 Tavistock Square**
    This was the home of the Woolfs from 1924 to 1939 and was where Virginia wrote *Mrs Dalloway, To the*

Lighthouse and *A Room of One's Own*. It is now the site of the Tavistock Hotel.

5. 44 Bedford Square

Lady Ottoline Morrell was an eccentric but generous hostess at her Oxfordshire country house, Garsington Manor, entertaining everybody who was anybody in the literary world, from DH Lawrence to TS Eliot and Aldous Huxley to Bertrand Russell. She was a friend to most of the members of the Bloomsbury Group. Many of the writers repaid her by creating thinly disguised and cruelly satirical portraits of her in their works. No. 44 Bedford Square was Lady Ottoline's London home.

6. 51 Gordon Square

The home of the critic and biographer Lytton Strachey from 1909 to 1924, 51 Gordon Square was where the strange triangular relationship between Strachey, the painter Dora Carrington and her husband, the writer Ralph Partridge began. It continued when the three leased Ham Spray House in Wiltshire together and lasted until Strachey's death in 1932. Carrington, overcome by grief, killed herself.

7. Clifford's Inn

Virginia Woolf and her husband Leonard lived in the Inn in 1912–13. It was the scene of her first bout of mental illness and her first attempt at suicide.

8

SPORT

5 ALL-LONDON FA CUP FINALS

13 LONDON FOOTBALL LEAGUE CLUBS IN ORDER OF FOUNDATION

10 NOTABLE FOOTBALL MATCHES AT WEMBLEY

7 LOST LONDON SPORTING VENUES

15 CELEBRITIES WHO HAVE RUN THE LONDON MARATHON AND 1 WHO

TRIED BUT DIDN'T

6 SURPRISING EVENTS AT THE 1908 LONDON OLYMPICS

26 SPORTS TO BE FEATURED AT THE 2012 LONDON OLYMPIC GAMES

5 ALL-LONDON FA CUP FINALS

Of all the FA Cup finals contested since 1872, only five have been between two London sides. These are:

1. 1967: Tottenham Hotspur 2, Chelsea 1
2. 1975: West Ham 2, Fulham 0
3. 1980: West Ham 1, Arsenal 0
4. 1982: Tottenham Hotspur 1, Queen's Park Rangers 0 (replay after the first match ended 1–1 after extra time)
5. 2002: Arsenal 2, Chelsea 0

13 LONDON FOOTBALL LEAGUE CLUBS IN ORDER OF FOUNDATION

1. **Fulham, 1879**
   The team began as a church side, St Andrews of West Kensington, becoming professional nineteen years later.

2. **Leyton Orient, 1881**
   Starting as the football team of the Glyn Cricket Club in East London, the side took the Orient into the name in 1888 at the suggestion of a player who worked for the Orient Shipping Line. Known as Clapton Orient from 1898, they moved to Leyton in the 1930s.

3. **Barnet, 1882**
   Founded as Woodville FC by former students of two schools in the area, the team became New Barnet FC in 1885 and simply Barnet FC three years later.

4. **Tottenham Hotspurs, 1882**
   Formed by boys from the Hotspur cricket club and from

the local grammar school and named Hotspur FC, the side took the name of Tottenham Hotspur Football and Athletic Club in 1884.

5. **Millwall, 1885**

The team was founded as Millwall Rovers in the summer of 1885 by workers at Morton's Jam Factory on the Isle of Dogs.

6. **Queen's Park Rangers, 1886**

The club was formed when a team called St Judes combined with a team called Christchurch Rangers in 1886.

7. **Arsenal, 1886**

The Gunners began life as 'Dial Square' when a group of workers at the Woolwich Arsenal Armament factory formed a team of that name and played their first game on 11 December 1886. In 1891 the Club turned professional and changed its name to Woolwich Arsenal, joining the Football League two years later.

8. **Brentford, 1889**

The team was founded as an offshoot of the Brentford Rowing Club. Once it was established, there was a debate at one of the earliest meetings about whether the team should play Association football or Rugby football. Association won by eight votes to five.

9. **Wimbledon, 1889 (now the MK Dons)**

Formed as the Wimbledon Old Centrals, they played their first matches on the Common.

10. **West Ham United, 1895**

The Hammers were founded as the works team of the Thames Ironworks and Shipbuilding Co. Ltd.

11. **Charlton Athletic, 1905**

The team was created by a group of teenagers who all lived in and around Eastmoor Street, SE7, and did not become a senior side for another eight years.

12. Chelsea, 1905

Two businessmen called Mears bought the athletics stadium at Stamford Bridge with the intention of staging football matches but they did so before they had a team to play there. After approaching Fulham to see if they wanted to move in (they didn't) the brothers chose to form a new club from scratch. Chelsea were founded on 14 March 1905 in what was then the Rising Sun pub opposite the main entrance to Stamford Bridge on Fulham Road. Voted into the Football League for the 1905–06 season, they became the only team ever to enter the League before they'd played a match.

Chelsea FC, 1905 team

13. Crystal Palace, 1905

Founded as a team to play at the sporting facilities at the old Crystal Palace which stood on Sydenham Hill, the side won the Southern League Division Two championship in their first season.

10 NOTABLE FOOTBALL MATCHES AT WEMBLEY

1. ### Bolton Wanderers 2 West Ham United 0, 20 April 1923

   At the very first FA Cup final played at the then new Wembley Stadium, a crowd estimated at nearly 200,000 people crammed into a ground intended to hold 127,000. It took 45 minutes for mounted police, including the officer on the white horse who became a Wembley legend, to clear spectators from the pitch and allow the match to go ahead. Even then, players taking corners were so close to the crowd that it was impossible for them to take a run up until the police had pushed back fans encroaching on the pitch.

2. ### Cardiff City 1 Arsenal 0, 9 May 1927

   This was the first and only time that the FA Cup has been won by a non-English club. It was also the first final at which 'Abide With Me' was sung before the game. The pre-match singing of the hymn became a tradition.

3. ### Scotland 5 England 1, 31 March 1928

   England's first defeat at Wembley took place in only the second international match they played there. (The first, also against Scotland, had ended in a draw.) The Scottish team, later dubbed the Wembley Wizards, were led to victory by the legendary winger Alex James who scored three of his side's five goals.

4. ### Blackpool 4 Bolton Wanderers 3, 2 May 1953

   Known as the Matthews Final (although it was Stan Mortensen who scored three goals, not Stanley Matthews), this was the game in which Blackpool seemed to be heading for a third defeat in the FA Cup final until Matthews turned on the magic and his team scored twice in the last three minutes to win.

5. **Hungary 6 England 3, 25 November 1953**

England had never lost to a team from outside Britain until they met the Hungarian side led by Ferenc Puskás. The portly Puskás was an unlikely looking footballer. 'Look at that little fat chap,' one of the England players is supposed to have said before the match. 'We'll murder this lot.' In the event it was Puskás and his team-mates who gave England a masterclass in skilful passing football and ruthless finishing. Tongue in cheek, England's goalkeeper Gil Merrick later said. 'It's just as well I was in form that day, otherwise they'd have scored twelve.'

6. **Tottenham Hotspur 2 Leicester 0, 6 May 1961**

This was the match in which Spurs became the first side to complete the double (winning both League Championship and Cup in the same season) in the twentieth century. The last team before Spurs to achieve the double were Aston Villa in 1897.

7. **England 4 West Germany 2, 30 July 1966**

England's finest footballing moments came at Wembley when they won the 1966 World Cup. The match is remembered for many things but, perhaps most famously, for the controversial third England goal (Oxford University researchers in the 1990s used advanced computer analysis of footage from the game to 'prove' that the ball never crossed the line and the goal should have been disallowed, something Germans have been claiming ever since the Russian linesman said Geoff Hurst's shot went in) and for commentator Kenneth Wolstenholme's words ('some people are on the pitch … they think it's all over … it is now') as Hurst scored the clinching fourth goal.

8. **Manchester United 4 Benfica 1, 29 May 1968**

Manchester United became the first English team to win the European Cup in this Wembley final. The score was

1–1 at full time but, in extra time, Matt Busby's Manchester team, which included such legendary players as Bobby Charlton, George Best and Denis Law, scored three goals in less than ten minutes to ensure victory. Benfica, defeated by AC Milan in 1963, are the only team to lose twice in a European Cup final at Wembley.

9. **Scotland 2 England 1, 4 June 1977**

Some of the most exuberant celebrations in Wembley's history followed Scotland's victory over the auld enemy in 1977. Thousands of elated Scotsmen invaded the pitch, swung on the goalposts until they collapsed and dug up lumps of the turf to transport home as souvenirs of their triumph.

Scotland v England, June 1977

10. **Germany 1 England 0, 7 October 2000**

This was the last international match played at Wembley and the goal, scored by Germany's midfielder Dietmar Hamann, was the last goal scored in the old stadium.

7 LOST LONDON
SPORTING VENUES

1. **White City**

Built in 1908 for the London Olympics of that year, the stadium was in existence for more than 70 years. Best known for greyhound racing and speedway, White City Stadium was also the venue for a number of other sports. It was Queen's Park Rangers' home ground in the early 1930s and again briefly in the 1960s. The match in the 1966 World Cup between Uruguay and France was originally scheduled to be played at Wembley but the owners of that stadium unsportingly refused to cancel a regular greyhound meet and the match had to transfer at short notice to White City. The stadium was demolished in 1985 and BBC White City now stands on the site.

2. **The Hippodrome, Notting Hill**
    Between 1837 and 1842 there was a racecourse in Notting Hill and the still-existing street name Hippodrome Place is a reminder of it. The spectators at the course stood on the sides of the hill and watched the horses race around a circuit around its base. Described by a contemporary magazine as 'a racing emporium more extensive and attractive than Ascot or Epsom', the Hippodrome nonetheless lost money for its owners and was closed after only five years.

3. **Lord's, Dorset Square**
    Opened by Thomas Lord in 1787 on what was then fields and is now Dorset Square, the ground saw its first match (between Middlesex and Essex) played on 31 May that year. It continued to be in use until 1809 when the land, which Lord had only leased, was sold and he moved to St John's Wood. One of those who played on the old ground was the poet, Lord Byron, who appeared for Harrow in the first Eton v. Harrow match in 1805. A plaque now commemorates the old Lord's.

4. **Lillie Bridge Grounds, West Brompton**
    Opened in the late 1860s, the Lillie Bridge grounds hosted a wide variety of sporting events from bicycle racing to boxing. In 1873, it was the venue for the second FA Cup final between Wanderers and Oxford University, the match kicking off at 11.30 a.m. so spectators could watch the Boat Race later the same day. Wanderers won 2–0, their second goal being scored when Oxford made the mistake of moving their goalkeeper into the attack, leaving the goal undefended for long periods. The varsity

athletics matches between Oxford and Cambridge were held here from 1867 to 1887. In the latter year a crowd of several thousand at another athletics meeting, provoked by a gang involved in betting on the races, ran riot and destroyed the track and grandstand. The Lillie Bridge grounds never recovered from the riot and closed the following year.

5. **Prince's Club**

Founded by two sporting brothers called Prince in the late 1850s, the grounds owned by the club were one of Victorian London's major sporting venues, important in the history of both cricket and lawn tennis. Marylebone Cricket Club played there for four years in the 1870s. Batsmen were obliged to be wary when playing the ball to square leg since the ground adjoined a skating rink and there was a danger of hitting skaters. MCC left for St John's Wood in 1876 but the ground continued to host major matches, Australia playing there during their 1878 tour. Tennis was introduced in the mid-1870s and the club did much to formalise the rules of the game, establishing both the height of the net and the method of scoring still in use today. Overhead service was first introduced at the Prince's Club grounds in 1881, at which time the annual championship there was as renowned and as prestigious as the rival championships at Wimbledon. The grounds closed in 1886 and the site is now covered by Lennox Gardens, SW1.

6. **The Ring, Blackfriars**

The pub called The Ring in Blackfriars Road is a reminder of the Ring boxing arena, which was sited just opposite. Originally built as Surrey Chapel for an eccentric preacher called Rowland Hill, it was transformed into a place of entertainment in 1881 and became a boxing venue in 1910 when it was bought by a former British lightweight champion called Dick Burge. It was destroyed in the Blitz in 1940.

7. **Jack Broughton's Amphitheatre**
Established in 1743 in Cockspur Street by Jack Broughton, self-styled boxing champion of England, who was one of the first men to try and impose some kind of code of rules on prize fighting. His own past career in bare-knuckle fighting, during which he killed a man in the ring, gave Broughton an incentive to introduce what became known as the London Prize Ring Rules. His amphiteatre was the first place where a form of boxing gloves were used, that would, in the words of a contemporary, 'effectually secure the fighters from the inconveniency of black eyes, broken jaws and bloody noses'. Nonetheless, the amphitheatre was the scene of some bloody spectacles in the eleven years that it was open, including bear baiting and what were known as Broughton's Battles Royal, in which one man would take on up to seven others at a time. Broughton died in 1789, in his late eighties, and is buried in Westminster Abbey.

15 CELEBRITIES WHO HAVE RUN THE LONDON MARATHON AND 1 WHO TRIED BUT DIDN'T

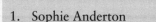

1. Sophie Anderton
2. Jeffrey Archer
3. Floella Benjamin
4. Jo Brand
5. Frank Bruno
6. Alastair Campbell
7. Ranulph Fiennes
8. Rebecca Loos
9. Nell McAndrew
10. Jonny Lee Miller
11. Matthew Pinsent
12. Gordon Ramsay
13. Sir Steve Redgrave
14. Jimmy Savile
15. Anthea Turner

and

1. Jade Goody
   The former Big Brother star set off on the 2006 Marathon but her training programme had not been rigorous enough. She collapsed with exhaustion after 18 miles and had to be rushed to hospital.

6 SURPRISING EVENTS AT THE 1908 LONDON OLYMPICS

1. **Tug of War**
   The tug of war was an Olympic event from 1900 to 1920. The victor in the 1908 competition was a team from the City of London police force. The silver medal went to a team from the Liverpool police and the bronze to a team from the Metropolitan police. British police officers might not have had it all their own way if the American team had competed but the Americans had accused the Liverpudlian team of wearing illegal boots and, when their objection was overruled, they withdrew from the contest.

2. **Jeu de Paume**
   This was the only Olympics in which jeu de paume, or 'real tennis', the game enjoyed by earlier English monarchs like Henry VIII and Charles II, was included. The gold medal was won by an American, Jay Gould, the grandson of the ruthless financier of the same name who was one of the group of late nineteenth-century businessmen nicknamed 'the robber barons'.

3. **Polo**
   The game was part of the Olympics programme until Berlin in 1936. In 1908 both gold and silver medals were taken by teams from Great Britain, first place going to the

Roehampton Club and second to the Hurlingham Club.

4. **Rugby**

Rugby Union has been an Olympic sport on four occasions although it has never attracted many teams to compete for the gold medal. In the 1908 Games there were precisely two. In the only match in the competition – both opening round and grand final – Australia beat Britain 32–3.

5. **Standing Jumps**

Ray Ewry

One of the great Olympic athletes of the early part of the twentieth century has been largely forgotten because the events in which he excelled have long since been dropped from the Olympic programme. The American Ray Ewry won eight gold medals in the 1900, 1904 and 1908 Olympic Games, competing in the standing jumps. These were the same disciplines – long jump, high jump, triple jump – that exist today but competitors were not allowed to take any kind of run-up before jumping. They jumped from a standing position. Ewry's Olympic record for the standing high jump was 1.65m (the current world record for the high jump is 2.45m) and, for the standing long jump, 3.47m (the current world record is 8.95m).

6. **Water Motorsports**

The 1908 games were the only Olympics which included motorsports. The gold medal for Motor Boating Open Class, Forty Nautical Miles went to a Frenchman, Emile Thoubron which was unsurprising since he was the only competitor to complete the course.

Perhaps the most surprising thing about the 1908 Olympics for a Briton of today reading about it was the final medals table. Britain took 56 gold medals. The USA, in second place, won only 23.

26 SPORTS TO BE FEATURED AT THE 2012 LONDON OLYMPIC GAMES

Athletes at the 2012 Olympic Games will compete for medals in the following sports. Two sports (baseball and softball), which were part of the 2004 Athens Olympics, have been dropped from the programme. Squash and karate were scheduled to replace them but received the thumbs down from voting members of the International Olympic Committee.

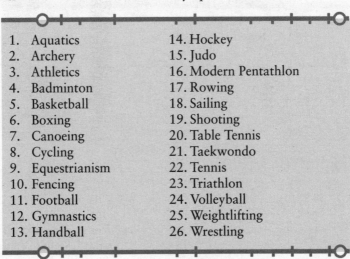

1. Aquatics
2. Archery
3. Athletics
4. Badminton
5. Basketball
6. Boxing
7. Canoeing
8. Cycling
9. Equestrianism
10. Fencing
11. Football
12. Gymnastics
13. Handball
14. Hockey
15. Judo
16. Modern Pentathlon
17. Rowing
18. Sailing
19. Shooting
20. Table Tennis
21. Taekwondo
22. Tennis
23. Triathlon
24. Volleyball
25. Weightlifting
26. Wrestling

9

MISCELLANY

9 Miscellaneous London Firsts

14 Names By Which London Is Known In Other Languages

8 Other Londons

14 of the Strangest Things Found in Transport for London Lost Property Offices (From *The Book of Lists*)

8 Items from the Time Capsule in Cleopatra's Needle 1879

8 Items from the Blue Peter Millennium Time Capsule 1998

6 Strange London Deaths

10 London Ghosts

London's Population at the Time of 5 Censuses

10 London Census Statistics

12 London Trees

5 Famous Animals at London Zoo

6 Animals Now Extinct in Britain Whose Bones Have Been Found in London (plus 1 that is extinct everywhere)

8 Commonest Birds in London

8 Rarest Birds that have been Spotted in London since 1800

15 Fish that have been Caught in the Thames

6 Extreme Weather Events in London

7 London Onlys

5 London Lasts

9 MISCELLANEOUS LONDON FIRSTS

1. ### First Demonstration of Television

The Scotsman John Logie Baird began his research into the transmission of visual images in Hastings in the early 1920s but moved to London in 1924. He rented an attic room at 22 Frith Street, Soho, to use as a workshop and it was there on 26 January

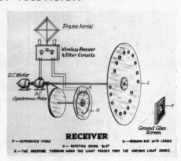

John Logie Baird's receiver

1926 that members of the Royal Institution made up the first television audience. The room was above what is now Bar Italia. The world's first sale of a television set took place at Selfridge's in 1928.

2. ### First Indian Restaurant in London

The Hindostanee Coffee House opened off Portman Square, London, in 1809. Its owner was a remarkable man called Dean Mahomet who had arrived in London from India two years earlier. Mahomet's establishment offered, in the words of one of its advertisements, 'India dishes in the highest perfection' but, sadly, the public wasn't ready for them and the Hindostanee went bust in 1812. Mahomet then moved to Brighton where he opened a private bathhouse that was patronised by the Prince Regent. He died in Brighton in 1850, aged ninety-one.

3. ### First London Telephone Directory

The first known telephone directory was issued by the London Telephone Company in January 1880. It was six pages long and included 255 names.

4. First Known Representation of London

This can be seen on a gold medallion found in Arras, France, and now in the British Museum. The Roman emperor Constantius Chlorus, father of Constantine the Great, is shown being welcomed by a figure with outstretched arms, kneeling in front of a gate of the walled city. Ironically the fortified gateway shown on the medal was probably based not on anything a contemporary visitor could have seen in London but on the Porta Nigra at Trier which was where the medallion was minted.

5. First London Escalator

The first escalator in the city was installed in Harrod's in 1878. The store management was so concerned that customers might be overcome by the experience of travelling on it that a member of staff was on hand at the top with brandy and smelling salts to revive them. Possibly their worries were justified since the escalator was not a moving staircase with steps but a smooth slope with a handrail at the side to which to cling.

6. First London A-Z

A young woman called Phyllis Pearsall compiled the first edition in the 1930s. She rose at 5.00 in the morning each day and walked 18 miles through the streets, taking notes, eventually completing 23,000 individual street entries which she kept in shoeboxes under her bed. No publisher was interested so she published it herself, delivering copies to branches of WH Smith in a wheelbarrow. By the time of her death in 1996, the A–Z had sold millions of copies.

7. First Metropolitan Police Officer Killed on Duty

PC Joseph Grantham was kicked in the head while attempting to make an arrest during a drunken disturbance in Somers Town, Euston, in 1830, a year after the Metropolitan Police was founded. Another early police fatality had an even more undignified demise. In 1832 PC Thomas Hart was drowned when a stray cow he was trying to return to its owner knocked him into the River Brent. In the early days of the force the police were extremely unpopular. Three years later another police officer, PC Robert Culley, was killed during a riot in Coldbath Fields, Grays Inn Road. The coroner's jury returned a verdict of 'justifiable homicide'.

8. **First Railway Murder**
On 9 July 1864 Franz Müller, a German living in London, attacked an elderly man called Thomas Briggs on a train between Bow and Hackney Wick and threw him out of the window. Briggs died of his injuries the following day. Not very cleverly, Müller took his victim's hat instead of his own, leaving the latter for the police to find. They were able to trace it to Müller and a jeweller in Cheapside identified the German from a photograph as the man who had tried to sell him a gold chain belonging to Briggs. Müller had fled to New York but was brought back to England to face trial. His defence was that he was with a prostitute at the time of the murder but prosecuting counsel loftily dismissed this with the remark that 'little reliance should be placed on a clock in a brothel'. The jury did not believe Müller's story and he was hanged on 14 November 1864.

9. **First Ferris Wheel**
Built by JR Whitley on the site of what is now Earl's Court Exhibition Centre, the giant wheel had a diameter of 300 feet and was opened to the public in July 1895. In May of the following year, the wheel became stuck in mid-rotation and dozens of passengers were stranded on it, some of them overnight. They were given generous compensation in the form of a £5 note and, curiously, the breakdown increased the wheel's popularity. The next day thousands of people queued to get on it, many of

them hoping that it would come to a halt again and they too would be compensated. The wheel finally closed and was demolished in 1907.

14 NAMES BY WHICH LONDON IS KNOWN IN OTHER LANGUAGES

1. Londýn (Czech)
2. Londen (Dutch)
3. Londono (Esperanto)
4. Lontoo (Finnish)
5. Londres (French)
6. Λονδίνο (Greek)
7. Lundúnir (Icelandic)
8. Londra (Italian)
9. Rondon (Japanese, transliterated into Roman alphabet)
10. Londinium (Latin)
11. Londona (Latvian)
12. лондон (Russian)
13. Lunnainn (Scots Gaelic)
14. Llundain (Welsh)

8 OTHER LONDONS

There are more than thirty other Londons around the world. The following are eight examples:

1. **London, Ontario, Canada**
   Originally named by an eighteenth-century Lieutenant-Governor of Canada, John Graves Simcoe, the settlement did not really develop until the 1820s, and was finally incorporated as a city in 1855. With a population of nearly

half a million, it is much the largest of the other Londons around the world. It parallels many of the landmarks in the original London. It has its own St Paul's Cathedral and its own Blackfriars Bridge, as well as a suburb called Ealing and a market called Covent Garden.

2. **London, Ohio, USA**
The county seat of Madison County, the town was established in 1810 and given the name by its founding fathers. Its current population is just less than 9000.

3. **London, Kentucky, USA**
The county seat of Laurel County, it was founded in 1826 and has a population of just less than 6000. Colonel Sanders' original Kentucky Fried Chicken restaurant was in Laurel County and London now plays host to an annual World Chicken Festival.

4. **London, Equatorial Guinea**
A small settlement in this West African country still bears the name given to it in the nineteenth century, when Britain leased land on its coast to use as bases in the campaign against the slave trade.

5. **London, Limpopo Province, South Africa**
The largest of three villages in South Africa that have the name.

6. **London, Belize**
There is a small village in the former colony of British Honduras that was named after the imperial city in the early nineteenth century.

7. **London, Nigeria**
Another small village that takes its name from London.

8. **London, Kiritimati (Christmas Island)**
Most of the place names on the Pacific island were invented by a French priest, Father Emmanuel Rougier, who leased the island from 1917 to 1939 in order to grow coconut

trees. He lived in a small settlement he called Paris and named the port on the opposite side of the main entrance to the lagoon Londres, or London. It is now the main settlement on the island.

Christmas Island

14 OF THE STRANGEST THINGS FOUND IN TRANSPORT FOR LONDON LOST PROPERTY OFFICES

1. Two-and-a-half hundredweight of sultanas
2. Lawn mower
3. Breast implants
4. Theatrical coffin
5. Stuffed eagle
6. 14-foot long boat
7. Divan bed
8. Park bench
9. Garden slide
10. Jar of bull's sperm
11. Urn of ashes
12. Dead bats in container
13. Vasectomy kit
14. Two human skulls in a bag

Taken from *The Book of Lists*, by David Wallechinsky and Amy Wallace

8 ITEMS FROM THE TIME CAPSULE IN CLEOPATRA'S NEEDLE, 1879

The obelisk, originally erected in front of an Egyptian temple in the second millennium BC, was offered to Britain in 1819 by Mehemet Ali, the Turkish Viceroy in the country. However, the task of transporting it seemed so daunting that it was left to lie in the sands at Alexandria for another sixty years before, in 1877, General Sir James Alexander arranged to load it on a pontoon and have it towed to London. During a storm in the Bay of Biscay en route, the obelisk was nearly lost when the pontoon broke free and several seamen died in the struggle to rescue it. Plaques mounted around the base show scenes from the journey and commemorate the men who lost their lives. In its plinth are buried a number of items from 1879, the year in which it was finally erected on the Embankment. These include:

1. The day's newspapers
2. A box of cigars
3. A copy of Bradshaw's *Railway Guide*
4. A portrait of Queen Victoria
5. Pictures of twelve of the country's leading beauties
6. Several bibles
7. A complete set of British coins from that year
8. A copy of the 1878 *Whitaker's Almanack*

8 ITEMS FROM THE *BLUE PETER* MILLENNIUM TIME CAPSULE 1998

During the construction of the Millennium Dome, the children's TV programme Blue Peter arranged for a time capsule to be buried beneath the Dome's floor. Amongst other things it contained:

1. A *Blue Peter* badge
2. A set of Teletubby dolls
3. An insulin pen
4. A France '98 World Cup football
5. A Spice Girls CD
6. A photograph of Princess Diana
7. A cub's scarf and toggle
8. A tamagotchi

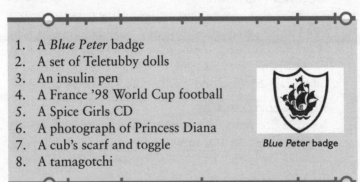

Blue Peter badge

6 STRANGE LONDON DEATHS

1. **Thomas May**

   The seventeenth-century poet and historian died in November 1650. A well-known boozer and very fat, he had gone to bed drunk and met his death there, brought about, according to the contemporary gossip Anthony à Wood, 'by tying his nightcap too close under his fat cheeks, which choked him when he turned on the other side'.

2. **Robert Cocking**

   Cocking was the first man in history to die in a parachute jump. After long years of experimentation he produced designs for what he believed was an improved version of a parachute that had been used successfully for descents early in the nineteenth century and, in 1837, crowds gathered in Vauxhall Gardens to watch him go up in a balloon to a height of 5000 feet. Sadly, when he came to release himself and the parachute, he found that his invention let him down. It failed to open properly and he died soon after hitting the ground.

3. **Colonel Pierpoint**

London's first traffic island was put in St James's Street in 1864 at the personal expense of a Colonel Pierpoint, who was afraid of being run over on his way to his Pall Mall club. When it was finished, he dashed across the road to admire his creation and was knocked down by a cab.

4. **PC Joseph Daniels**

In 1892 this brave police constable responded to the call of duty when he ran to assist in an arrest in Holborn. Unfortunately the act of running loosened his ill-fitting false teeth and he choked to death on them.

5. **Chung Ling Soo**

William Robinson was an American magician who worked under the stage name of Chung Ling Soo. His most famous trick involved assistants apparently shooting bullets at him which he caught in his mouth and spat out onto a plate. In 1918, while playing the Wood Green Empire, the rigged firearm which allowed him to perform the illusion went wrong, and a real bullet headed towards him. He was unable to catch it and it him in the chest. He died in hospital the next day.

6. **Stephen Milligan**

The Conservative MP Stephen Milligan was found dead in his Chiswick flat in February 1994. He was naked save for stockings and suspenders, had an electrical flex tightened in a noose around his neck and a segment of an orange in his mouth. In the absence of any other even halfway plausible explanation (conspiracy theories about murder can be dismissed), it has been assumed that he died during an act of auto-erotic asphyxiation that went badly wrong.

10 LONDON GHOSTS

1. **The Cock Lane Ghost**

Perhaps the most famous of all London ghost stories began in January 1762 when Elizabeth, the twelve-year-old daughter of a parish clerk called Richard Parsons, seemed to become the conduit through which a murder victim could accuse her killer from beyond the grave. Communicating largely through the standard system of coded knocks (one for yes, two for no), the ghost of Fanny Kent, a former lodger with the Parsons, told how she had been poisoned by her common-law husband, William Kent. The story reached the newspapers and the Parsons' home in Cock Lane, near St Paul's, was besieged by journalists, clergymen and sightseers. For a time Cock Lane became as popular a destination for sensation-seekers as the lunatic asylum at Bedlam. Fanny, or Elizabeth, did not disappoint her audiences. When William Kent was brought to the house, he was greeted by a flurry of knockings, accusing him of doing away with his wife. Unsurprisingly, he denied it all. Visitors continued to flock to the house. One was the writer Oliver Goldsmith, who left an account of what he saw. 'The spectators ... sit looking at each other, suppressing laughter, and wait in silent expectation for the opening of the scene. As the ghost is a good deal offended at incredulity, the persons present are to conceal theirs if they have any, as by this concealment only can they hope to gratify their curiosity. For if they show, either before or when the knocking is begun, a too prying inquisition, or ludicrous style of thinking, the ghost continues usually silent, or to use the expression of the house, Miss Fanny is angry.' Eventually a committee was formed to conduct a semi-official investigation into the haunting. Members included an eminent physician, the matron of a maternity hospital and the poet, lexicographer and all-round literary luminary, Dr Samuel Johnson. Fanny, in the shape of Elizabeth Parsons, proved largely uncooperative and the committee was unimpressed by the idea that a murdered woman had returned to call for revenge on her killer. As Dr Johnson wrote in *The Gentleman's Magazine*, 'It is … the opinion of the whole assembly, that the child has some art of making or counterfeiting particular noises, and that there is no agency of any higher cause.' By the summer of 1762 William Kent had wearied of this ghostly attack on his good name and he brought a court case against Richard Parsons and others, claiming a conspiracy against him. A jury returned a verdict in his favour and Parsons was sentenced to spend time in the pillory. The Cock Lane ghost disappeared from the headlines.

2. **'The Man in Grey', Theatre Royal, Drury Lane**
    Most London theatres of any age have at least one ghost which haunts the auditorium or appears suddenly in a dressing room to scare the wits out of an unsuspecting actor. The Adelphi Theatre, for instance, is reputed to be haunted by the ghost of William Terriss, an actor who, in 1897, was stabbed to death by a deranged rival just outside the stage door. The nineteenth-century clown, Joseph Grimaldi, has been seen at Sadler's Wells, still wearing the make-up he made famous. Grimaldi has also been spotted at the Theatre Royal, Drury Lane, but the most famous ghost seen there is the so-called 'Man in Grey'. Dressed in a long grey coat, and wearing a tricorn hat, the ghost is unusual in that, unlike the majority of spooks, who await the witching hour, it appears during the daytime. Seeing the man in grey at rehearsals for a

production is said to augur well for the show's success. No one seems sure who the ghost might be, although some claim he is a man who was murdered in the theatre in 1780.

3. **50 Berkeley Square**

Once described as London's most haunted house, 50 Berkeley Square was reputed to be home to a supernatural creature so horrible that it drove those who saw it insane. The most frequently repeated story tells of two sailors who, some time in the middle decades of the nineteenth century, broke into the then unoccupied house in order to find a place to sleep. They had chosen their resting place unwisely. In the morning one of the sailors was found dead, impaled on the railings outside the house. The other sailor was still inside the house but had been reduced to a babbling lunatic. Further stories of foolhardy individuals agreeing to spend the night alone in the house and being found as gibbering wrecks were told in Victorian books and magazines. Various theories were advanced to explain the ghost. Perhaps it was the spirit of a former tenant, a Mr Myers, 'an odd cross between Scrooge of *A Christmas Carol* and Miss Havisham of *Great Expectations*', who had become a miserly recluse after he was jilted on his wedding day. Perhaps it was the ghost of another tenant's lunatic brother, who had been shut away in the attic. The trouble with all the stories about 50 Berkeley Square is that they owe more to literature than to historical reality. Lord Lytton's story, 'The Haunted and the Haunters', first published in 1859, with its tale of a man agreeing to pass a night in a haunted house that sounds remarkably similar to 50 Berkeley Square, may well have influenced later stories told as if they were fact. 50 Berkeley Square is currently home to the antiquarian booksellers, Maggs & Co, and they report no supernatural activities on their premises.

4. ## British Museum Ghost

    Lurid tales of a mummy's curse and the spirits of long-dead Ancient Egyptians haunting the rooms of the British Museum have been told for decades. One particular mummy, that of a young girl who served the god Amon-Ra, has been the focus of many stories. Security staff claimed that, during their night patrols, they could sense a horrible presence close to the mummy. A photographer who took pictures of the mummy's case killed himself after he developed them in his dark room and saw what the camera revealed. The old British Museum Underground station, no longer in use, was also reputed to be haunted by the ghost of an Ancient Egyptian, inadequately dressed for English weather in a loincloth and ceremonial head-dress.

5. ## Tower of London ghosts

    So many people have been imprisoned in the Tower and so many have been executed either within its walls or on Tower Green, that it is little wonder that the place has so many ghost stories attached to it. Among the more famous of the Tower's reluctant guests who have been spotted still walking its rooms and corridors are a headless Anne Boleyn, Sir Walter Raleigh, Guy Fawkes and the Princes in the Tower. The most dramatic of the Tower's multiple hauntings is the ghostly re-enactment of the bungled execution of the Countess of Salisbury which is said to take place on the anniversary of her death in 1541. The elderly countess was condemned to death by Henry VIII, largely because of her son's treason and because she had a remote claim to the throne. She went to her death very unwillingly and had to be chased around the block by the executioner, who struck at her repeatedly with his axe before she finally fell.

6. ## Ghost of a Bear in Cheyne Walk

    Not all London ghosts are human. A ghostly bear was regularly seen in the garden of one of the houses in

Cheyne Walk, Chelsea, in the nineteenth century and the early decades of the twentieth century. The creature was supposed to be one of the bears baited to death on the site in the sixteenth century but the story may have its origin in the menagerie of exotic animals kept at 16 Cheyne Walk in the 1860s by the poet Dante Gabriel Rossetti. Rossetti owned kangaroos, armadillos, zebus, a Brahmin bull and a somewhat mangy black bear, all of which had the run of the garden of his house. Tales of the poet's weird pets may have contributed to the sightings of a spectral bear padding around the back gardens of Chelsea.

7. **University College Hospital – Ghost of a Nurse**
Unsurprisingly, hospitals regularly attract ghost stories. Most seem to be nurses returning to their old workplaces. The Grey Lady of St Thomas's Hospital appears to patients who are about to die and is usually seen only from the knees upwards, supposedly because she materialises in a ward where the floor levels have been altered over the years. University College Hospital in Gower Street also has its own spectral visitor. Said to be the ghost of a nurse who accidentally gave a patient an overdose of morphine and was so traumatised by her mistake that she killed herself, the spirit regularly shows itself to both patients and staff. Dressed in a noticeably old-fashioned uniform, the ghost still has the best interests of the patient at heart and many have praised the kind treatment they have received from a nurse that no one else can see.

8. **Collins Music Hall, Islington Ghost**
Sam Vagg was a London chimney sweep who reinvented himself as an 'Irish' singer called Samuel Collins in the pubs and music halls of mid-Victorian England. In 1862 he took over a pub called The Lansdowne Arms on Islington Green and re-launched it as Collins Music Hall. Although Collins himself died three years later, at the age of only thirty-nine, his theatre thrived and most of the great

names of music hall played there at some point in their careers. Gracie Fields made her London debut at Collins in 1912. For many years the founder seemed unwilling to tear himself away from the theatre that bore his name and his ghost was regularly seen in the offices where the day's takings were counted. Collins was destroyed by fire in 1958 and never rebuilt. A branch of Waterstone's now stands on the site.

9. **Bank of England Ghosts**
In 1933, during excavations connected to the rebuilding of the Bank, a coffin was unearthed in the old Garden Court. Seven-and-a-half feet long, the coffin belonged to a clerk at the Bank called William Jenkins, who had died in 1798. Unusually tall for his time – he was over 6 foot 7 inches – Jenkins had been obsessed during his final illness with the idea that body-snatchers would seize his corpse for its curiosity value and sell it to surgeons for dissection. His friends persuaded the Bank's directors that, as a long-serving employee, Jenkins deserved the Bank's protection post mortem, and he was buried in the Garden Court one morning before business began. Jenkins's tall ghost is still said to walk the Bank's corridors.

Outside the Bank, in Threadneedle Street, late-night passers-by have occasionally been confronted by a woman in early nineteenth-century dress asking whether or not they have seen her brother. This is the ghost known as 'the Bank Nun'. In 1812 a clerk at the Bank called Whitehead was tried for forging a bill and hanged. For twenty-five years after this, his sister Sarah, driven insane by her brother's death, came each day to the bank, convinced that he still worked there. She became a familiar sight to the bank workers, who dubbed her 'the Bank Nun' because of the long black dress she always wore. Sarah Whitehead's ghost has also been seen in Bank Underground station.

10. The Phantom Bus of Ladbroke Grove

One of the longest-lasting urban legends of west London tells of a ghostly bus that, in the mid-1930s, was frequently seen careering along the roads of Ladbroke Grove in the early hours of the morning. The bus was usually sighted at the junction of St Mark's Road and Cambridge Gardens and dozens of people claimed to have seen it. 'I was turning the corner,' one witness said, 'and saw a bus tearing towards me, the lights of the top and bottom decks and the headlights were full on but I could see no crew or passengers.' The junction, with a blind bend in both directions, had a reputation as an accident black spot and, initially, the phantom bus only added to this. Several car crashes were blamed on the shock drivers experienced when seeing it. Eventually, the council straightened the road at the junction and the ghostly red double-decker was seen no more.

10 LONDON CENSUS STATISTICS

All these figures come from the 2001 Census, the most recent one conducted.

1. Population of London – 7.4 million
2. Percentage increase in London population from 1981 to 2001 – 8.6%
3. Percentage of the UK population living in London – 12%
4. Percentage of London population aged sixteen or under – 19.5% (19.7% in the UK as a whole)
5. Percentage of London population aged between twenty-five and forty-four – 36.5% (28.8% in the UK as a whole)
6. Percentage of London population of pension age or over – 14% (18.5% in the UK as a whole)
7. Percentage of population belonging to a minority ethnic group – 29%
8. Number of yearly births in London – 104,200
9. Number of yearly deaths in London – 58,600
10. Infant mortality rate – 5.7 per thousand births (5.3 per thousand in the UK as a whole)

Source: National Statistics Online

LONDON'S POPULATION AT THE TIME OF 5 CENSUSES

The first British census took place in 1801 and has been conducted in the first year of every decade since that date, apart from 1941. The following figures from five censuses at intervals of half a century provide snapshots of London's population. The most striking fact is the colossal rise in the population of the city between 1851, the year of the Great Exhibition and 1901, the year of Queen Victoria's death.

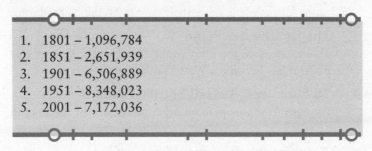

1. 1801 – 1,096,784
2. 1851 – 2,651,939
3. 1901 – 6,506,889
4. 1951 – 8,348,023
5. 2001 – 7,172,036

12 LONDON TREES

'We may say that London begins where tree trunks commence to be black.' (Ford Madox Ford)

1. The Lucombe Oak, Kew Gardens
Originally raised in the eighteenth century by a Mr Lucombe, this cross between two other types of oak was first planted at Kew in 1773. Lucombe loved his tree so much that he wanted to be buried in a coffin built from its wood, and he felled one of his first examples for this purpose.

2. Maidenhair Tree, Kew Gardens
One of the oldest trees in Kew, this gingko was planted in 1762, only a few decades after the first specimens had been introduced to Europe from China.

3. Corsican Pine, Kew Gardens
Situated just inside the main gate, this is one of the hardiest specimens at Kew, since it has survived several lightning strikes and an accident in the pioneer days of aircraft when a biplane crashed into the top of it.

4. **The Wembley Elm**
    In front of the Greyhound pub, this was long a meeting point for people making their way to Wembley Stadium.

5. **The Dorchester Plane**
    Planted outside the Dorchester Hotel at the time it was built, it has become a West End landmark.

6. **TS Eliot Tree, Russell Square Gardens**
    An Irish Yew was planted here in memory of the poet in 1996.

7. **Anne Frank's Tree, New Row, WC2**
    This was planted in New Row in 2001 by the actress Hannah Gordon and dedicated by Sir Ben Kingsley to mark the tenth anniversary of the Anne Frank Trust and, according to the plaque by it, 'as a place to reflect on all the children who have died owing to the wars and persecution in the last century'.

8. **Storm Tree, The Strand**
    A year after the Great Storm of 1987, this tree was planted by the City of Westminster to commemorate a destructive event in which nearly 250,000 trees were lost in the Greater London area. (*See also* **7 Extreme Weather Events,** p.296.)

9. **St James's Church Indian Bean Tree, Piccadilly**
    An example of a rare species of tree in the heart of the West End.

10. **Fulham Palace Oak**
    Five centuries old, the tree was planted at much the same time as many of the buildings in Fulham Palace were erected.

11. **Barn Elms Plane**
    London is renowned for its plane trees and this massive specimen, in Barn Elms Park, Barnes, is the oldest of them all.

12. Charlton House Mulberry

Planted in the early years of the seventeenth century, the tree is a reminder of the silk trade that flourished in outlying areas of London.

5 FAMOUS ANIMALS AT LONDON ZOO

1. Jumbo the Elephant

The original Jumbo was an African bull elephant who arrived at the Zoo in 1865. He rapidly became enormously popular and, for nearly twenty years, gave thousands of rides to delighted children. He was seen as a national institution and there was outrage when the Zoo proposed to sell Jumbo to the American showman

Jumbo the elephant

Phineas T Barnum. The wily Barnum, scenting publicity, encouraged the controversy and Jumbomania swept Britain. Letters were written to *The Times* and other newspapers. Lawsuits were threatened. Even the Queen appealed to the Zoo not to go ahead with the sale. Jumbo made his own contribution to the unfolding saga by refusing to enter the box in which he was supposed to make his transatlantic passage. Barnum, however, was adamant that the sale should go ahead. Jumbo, who was to be accompanied by his favourite keeper, was eventually tempted into his travelling cage and was shipped to the United States to become as big a star in New York as he had been in London. Tragedy, however, was waiting in the wings. Three years after making the journey across the Atlantic, Jumbo was killed in a train accident when travelling with the Barnum show. Barnum, never one to lose an opportunity for profit, had Jumbo stuffed and continued to display him around the country for several more years.

2. **Guy the Gorilla**

Guy the Gorilla, so called because he arrived in the Zoo on Guy Fawkes Day 1947, remained one of the most popular attractions for more than thirty years. He grew from a tiny baby to a giant adult male in captivity but his fearsome appearance disguised a sweet temperament. When he died of a heart attack in 1978, following an operation to remove a tooth, he was mourned by many who had seen him over the years. The Zoo commissioned the sculptor William Timym to create a more-than-lifesize statue of Guy which still stands near the main entrance.

3. **Goldie the Golden Eagle**

The Zoo's great escape occurred in 1965 when a golden eagle known as Goldie exited his cage as keepers were cleaning it and headed for the trees in Regent's Park. For nearly twelve days he eluded all would-be captors and became a national celebrity. He appeared on the front pages of all the newspapers and traffic jams were caused by the thousands of cars carrying people to the Park to watch him enjoying his freedom. He was even mentioned in a debate in House of Commons, where his name was greeted with cheers and shouts of approval. Goldie was eventually recaptured when he was lured by the prospect of his favourite food. Deputy Head Keeper Joe McCorry tied a dead rabbit to a rope near one of the eagle's regular haunts and, when Goldie swooped down to tuck in, McCorry seized him.

4. **Obaysch the Hippopotamus**

The first live hippopotamus to be seen in Europe since the time of the Roman Empire, Obaysch arrived at the Zoo as a one-year-old in 1850. He had been brought there by Sir Charles Murray, British Consul-General in Egypt and soon became the Zoo's greatest attraction. Visitors to the Zoo more than doubled in the first year after Obaysch's arrival. Victorian London went hippo mad. Cartoons appeared in *Punch*, silver models of Obaysch were sold in the shops and a 'Hippopotamus Polka' was one of the music hits of the season. Murray would occasionally visit his protégé in the Zoo, calling to him in Arabic, and Obaysch would lumber towards the sound of his former master's voice, grunting in recognition.

5. **Belinda the Mexican Red-kneed Bird-eating Spider**
Belinda, who died at the age of twenty-two in 1993, was one of the more surprising stars of London Zoo, appearing on TV programmes from *Blue Peter* to the national news and taking a lead role in one of the Zoo's advertising campaigns. She was also used by hypnotherapists to help people overcome their arachnophobia.

6 ANIMALS NOW EXTINCT IN BRITAIN WHOSE BONES HAVE BEEN FOUND IN LONDON (PLUS 1 THAT IS EXTINCT EVERYWHERE)

1. **Wolf** in Cheapside
2. **Crocodile** in Islington
3. **Hippo** in Trafalgar Square
4. **Brown Bear** in Woolwich
5. **Lion** at Charing Cross
6. **Elephant** in Whitehall
+1. **Mammoth** in King's Cross

8 COMMONEST BIRDS IN LONDON

1. Starling
2. House Sparrow
3. Feral Pigeon
4. Woodpigeon
5. Blackbird
6. Swift
7. Crow
8. Rook

Source: London Bird Report

8 RAREST BIRDS THAT HAVE BEEN SPOTTED IN LONDON SINCE 1800

1. Iberian Chiffchaff (first recorded sighting in UK was at Brent Reservoir in London)
2. Naumann's Thrush (first recorded sighting in UK was at Chingford, Greater London)
3. Sooty Tern
4. Tengmalm's Owl
5. Hermit Thrush
6. Crested Lark
7. Western Sandpiper
8. Lesser Kestrel

Source: London Bird Report

15 FISH THAT HAVE BEEN CAUGHT IN THE THAMES

Since 1964 specimens of 121 species of fish have been caught in the Thames between Fulham and Tilbury. The following are fifteen examples:

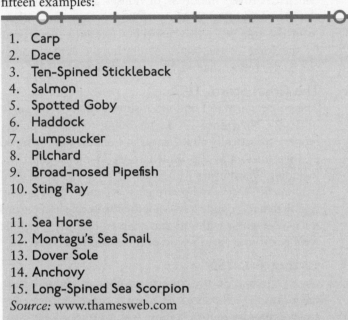

1. Carp
2. Dace
3. Ten-Spined Stickleback
4. Salmon
5. Spotted Goby
6. Haddock
7. Lumpsucker
8. Pilchard
9. Broad-nosed Pipefish
10. Sting Ray

11. Sea Horse
12. Montagu's Sea Snail
13. Dover Sole
14. Anchovy
15. Long-Spined Sea Scorpion

Source: www.thamesweb.com

6 EXTREME WEATHER EVENTS IN LONDON

1. **Tornado, 1091**
   On 30 October 1091 a tornado swept through the city which destroyed hundreds of houses and a number of churches including St Mary le Bow where four rafters from the roof were driven twenty feet into the ground by the force of the wind. Astonishingly, contemporary chronicles report that only two people were killed.

2. **The Great Storm, 1703**
   The worst storm in London's history struck on the night of 26–27 November 1703. According to contemporary reports, 'practically all the roofs in London were stripped of their tiles' and the leaden roofs of many churches, including Westminster Abbey, were 'rolled up like skins of parchment'. Defoe, who wrote an account of the storm, revealed that 'nobody durst quit their tottering habitations for it was worst without' and claimed that many people were convinced that the end of the world had come.

3. **Earthquake, 1750**
   On 8 March 1750 the city was awoken at about 5.30 in the morning by the shock of an earthquake. According to a contemporary report, 'a noise was heard resembling the roaring of a great piece of ordnance, fired at a considerable distance, and then instantly the houses reeled, first sinking, as it were, to the south, and then to the north, and with a quick return to the centre'. In the Thames the water was so agitated that fish were seen to leap half a yard above its surface. Many preachers were eager to seize upon the event as an indication of God's wrath with a sinful city. Charles Wesley proclaimed that 'of all the judgments which the righteous God inflicts on sinners here, the most dreadful and destructive is an earthquake' and that 'this He has lately brought on our part of the earth, and

thereby alarmed our fears, and bid us "Prepare to meet our God!"'

4.   **Floods, 1928**

The last time that central London flooded was in 1928. On 6 and 7 January heavy rainfall, a rapid snow melt and a spring tide combined to cause the Thames to break its banks at several points. A section of embankment near Lambeth Bridge collapsed and water rushed into nearby houses, drowning fourteen people.

5.   **Great Smog, 1952**

Fog has long been a regular hazard in London. Accounts of its peculiar density date back centuries. Often it was made worse by the burning of coal. In the seventeenth century the diarist John Evelyn wrote of the 'hellish and dismall cloud of sea-coale' that lay over the city. However, in the late nineteenth century and the first half of the twentieth, the combination of fog, household fires burning coal and the emissions from factory chimneys produced the dreadful 'peasoupers' which were a serious threat to the health of Londoners. The worst was in December 1952. Transport was brought almost to a standstill as visibility reduced to a matter of inches rather than feet. At Sadler's Wells a performance had to be abandoned because the fog in the auditorium made it impossible for the audience to see and the cast to continue. Approximately 4000 people died as a direct result of bronchial and cardiovascular illnesses exacerbated by the smog but many other deaths may have been related to its effects. The consequences of the Great Smog were so dire that legislation in the form of Clean Air Acts were passed to limit smoke emissions of all kinds and the London smog was largely consigned to history.

6.   **The Great Storm of 1987**

Famously unpredicted by the Met Office, the great storm

that swept the south of England on the night of 15/16 October 1987 had devastating effects in London. Gusts exceeding 80 knots were recorded at the London Weather Centre and at Heathrow and Gatwick Airports. Nearly a third of the trees in Kew Gardens, many of them rare and valuable specimens were uprooted or destroyed. The storm was the worst to hit the capital since 1703. (*See* **12 London Trees,** p. 288)

7 LONDON ONLYS

1. ## Only Remaining Independent Bank
    C. Hoare and Co was founded in Cheapside in 1672 by a goldsmith called Richard Hoare and moved in 1690 to Fleet Street, where it still remains. Famous customers at Hoare's over the centuries have included Samuel Pepys, David Garrick, Lord Byron and Jane Austen.

2. ## Only Surviving Galleried Inn
    The George in Borough High Street is a short distance from the long-vanished Tabard where Chaucer's pilgrims gathered before setting off for Canterbury. First recorded in the 1540s, when it was owned by the MP for Southwark, it was rebuilt in the seventeenth century. Two of the wings were demolished in 1889. The inn is now owned by the National Trust.

4. ## Only London Lighthouse
    A small lighthouse still stands at Trinity Buoy Wharf, which was built in the nineteenth century as a training station for lighthouse keepers before they were despatched to lonelier locations. Trinity Buoy Wharf is now an arts centre.

5. ## Only Statue Carrying an Umbrella
    The statue of Sir Sydney Waterlow in Waterlow Park, Highgate depicts him leaning on his umbrella.

5. ## Only Building to be a Church, Synagogue and Mosque

The Jamme Masjid Mosque in Fournier Street, Spitalfields, was built in 1742 as a Huguenot chapel, then became Spitalfields Great Synagogue in 1898 and converted to a mosque in the 1990s.

6. ## Only Monument in St Paul's to Survive the Great Fire

The monument to John Donne is situated in the south choir aisle and shows him wrapped in a shroud and standing on an urn. All the other memorials in the cathedral were destroyed in the fire.

7. ## Only London Interior Designed by a Nazi War Criminal

Several of the houses in Carlton House Terrace have connections with Nazi Germany. Nos. 8 and 9 were converted into a single building to house the German ambassador to London, Joachim von Ribbentrop, in 1936–37. Hitler's architect Albert Speer, later tried and sentenced at the Nuremberg War Trial, visited Carlton House Terrace twice during the renovation and, although not all the interior was his work, he designed many of the features.

5 LONDON LASTS

1. Last Man Executed at the Tower of London

The last person to be executed at the Tower was Josef Jakobs, a German intelligence agent who was parachuted into southern England on 31 January 1941. Injured in landing, he was easily captured and the equipment he was carrying clearly proved that he was a spy. After a swift court martial he was executed by firing squad on a miniature rifle range in the King's House. Because of his injuries, he was unable to stand and met his death sitting in a brown Windsor chair.

2. Last Toll Gate in London

Until the 1860s there were more than 100 toll gates within a six-mile radius of Charing Cross, but most were removed in the middle of that decade. The last remaining tollgate in London is on College Road, Dulwich, which is owned by the nearby school. The old board showing the tolls, which dates from the end of the eighteenth century, is still there. Taking a flock of sheep through the gate costs 2d. Pedestrians can pass through it for free.

3. Last Bomb to Fall on London in World War II

On 27 March 1945, less than two months before VE Day, the last V2 Flying Bomb struck two of the blocks of flats at Hughes Mansions, Vallance Road, Stepney. More than 130 people, many of them Jewish, died in the attack which took place on the day before the Passover.

V2 rocket

4. Last Texan Embassy in London

A short alleyway off St James Street, by the side of the wine merchants Berry Bros & Rudd, leads to a tiny courtyard called Pickering Place. Here there is a plaque that marks the site of the Legation from the Republic of Texas to the Court of St James between 1842 and 1845. The short-lived Texan Republic ended when the state became the twenty-eighth in the United States.

5. ## Last Coin Minted in London

Coins were minted in London from at least the ninth century and King Alfred's reign. For hundreds of years the Royal Mint was in the Tower of London and, even when it was decided to find a new home for it in 1810, it moved only a short distance, to a site on Tower Hill. However, by the 1960s, with decimalisation and the minting of hundreds of millions of new coins planned, it was clear that the Tower Hill premises could not cope. A new Mint was opened in Llantrisant, South Wales. Seven years later the very last coin to be minted in London, a gold sovereign, was struck.

INDEX

INDEX

INDEX

INDEX

INDEX

Twelfth Night
(Shakespeare) 235
Tyburn, River 161

Underground *see* Tube
University College
Hospital ghost 283
unlikely Londoners
54–7
Upstairs, Downstairs
(TV) 216

Van Gogh, Vincent
55–6
Vauxhall Bridge 24
Verlaine, Paul 54
Victoria, Queen 111–
12, 180
Vietnam 230
visitors 60–3, 63–5
Voltaire 54

Wain, Louis 80–1
Waiting for Godot
(Beckett) 238
Wakefield Tower 33
Walbrook, River 161
Waltham Forest 9
Walworth, Sir William
73–4
Wandsworth 9
Wardrobe Tower 33

water motorsports 266
Waterloo Bridge 24
Waterlow, Sir Sydney
296
Watkin's Tower 15
Waugh, Evelyn 209–10
*We Are the Lambeth
Boys* (film) 233–4
weather, extreme 294–6
Well Tower 33
Wellington, Duke of
156
Wellington, HQS 188
Wells, HG 195
Wembley Elm 288
West Germany 260
West Ham United 257,
259
Westbourne, River 161
Westminster Abbey
220–2
Westminster Bridge
22–3
Westminster, City of 6
Wharton, Sir George
153
White, Antonia 81
White City 261–2
White Hart Yard 199
White, Marco Pierre
90–1
White Tower 33

whitebait 165
Whitechapel Bell
Foundry 59
Whiteley, William 87
Whittington, Dick 74
whores 117–20
Widow's Son (pub)
11–12
Wild, Jonathan 131
Wilkes, John 75
Will's (coffee house)
168–9
Wilson, Colin 65
Wilson, Harriette 119
Wilson, Sir Henry
109–10
Wimbledon FC 257
Wimbledon Station 249
Wimpole Street 244
Winchilsea, Lord 156
Wood, Haydn 242
Wood Lane (tube) 185
World War II 207–10,
298
Worth, Adam 132
Wragg, Harry 69
Wren's Giant Pineapple
15
writers' addresses
216–20

zoo 289–91